AFRICAN IDENTITIES

This fascinating and well-researched study explores the historical meanings generated by 'Africa' and 'Blackness'. Using literary texts, autobiography, ethnography, and historical documents, Kanneh suggests that 'discourses of Africa' are crucial for any analysis of modernity, nationhood and racial difference.

In *African Identities* Kanneh locates Black identity in relation to Africa and the African Diaspora. Kanneh discovers how histories connected with the domination, imagination and interpretation of Africa are constructive of a range of political and theoretical parameters around race.

Moving from more historical material to modern literatures the book aims to highlight the connections between history, cultural analysis and literary texts. The originality of this research lies in its historical range and the connections it makes between continents and times.

For anyone interested in literature, history, anthropology, political writing, feminist or cultural analysis, this book will open up new areas of thought across disciplines.

Kadiatu Kanneh is lecturer in English at the University of Birmingham.

AFRICAN IDENTITIES

Racc, Nation and Culture in
Ethnography, Pan-Africanism and
Black Literatures

Kadiatu Kanneh

London and New York

First published 1998
by Routledge
11 New Fetter Lane, London EC4P 4EE

© 1998 Kadiatu Kanneh

The right of Kadiatu Kanneh to be identified as the author of this
work has been asserted by her in accordance with the Copyright,
Designs and Patents Act 1988

Typeset in Baskerville by
BC Typesetting, Bristol
Printed and bound in Great Britain by
T.J. International Ltd, Padstow, Cornwall

British Library Cataloguing in Publication Data
A catalogue record for this book is available from the British Library ·

Library of Congress Cataloging in Publication Data
A catalogue record for this book has been requested

ISBN 0–415–16445–1

CONTENTS

v

CONTENTS

INTRODUCTION

The argument of this book has grown out of an attempt to formulate what it means to be Black in the twentieth century. W.E.B. DuBois wrote in 1903 that 'the problem of the twentieth century is the problem of the *color-line*'; that race and its variously *linear* parameters (borders, passages, journeys; traditions and origins; demarcations and discriminations) are still politically central at the end of the century serves as a reminder that the urgency of this message has in no sense diminished. Situating the politics of race and racism as *the* problem that haunts and constructs the discourses of modernity, the subjectivities we inhabit and the times in which we live, makes dramatically apparent the ways in which 'race' has become the founding illusion of our identities.

DuBois published *The Souls of Black Folk* on the threshold of the twentieth century, and his declaration on its future had its roots in the events, the dreams and the thoughts of the century that had just closed. What he meant by 'Negro' identity cannot be exactly mapped onto the ideologies, the debates and the times out of which Black identities are understood and enacted today. However, the differential and highly contextualised meanings of Blackness (and of Whiteness) are still closely and significantly bound to the histories inhabited and analysed by DuBois, and cannot be adequately interrogated without those histories.

Throughout this book, I locate Black identity in relation to Africa and the African Diaspora, in order to discover how histories connected with the domination, the imagination and the interpretation of Africa are and have been constructive of a range of political and theoretical parameters around race. This book will pay detailed attention to not only the various histories that inform and inspire ideas of Africa and African identities, but also the *connections* between these diverse discourses, disciplines and times. Revisiting debates within ethnography, historical inquiry, autobiography and literary text, the argument examines *how* these various textualities interconnect, continue, re-interpret or contradict each other. Through such divergent disciplines and genres the political meanings of Black Africa and its Diaspora are explored.

Moving within the historical era that stretches from the mid-eighteenth century to the present, the argument seeks to make it clear that analyses of ethnographic, literary or theoretical texts – for a reading of how Africa and Blackness becomes meaningful – demand attention to the historical traces that form these texts. Making new connections between habitually separated disciplines, geographies and times, the argument of the thesis foregrounds how meaning is and has been constructed *across*, between and in (conscious or unconscious) reference to other, related, times, spaces and texts.

Chapter 1 begins the inquiry into interpretations of Africa as a cultural, racial and philosophical whole by reading how ethnographies have interacted with and developed from the colonial politics of the nineteenth and twentieth centuries. The chapter opens with an analysis of V. S. Naipaul's *A Bend in the River*, a reading of a late twentieth-century literary text that facilitates an immediate recognition of the *range* of discourses and histories that can form the meanings of such a narrative. Examining the various sources and resources of the novel leads to an analysis of colonial ethnographies, modern African literatures and African ethnographies, whereby it becomes apparent how dense and significant are the interdisciplinary connections between political and imaginative constructions of Africa.

Chapter 2 pursues the inquiry into the cultural and racial construction of Africa in literatures and ethnographies by focusing on the history of Britain's first African colony. This analysis of Sierra Leone as a settler colony and protectorate acts as a base from which to explore and make connections between a range of diasporic histories and politics, from pan-Africanist nationalisms to the confessional slave narratives. Charting the chronologies of colonialism, slavery and resistance, the argument reads the debates around race, culture and modernity as historical and geographical continuities. By allowing theoretical interpretations of African subjectivities and nationalisms to emerge from these spatial and temporal connections, this chapter can look more sensitively and imaginatively at representations of Africa, of race and of nation in twentieth-century African literatures and political writings.

The third chapter moves from the historical investigations of the second to discover how modern diasporic literatures and politics revisit the territories of the past in order to imagine and reconstruct identities that in some way 'connect' with Africa. Discussing the role of the United States as a national context, and moving on from the Caribbean and American pan-Africanisms invoked in Chapter 2, the argument investigates how modern African-American pan-Africanisms *appropriate* ideas of 'Africa' for American agendas. I suggest that some African-American feminisms have become implicated in structures of domination towards Africa and African cultures in ways that uncomfortably echo the colonial ethnographies and nationalisms of the preceding century.

The passage from third to fourth chapter shadows Olaudah Equiano's triangular journey from Africa to the Americas and finally to England (discussed in Chapter 2), by focusing the argument on postmodern analyses of Black identities in Britain, with a study of how Caribbean migrations to Britain have served to construct the politics of British nationality and nationalisms. This final chapter extends the analyses of Black British identities by exploring how racial theories have become implicated in the theories and politics of sexuality and sexual identity. Reading twentieth-century literary and theoretical texts from Africa, the United States and Britain, the argument draws on the historical and geographical mappings of the preceding chapters to suggest how inter-racial sexual encounters and mixed race subjectivities delineate the difficulties, fantasies and politics of race in the modern world.

For my mother, Megan Kanneh,
and in memory of my father, A.B. Kanneh,
1930–1970

ACKNOWLEDGEMENTS

The arguments and ideas in this book have emerged, not only from individual research, but also from dialogue, debate, help and advice from a number of sources. My first debt of gratitude is owed to Homi K. Bhabha, who supervised the doctoral thesis on which this book is based. His constant support, encouragement and faith in me have been invaluable. My thanks also go to Norman Vance, whose constructive and detailed comments on my work made all the difference, and whose friendship and institutional support have been very much appreciated. I am also grateful to Lynn Innes and Cedric Watts for their very useful discussion of the text.

Two colleagues and friends of mine from the University of Sussex have been especially helpful for writing this book. My deep gratitude and affection go to Denise deCaires Narain for her insightful ideas and for our frequent sessions of mutual 'thesis-babble'. The friendship of Roland-François Lack has been vital, particularly during the final stages of completion. François' practical help, his endless patience and untiring generosity have been crucial. My warmest thanks are due to him.

Many friends and teachers have given me sustained encouragement, warmth and intellectual support during the time of writing. I am grateful in particular to Isobel Armstrong, Tony Crowley and Robert Young.

My deepest and most loving acknowledgements are given to my family. My thanks to my grandparents, James and Ivy Edwards, my mother, Megan Kanneh, and Steven, Isata, James, Rhiannon Kadiatu and Idris Kanneh.

Thanks and love, of course, to Stuart, to Isata Megan and to Braimah Sean.

Sections of Chapter 1 of this book incorporate material revised from the following previously published pieces: Kadiatu Kanneh, 'What is African Literature? Ethnography and Criticism', in Paul Hyland and Mpalive-Hangson Msiska (eds), *Writing and Africa* (Harlow: Longman, 1997), reprinted by permission of Addison Wesley Longman Ltd; '"Africa" and Cultural Translation: Reading Difference', in Keith Ansell-Pearson, Benita Parry and Judith Squires (eds), *Cultural Readings of Imperialism: Edward Said and the Gravity of History* (London: Laurence & Wishart, forthcoming).

ACKNOWLEDGEMENTS

Sections of Chapters 3 and 4 of this book incorporate material revised from the following previously published pieces: 'Place, Time and the Black Body: Myth and Resistance', in Robert Young (ed.), 'Neocolonialism' (Special issue), *Oxford Literary Review* 13 (1991); 'Love, Mourning and Metaphor: Terms of Identity', in Isobel Armstrong (ed.), *New Feminist Discourses* (London: Routledge, 1992); 'Racism and Culture', in Richard H. King and Patrick Williams (eds), *Paragraph* 16(1) (1993); 'Mixed Feelings: When My Mother's Garden is Unfamiliar', in Sally Ledger, Josephine McDonagh and Jane Spencer (eds), *Political Gender: Texts and Contexts* (Hemel Hempstead: Harvester Wheatsheaf, 1994); 'The Difficult Politics of Wigs and Veils: Feminism and the Colonial Body', in Bill Ashcroft, Gareth Griffiths and Helen Tiffin (eds), *The Post-Colonial Studies Reader* (London: Routledge, 1995); 'The Death of the Author? Marketing Alice Walker', in Kate Fullbrook and Judy Simons (eds), *Writing: A Woman's Business* (Manchester: Manchester University Press, 1998).

1

THE MEANING OF AFRICA
Texts and histories

> To know how I am and how I have fared, you must understand
> why I resist all kinds of domination, including that of being
> given something.
>
> (Nuruddin Farah, *Gifts*)

The argument of this chapter is framed within a problematic that relates
nineteenth-century and early twentieth-century discourses to the complicated textualities of late twentieth-century 'African' writing. In order to
investigate the meanings of 'African identity' in the present, in order to examine how 'Africa' operates as a referent and as a politics in modern ideologies
of race, culture and nation, this chapter unpacks the implicit dialogue
between dispersed times and places. Revealing the links between a range of
disciplines that have constructed 'Africa' as a discursive object invested with
meanings, I argue that an analysis of how African identities are made meaningful relies on attention to the construction of Africa *across* and *between* disciplines. Discourses of Africa are significant in relation to the politics of Black
identities and cultures in the African Diaspora, and any theorisation of these
constructions and subjectivities needs to recognise, not only the interrelatedness of disciplines in the present, but also the ways in which the present has
been constructed by its historical traces. Recognising the multivocal structure
of texts and discourses, I argue that an analysis of the connections between
times, places and disciplines reveals both how meaning emerges from and
accrues to the discursive object, 'Africa', and how 'Africa' becomes located
and defined as object of knowledge.

The chapter frames the reading of twentieth-century texts within and
against *histories* of African knowledge that *condition* the discursive parameters
of modern knowledge. The movement between African and European contexts reveals how Africa and its identities have been crucially informed by
the impact of knowledges and interests from *outside* the continent. The reading
of literary texts alongside and against theoretical, political and ethnographic
writings is intended to emphasise, not the *formal* or stylistic interchangeability
of genres, but the necessity of approaching literary texts as a nexus for the re-
articulation of – culturally and socially mediated – ideological material.

Interrupting the interconnections between various textual histories in constructing discourses of Africa and African identity, the chapter focuses on the analysis of these active cross-references, whose conjunctions are far from innocent. These textual histories are located in the disciplines and genres of colonial anthropologies, travel narratives, ethnophilosophies and literary representations, to reveal how the histories of colonial narratives locate and imagine the concept of Africa. The use of *very specific* colonial ethnographies in this chapter does, for example allows numerous connections to be made with earlier or later colonial or ethnographic discourses, and clearly demonstrates how individual and localised texts inform and are informed by a network of cultural, historical and social realities.

The examination, in this chapter, of African ethnographies and literatures is taken up in the following chapter by a closer inquiry into colonial history and early pan-Africanism, laying a necessary foundation and reference point for the later analyses of race and sexuality. The symbiosis of place and time operates as a recurring motif in my argument, and serves to show how these concepts or referents have been continually mapped onto each other in colonial histories, how this 'mapping' constructs theories of race, nation and culture, and how late twentieth-century writing re-articulates and re-imagines these links.

Looking for Africa: 'Cultural translation' and African ethnographies

By way of introduction to the arguments of this chapter, I shall discuss a late twentieth-century literary text that engages with the problematics of cultural interlocution and history in relation to Africa. V.S. Naipaul's *A Bend in the River* (1979) offers an important angle of vision on the ethnographical issues which the chapter interrogates. Naipaul's particular position vis-à-vis Africa as both a cultural other and a national from Britain's colonial margins places him at a curious and productive intersection of historical and cultural ideas. Salim, the main character of *A Bend in the River*, is positioned in a similarly complicated cultural space. As a *South Asian* African, Salim's consciousness as native *and* settler allows the novel to explore the production of cultural knowledge in a liminal space between identities. This fraught and *un*-settled angle of vision is peculiarly productive of the questions and insights that pre-occupy ethnographic texts.

I choose to discuss this text precisely because it demonstrates, in its own self-conscious narrative, both the difficulties of representing or defining cultural others, and the inevitable historical and textual complicities underlying the location and legitimation of otherness. What the novel manages to enact, from the site of an implicated, yet detached authority, in anxious control of a subject which keeps slipping out of sight, is a sustained grappling with the *idea* of Africa. From an obsessive focus on the intense physicality of an African landscape, massively alive, massively secretive, to the repeated invocation of an African history without narrative structure, *A Bend In the River* deliberately writes itself against and alongside Joseph Conrad's *Heart of Darkness* (1902), which represents what becomes a sustained metaphorical reference in Naipaul's text:

> Going up that river was like traveling back to the earliest beginnings of the world, when vegetation rioted on the earth and the big trees were kings. An empty stream, a great silence, an impenetrable forest.[1]

The perplexity of the text lies in its constant engagement with cliché – the mystery, the violence, the impenetrability of African forest and African native – and, at the same time, its insistence on re-examining and dismantling the origins and meanings of cliché away from the dominating stance of 'foreign fantasy', a fantasy that originates in the colonial metropolis.[2] What becomes clear is that the novel's subject and project is profoundly *textual*. Unable to represent an Africa which recedes behind the threat of bush and river, the novel lays contesting clichés, one against another, which compete bewilderingly against a backdrop of resolute mystery. Barred from the possibility even of *imagining* a direct engagement with the text's ostensible subject, the novel insistently foregrounds the monologue of its own displaced, post-colonial narrative, locked in the long history of European colonial encounter.

Exactly because the 'lost' and 'hidden' *meaning* of Africa is projected as lying behind the *presence* of African natural geography, African modernity becomes impossible to imagine. To make 'the land' (p. 8) 'part of the present' (p. 9), 'this land of rain and heat and big-leaved trees – always visible' (p. 42), its *visibility*, its offensive encroachment, must itself be annihilated. The precarious temporality of modernity in Africa relies on European order and is perpetually threatened by a violence and rage which is both historically necessitated (pp. 26, 81) and part of 'some old law of the forest, something that came from Nature itself' (p. 80).

The familiar colonial rhetoric of the timelessness of Africa, the emptiness of village life, locked in a fixed and lost dimension, the primitive savagery energising the episodic destruction of order, lies against another familiar rhetoric of celebration which is positioned as another object, distanced from the narrative voice. The character, Father Huismans, a Belgian priest and self-made anthropologist, and occupying the space of missionary and ethnographer, re-interprets the same Africa 'of bush and river' (pp. 62–3) as, 'a wonderful place, full of new things'.

The crucial difference of Huismans' idea of Africa lies in his particular understanding of history as a dominating narrative destiny, intent on over-riding and writing over what is, for him, *essentially* African. His veneration of Africa is actually a veneration of his own ability to seek out, to 'witness' (p. 65) African cultural objects and, by placing them in his museum, located on the site of the European school, to *interpret* them. The force of European history, its power to exterminate Africa in the name of its own logic, becomes embodied by Father Huismans:

> True Africa he saw as dying or about to die, that was why it was so necessary, while that Africa still lived, to understand and collect and preserve its things.
>
> (p. 64)

The African masks in Father Huismans' museum become the locus of a war of interpretation, staged between the intense narcissism of the novel's own narrative and the clichéd philosophy of Father Huismans. Focusing on a carved African statue, the non-African, non-European narrator, Salim, opposes Father Huismans' celebration of the artwork as 'imaginative and full of meaning', with an interpretation which insists on deeper ethnographical understanding. Salim's recognition of the statue as 'an exaggerated and crude piece, a carver's joke' (p. 61) at once underlines the text's constantly *knowing* position as recogniser of clichés, and at the same time points to the subversive presence of other meanings beneath colonial discourse. These, in turn, disrupt and disturb any narrative certainty.

The previous reading of the African Ferdinand's face by Salim, which he confidently asserts was a 'looking . . . with the eyes of an African', and which compares Ferdinand's face with 'the starting point of certain kinds of African masks' (p. 37), must now be thrown under suspicion. This is a suspicion of which the narrative is very well aware and which it exploits in such a way that Africa's power, mystery and threat alternates with the mundane and the comic. Africa as a whole, represented by postcolonial Zaire – as a continuation of Conrad's Congo – both feared and mocked, is always superseded by the greater reality and textual order of Europe. Zaire, geographically situated in Central Africa, which, metonymically as well as spatially, represents the 'heart' of Africa, is used to portray an 'essential' Africa in both texts.

Independent, modern Africa, distanced from the hopeless, timeless secrecy of hidden forest villages, simply exists at the interchange of conflicting narratives, born of colonial discourse. Salim describes African modernity inconclusively as 'Europe in Africa, post-colonial Africa. But it isn't Europe or Africa' (p. 139).

Out of the constant self-referencing self-consciousness of Salim's narration, caught in his own idea of postcolonial displacement, and prey to his own object (p. 55), the novel identifies Africa as, inevitably, a site of its own narcissism: 'Those faces of Africa! . . . They were people crazed with the idea of who they were' (p. 269).

Sara Suleri's reading of Naipaul's novels and texts as indicative of a profound anxiety around the authority of *seeing* – of interpretation and judgement – is significant. She claims (to quote from her reading of *An Area of*

Darkness) that 'the text begins to acknowledge the narrator's bodily availability to interpretation, making it increasingly unclear whether the perceived or perceiving body is the greater redundancy on the narrative scene'.[3] The narrative of *A Bend in the River* returns obsessively to the narrator's position on the scene, constantly reiterating the priority of Salim's vision. What is perceived outside Salim's own body is repeatedly interpreted by and in connection with it, until (like *Heart of Darkness*) the landscape itself achieves the drama of consciousness:

> You heard yourself as though you were another person. The river and the forest were like presences, and much more powerful than you.
>
> (p. 8)

> This was how the place worked on you: you never knew what to think or feel. Fear or shame – there seemed to be nothing in between.
>
> (p. 76)

This presentation of the narrator as interpreter and the victim of interpretation, where the text's object insidiously returns in control of the narrative, foregrounds the impossibility of 'knowing' otherness before its reduction to the Same. The recognition of anxiety haunting the rhetoric of discourses which are invested in colonial values is a familiar one, and introduces a profound difficulty. *A Bend in the River* approaches the problem of representing otherness, both by entrenching the notion of absolute difference, impenetrable to the possibility of dialogue, and by claiming its purely textual or romantic existence against the reality of the banal. This constant engagement with the self, emphasising the limits of ethnology, exposes the necessary gap between mysterious difference and the knowable familiar. The predication of mystery allows the obliteration of dialogue, placing interpretation *only* within the narcissism of authority. Suleri's insistence that 'otherness as an intransigence . . . further serves as an excuse for the failure of reading' (p. 12) points suggestively to those moments in the text where forest and river present a wall beyond which life without rationality or self-expression (the requisite of mystery) will be superseded by modernity.

To begin with this reading of *A Bend in the River* is to introduce a literary presentation of the issues which coalesce around discussions of African identity or African culture. The temptation to continually move from an examination of the particular, the local, to an obsession with the whole, the continent, is prevalent in texts about Africa. What makes 'Africa' different from the 'West'? How, or can we discuss an African modernity? How have colonial discourses impinged on, or created, a modern understanding of African reality?

Naipaul's novel positions these issues as a problem of cultural interpretation, with a narrator who occupies the space of cultural interlocutor, or

ethnographer. In this way, a deliberate disjunction is made between interpretation and what is seen:

> So from an early age I developed the habit of looking, detaching
> myself from a familiar scene and trying to consider it as from a
> distance.
>
> (p. 15)

This distancing presents itself as a kind of privileged observation through
Salim's own radical cultural displacement as an East Indian in exile in
Zaire. Situated precariously on the edges of European colonial civilisation,
trading European goods with the African interior, Salim is able to comment
on the gaps between colonising and colonised cultures. What emerges, however, is not a transcendent narrative penetrating knowingly into pre-colonial
African societies, but a mystified gaze remaining transfixed on the mystery of
a doomed, deep forest. Repeatedly, the narrative revisits questions of time,
the writing of history and the problems of modernity from a standpoint
which recognises the permanence and ultimate authority of the written text,
and the inevitable obliteration of local intransigence. Travel and displacement become the focus for a modernity which insists on a perpetual and
unsentimental present, unstuck from the particularity of geographical place.
Having travelled from the east coast of Africa to its centre, in an ironic reversal of Marlow's journey from the west up the Congo in *Heart of Darkness*, and
from Zaire to Europe, Salim's view of an unknowable African specificity
gives way to an undifferentiated modern world:

> I was homesick, had been homesick for months. But home was hardly
> a place I could return to. Home was something in my head. It was
> something I had lost. And in that I was like the ragged Africans who
> were so abject in the town we serviced.
>
> (p. 107)

'Africa' becomes split between a dying, traditional past which is at once
hugely intrusive and obsolete, and a banal modernity which is obsessed with
interpreting an 'idea' of African identity. Salim's own preoccupations, yearn-
ings and exclusions decide and shape the nature of what he sees, until interpretation can only remain halted at the borders of a revelation which is
ultimately both elusive and illusive. This entrenched self-reflexivity opposes
itself to Father Huismans' enterprise of entering and preserving a 'true'
Africa by creating a museum of African masks. Rescued from the suffocating
timelessness of the forest where, removed from the present, they can *mean*
nothing, the masks become readable and contested cultural artifacts. This
'readability' can be premised only on the exclusion of a former context
which, under the imposed temporality of colonial knowledge, becomes

unreadable, without indigenous meaning. Sunday Anozie, however, attests to a differential semiotics of African masks outside the interpretive power of the museum:

> In Africa, the mask certainly constitutes an iconographic or semiotic system: as a system of signs, it also embodies language; in sub-Saharan Africa, there is an authentic mask language, known sometimes as 'juju' language, just as there is an authentic drum language.[4]

A Bend in the River is not an ethnographic text but a literary one. The novel's refusal to name its localities – whether countries, towns or villages – and to relate them only to the already metaphoric term, 'Africa', emphasises its intertextual relationship with preceding literary and anthropological texts. The realities to which it primarily refers are textual. This does not, however, wholly remove its concerns from those of ethnography. The novel's continual foregrounding of the uncertainty of an authorial voice, the concentration on culture and time, link it very clearly with the theoretical problems of ethnography.

The history of anthropology in Africa, to which *A Bend in the River* covertly refers, is closely implicated with colonial structures of knowledge. Emerging from a background of travelogues and conquest, including missionary narratives, anthropology in Africa has often constructed an African 'other' out of a conception of cultures as discrete entities, entirely separable from each other in space, and 'racially' as well as geographically distinct. The relationship between anthropology and imperialism, and its concomitant relationship with theories of unequal races, is well documented. Talal Asad, for example, associates anthropology directly with the 'unequal power encounter between the West and the Third World . . . an encounter in which colonialism is merely one historical moment'.[5] This 'encounter' has given rise to both a 'sustained physical proximity' (p. 17), and a structure of *exploitation* which ensured that observation, the taking of knowledge, and the writing of information, was always of, from and about the *non-European* other.

What is intrinsic to these theories of cultural difference is a notion of mapping *discrete* human groups at particular places on a path to modernity. This preoccupation with interpreting cultures in terms of a narrative of progress in (or through) time has particular implications for 'knowing' cultural others, and creates specific conditions for any encounter *across* cultures. Johannes Fabian's argument in *Time and the Other*, which explores the creation of anthropology as a discipline, a project and a profession, insists on a structural 'Politics of Time'.[6] Any 'knowledge of the other', in Fabian's discussion, is fundamentally informed by a politics of temporality which positions the object of anthropological investigation in a relationship *outside* the interlocutor's *present*, and dislocated from the possibility of contemporal *dialogue*. The concept of race which informs and lies behind the concept of separate human cultures within the history of anthropology is one which Fabian claims to rest on an idea of 'evolutionary time', where both *past* cultures and *distant*, living societies become 'irrevocably placed on a temporal slope, a stream of time – some upstream, others downstream' (p. 17). In order to view the contemporary human world, anthropological discourse has often resorted to a form of 'typological time' (p. 23) which allows different societies to be classified in terms of a quality of *states* rather than a measure of change or movement. In this way, the quality of dynamic *development* is one which is differentially attributed to particular societies. Thus, 'savage', 'tribal' and 'animist' cultures or races can be identified by anthropologists as *fixed* in their difference, outside or before history.

The relationship between ethnography about Africans and colonialism in Africa is evident in travelogues and novels often written by members of the British colonial service, and 'ethnophilosophy', which incorporates African literary criticism and presents itself as either resistance to, or resolution of, the problems of colonialism. An example of the British 'colonial travelogue' is Frederick Migeod's *A View Of Sierra Leone* (1926). Migeod is introduced as 'Colonial Civil Service, retired', and he presents in his Preface an account both of the reasons for his study of the people of the (then) colony and protectorate and some of the methodological problems involved. He classifies his own position repeatedly as 'the Anthropologist' and makes continual allusions to 'official publications', 'anthropological information' and the possibility of 'a general reference book to the colony',[7] making clear that his work is to be placed within and in dialogue with a politically sanctioned store of colonial literature and 'knowledge'.

In order to verify his generalisations about 'the simple savage', Migeod can glibly include an anecdote about a 'political officer in a distant colony' to illustrate a feature of Sierra Leonean 'native' activity. Yet, he insists on the significance of the *specific* landscape of a people in order to produce an accurate account of them: 'An anthropological student cannot draw just deductions unless he is perfectly acquainted with the environment of the tribe he is studying' (p. ix). This generalising tendency to reduce the totality of empire to a type of savagery *already known* and to simultaneously provide careful geographical detail concurs with Fabian's notion of how a particular (colonial) concept of time serves as an implicit method for 'studying' cultures dispersed in space. Lord Avebury's *On the Origin of Civilisation and Primitive Condition of Man* (1870) precedes Migeod's study by over fifty years. Lord Avebury, formerly Sir John Lubbock (1834–1913) holds a significant place in the history of anthropological writing. His celebrated and influential position in British public life in the late nineteenth and early twentieth century brought him into contact with a wide range of key issues and thinkers of his time. His close relationship with Charles Darwin clearly indicates the source of his ideas on evolution, and his work can be sited at the intersection of the natural and human sciences. His extensive European travels in search of the most recent innovations in anthropological thought make his work a valuable point of access to the ideas prevalent at this time.[8]

Narrowing the British empire into a sweeping 'study of savage life', Avebury spells out more clearly the meaning of Migeod's 'savage':

> The study of the lower races of men, apart from the direct importance which it possesses in an empire like ours, is of great interest . . . the condition and habits of existing savages resemble in many ways . . . those of our own ancestors in a period long gone by.
>
> (p. 1)

This evolutionary development of 'races' is not always an upwards movement, which illustrates how the civilising mission of colonialism gains part of its validity:

> It has been said by some writers that savages are merely the degenerate descendants of more civilised ancestors, and I am far from denying that there are cases of retrogression.
>
> (p. 3)

As with Migeod, dispersal in space is of less significance in terms of cultural and racial difference than the time schema of empire:

> Different races in similar stages of development often present more features of resemblance to one another than the same race does to itself in different stages of history.
>
> (p. 11)

If 'cultural difference' as a concept emerges from the 'culture gardens' in Fabian's discussion, or the higher and lower 'races' of anthropologists like Avebury, an approach to African literature which sees only otherness risks these totalising and essentialising strategies. Fabian's argument relies on a bid for 'Intersubjective Time' in anthropology, which refuses any absolute distinction between the temporalities of one culture and another, and relies instead on the dynamics of human interaction and communication (p. 24). However, in his insistence on 'coevalness', on a recognition that all societies are 'of the same age' (p. 159), Fabian cannot dismiss the reality of confrontation between 'cultures'. If coevalness rules out notions of divided evolutions, and disallows the identity of the present to be defined solely within the terms of Western modernity, it cannot rule out the violence of cultural domination and the negotiation of difference and resistance between and within human societies:

> What are oppposed, in conflict, in fact, locked in antagonistic struggle, are not the same societies at different stages of development, but different societies facing each other at the same Time.
>
> (p. 155)

James Clifford's question, asking how and if we *can* represent (other) cultures, is forced to move away from a reliance on exclusive totalities decipherable from each other[9] and to accept a more fluid but still active understanding of cultural identity as 'an ongoing process, politically contested and historically unfinished' (p. 9).

In this light, cultural difference cannot be an outdated preoccupation which needs to be pushed aside in favour of a more 'universal' or 'innocent' field of communication. Having been perceived and mapped by colonialist anthropologies, difference still operates in terms like 'modern' and 'traditional', which have become metaphors of contested space *within* and *between* societies, nations or 'cultures'. Although unequal power over resources of knowledge and dissemination of information has spawned documents like Migeod's 'view' of Sierra Leone, the struggle over representation emerges quite clearly within his text, where the generalised Mende, Temne or Limba 'native' informant constantly challenges the authority of Migeod's observations. For Migeod, the problem is partly the 'mercenary nature' of 'natives' who demand payment for giving information and, in this way, attempt to redress the balance of exploitation (p. ix). In addition, the control over knowledge is one which slips between the certainties of colonial power to the extent that anthropological study is at once reliant on and at the mercy of the native. The informant is never engaged in a dialogue of cultural give and take but is used as a *resource*. Recognising that the 'inquirer' is 'assuredly regarded as a very big fool by the simple savage', Migeod never accepts the possibility of a reciprocal conversation, or of the subversion behind the activities of the 'naughty' informant. His attitude and desire is succinctly revealed in a phrase which shows exasperation as well as a clear wish for human African resources to remain under the microscope:

> I have mentioned just a few incidentals connected with collecting information as regards the human species. The botanist, zoologist or geologist has an easy time in comparison. The objects of his research, if not passive, at least cannot lie to him.
>
> (p. x)

That accurate information often escapes the surveillance of Western eyes through the wit and evasion of human subjects is now a recognised fact of ethnographical study.[10] The relationship between the ethnographer and her material is fraught with relations of power and its subversion which seriously damage the edifice of 'cultural knowledge', but which also create the very

conditions of its existence. Literacy and *control* over information and interpretation always, however, remain securely on the side of the colonial anthropologist, who is able to outwit his native interlocutor by complicating the
simple pattern of interrogation, 'that is to preserve no sequence in one's
inquiries', and by being alert to the native's short attention span: 'after
twenty minutes questioning he gets tired' (p. ix). Sierra Leoneans themselves,
regardless of colonial education, or even of the fact that they have contributed
to Migeod's learned bibliography will never, in his view, be capable of understanding or interpreting 'anthropological information' about themselves
without British colonial interception: 'they would require guidance in how
to deal with their subject, and should confine themselves strictly to presenting
facts and draw no deductions' (p. xi). This approach to native literacy has
been informed by a developmental narrative which proposes limits on the
evolutionary potential of Africans through education. By this logic, the Freetown 'Creoles' – the hybrid people of the coast – through the 'generous'
supply of colonial schooling, have 'in all probability reached the highest
point to which the African black-man can attain' (p. 8). This is, of course,
not as high a point as the British, whose efforts to inculcate the speaking of
'good English' in the colony of Freetown are rewarded only with the 'cor-
rupted speech' of 'the Creoles' (which is called Krio).

Migeod opens his view of Sierra Leone with a claim that his book provides
'an account of what I saw' (p. ix), and this prioritising of visual observation
sustains a 'self-evident' discussion of the Mende people *as a race*. Migeod's
chapter, 'The Physical Characteristics of the Mende' derives from theories of
separate biological races, such as the 'pure Mende' (p. 203), who can be
easily distinguished by a science of physical appearance and phrenology into
'At least two types of Mende'. One has a 'dolichocephalic' head, rising 'high
above the ears', while the other is shorter with a 'more rounded' head.
Altogether, the Mende can boast 'twenty types of face' (p. 204), and these
visible qualities dictate a scientific table of character and behaviour, 'mental
capacity' and social tastes. Even education and literacy obtains a link with
a 'contraction of the forehead' (p. 211). This racial typology of the Mende,
specifically, is, then, casually confused with an ideology of race which can discuss 'The Fula' as 'not yet submerged in the flood of negroism' (p. 208).
'Negroism' is related to skin colour – the Fula being distinguished by their
fairness – although, in Sierra Leone, 'really black persons . . . are quite
unknown'. The barriers between Black and White races are rigid – fair-
skinned 'negroes' or 'red men' being distinctly separated from 'mulattoes' –
and the lengthy physical descriptions of the Mende seem significant mainly
to determine how 'useful' each 'type' is likely to be (p. 211).

Migeod's use of race and 'type' here appears to emerge from a confusion of
nineteenth-century racial theories. As Robert Young observes, 'type' 'came
into widespread use in the 1850s because it neatly brought together the implications of both species and race while dispensing with the theoretical and

terminological difficulties of both'.[11] Migeod uses 'type', however, as a sub-section of 'race' ('Mende' standing as a 'race'), with, it seems, 'Negro' operating as a kind of 'species'.

Interestingly, a discourse of nationhood seeps into the confused discourse of race, with Migeod 'looking for a national type' of Mende, while casual voyeurism allows him to include photographs of a Mende dwarf (p. 278) and the fact that 'albinos have brownish hair' (p. 208).

Migeod's statement that 'Sierra Leone was known to the ancients', that is, the Alexandrians (p. 1), makes it clear that 'knowledge' is a Western product, and extraneous to West Africa, even as it refers to it. Max Gorvie's *Our People of the Sierra Leone Protectorate* delivers knowledge of Sierra Leone by a 'native' (probably Creole) author. This text, published in 1944,[12] is part of a series of educational tracts, collectively named, 'Africa's Own Library', issued to colonial schools and training colleges in Sierra Leone throughout the 1950s by the United Society For Christian Literature. Colonial education and the propagation of Christianity frame the book's message, vilifying 'Mohammedan propagandists'[13] and presenting a blighted, savage Sierra Leonean past, ripe for colonialism. In a passage which puns on the country's name of 'Lion Mountain', Gorvie writes:

> The British Lion prowled over this part of the continent of Africa. . . .
> Suddenly beyond those mountain chains of Sierra Leone he gave a
> terrific roar that drove away far into the mountains the rapacious
> beasts disguised in the habiliments of human beings, known either as
> slave-dealers or cannibals. He suppressed their inhumanity.
>
> (p. 9)

Although this text is authored by a Sierra Leonean, the framework of publication and editorship, as well as the ideology which the series is intended to engender, places certain important qualifications on Gorvie's authorship. The Publishers' Note makes these qualifications and restraints clear:

> This series is designed to stimulate Africans to take an interest in
> reading of the great tribes and personalities of their continent.
> Many of the books are written by African authors, who, *as far as pos-
> sible*, are left to express their own views in their own words.
>
> (My emphasis)

The racial ideology informing the text is, again, a science based on observation of the natural world. 'Tribes' are described in terms of 'stock' and 'mongrel' progeny, tribal rulers were busy 'preying on each other as the baracuta preys on lesser fish' (p. 11), and their collective behaviour is reliant on the language of development and zoology:

The Loko is somewhat slow though not exactly lazy but yet not far removed from the drone. *It* is slow of action and slow to adopt new measures. Like the Sherbro, *it* seldom migrates.

(p. 29; my emphasis)

As with Migeod, this racial (and tribal) typology is presented as being directly relevant to the range of any 'advance of civilization and education'. In fact, the renaissance that British colonialism brings has helped to galvanise the 'tribes' into a change of architecture – described as an awakening:

The Temne is far behind the Mende in the art of architecture generally. Now that his country is being subjected to mineralogy, he is himself aroused to change from his age-old pyramid-shaped house. To-day he makes rapid strides in this direction.

(p. 27)

The continual references to passive, sleepy tribal people, who have been constantly preyed on by cannibals and 'Mohammedans', and who are slowly responding to the light of civilisation, is, at moments, interspersed with a recognition of native resistance. Similar to Migeod's account, this refusal of assent to colonial control is allowed to enter the text as part of a larger interpretation of native puerility, what Migeod would call the Temne 'want of politeness' (p. 21), and yet it remains to be read as a far more serious attack on colonial 'civilisation':

The Temne is . . . somewhat peevish and when once his anger is aroused it is difficult to talk him to reason. Doubtless this stern trait was partly responsible for the massacre of the '98 raid . . . when the various tribes pooled their forces unitedly and in one strong wave of patriotism gave vent to their dissatisfactions.

(pp. 26–7)

Known as the 'Mende Rising', or the 'House Tax War', and ignited by the Temne – or 'Timne' – sub-chief, Bai Bureh, the 1898 raid was a war between the protectorate and the Colony of Freetown over compulsory taxation. It was a war directed against White colonial authority,[14] making clear the need to claim Temne rudeness as a natural attribute, rather than as justifiable evidence of anti-colonial resistance.

William Vivian's *A Captive Missionary in Mendiland* (1899) is directly concerned with native resistance and its interpretation.[15] Published in 1899, and recounting the experiences of Rev. C.H. Goodman (pictured in the front of the book, sporting the perfect colonial helmet), the text foregrounds the glory of Christian redemption, both against the savagery of the Mende, and for the missionary's own deliverance from their uprising. As 'Late General

Superintendent of United Methodist Free Church Missions in Sierra Leone', Vivian presents the Mende within the Messianic scheme of redemption and Christian revelation. Being mentally and morally in 'aboriginal darkness' (p. 13), the Mende 'heathens' need Methodist enlightenment. This Christian narrative of salvation has a clear temporal schema which situates the Mende in a time before the modern age of Christian knowledge, and the 'earnestly aggressive' (p. 13) missionary societies are the harbingers of that modernity. This temporal mapping is also a starkly geographical one, which allows Vivian to discuss the 'strange and most impressive experience' it is to pass 'the bounds of civilization and plunge into African darkness for the first time' (p. 15). Again, the meaning of Mende resistance is disavowed in such a way that their 'unholy zeal' (p. 46) in utterly destroying the British colonial missions in 'Mendi country' only serves to legitimate the renewed vigour of missionary conversion and domination, the 'savage Mendies' having 'clearly demonstrated their great need of it' (p. v).

Nicholas Thomas places texts like Vivian's in a history of colonial writing where pre-modern or medieval thought discusses 'pagans or infidels' who lack salvation, and the mid-to-late eighteenth century sees the development of 'a distinctively *anthropological* discourse', with people ranked 'in an evolutionary natural history'.[16] Vivian's story of Mende resistance uncomfortably straddles a specifically Methodist ideology of universal redemption for all humanity, *and* a clear notion of evolution, which places the Mende in a time of undeveloped savagery. Vivian is able to hedge his bets by reporting (via Goodman) the odd 'gleam of humanity' (p. 47) among the 'pitiless' natives, and 'gleams of light' (p. 13) in the midst of gross depravity.

Gaining knowledge of other cultures is not a simple, uncomplicated matter of neutral translation from one social order to the direct relativity of another. Cultural translation, which is central to the creation of ethnographic texts, paradoxically insists on the possibility of cultural relativism and operates, at the same time, within a problematic which insists on radical non-relativity. Walter Benjamin's (1923) analysis of the task of the translator is useful here, and is regularly evoked in discussions of cultural anthropology.[17] His study of linguistic translation which, he claims, is 'only a somewhat provisional way of coming to terms with the foreignness of languages',[18] explores how meaning can be transmitted from one linguistic system to another. This transmission or communication can never be mimetic. Translation necessarily leaves a surplus of meaning, an *excess*, which cannot be communicated from the original to its translated form. This surplus, the particular property of the original text, is a quality of the relationship between meaning and its context which, in the process of translation, has inevitably to be lost:

> Even when all the surface content has been extracted and transmitted, the primary concern of the genuine translator remains elusive. Unlike the words of the original, it is not translatable, because

the relationship between content and language is quite different in
the original and the translation. . . . This disjunction prevents translation and at the same time makes it superfluous.

(p. 75)

This description of the 'genuine translator' seems, here, to indicate at least
a desire for mimetic accuracy, for a direct mirroring of content from the
original to its copy. This projection of linguistic similarity, although it
cannot overcome the entrenched nature of the *essence* of the original, still, in
Benjamin's analysis, attests to the ultimate reciprocity of languages: 'Languages are not strangers to one another, but are, a priori and apart from all
historical relationships, interrelated in what they want to express' (p. 72).
This reciprocity – this equality in difference – of languages cannot deny the
activity of radical separation which accompanies translation. Rather than
forging a mutual space or encounter, translation, on the contrary, forces a
more rigid interface between languages which closes off the possibility of
direct communication: 'Thus translation, ironically, transplants the original
into a more definitive linguistic realm since it can no longer be displaced by
a secondary rendering' (p. 75). This consequence emerges from the fact that
translation is a one-way movement of meaning from one language to another
without mutual change. The ideal translator insists that the secondary language – the translation's destination – itself undergo a rupture, a transformation of itself, under the onslaught of the original. In striving to approximate
the essence of meaning in the original, the translation has to act upon the
order and structure of the *second* language in order to produce a 're-creation'
– not a copy – of the first (p. 80).

In cultural translation, the foreignness of languages also remains resolute.
Vincent Crapanzano re-writes Benjamin's account of the desire for mimesis
as a more complicated, dual project. For Crapanzano, the ethnographer
aims, in his cultural translations, to 'communicate the very foreignness that
his interpretations . . . deny, at least in their claim to universality'. This idea
that the ethnographer must 'render the foreign familiar and preserve its
foreignness at one and the same time'[19] questions in practice the thesis of
linguistic interrelatedness. Insisting on the historical relationships which
Benjamin temporarily suspends, the *equal difference* of languages becomes,
in ethnography, *unequal disjunction*. The 'foreign' culture, which is made
meaningful *and* strange, is historically in a position of disadvantage – a disadvantage which is produced from specific global relations of power. In
this sense, cultural translation is also a form of cultural domination, or
rather, translation depends on the existing dominating stance of one politically and economically powerful culture over another.[20] Talal Asad's insistence on contextualising the practice of ethnography within power relations
creates a significant perspective on questions of relativism and professional
activity:

Given that this is so, the interesting question for enquiry is not whether, and if so to what extent, anthropologists should be relativists or rationalists, critical or charitable, toward other cultures, but how power enters into the process of 'cultural translation', seen both as a discursive and as a non-discursive practice.[21]

This moves discussion of cultural translation away from ethnographical *techniques*, or linguistic accuracy, to a *primary* consideration of external power imbalances. Conditions of power determine *which* culture will be translated into meaning for the other, while geographical distance metonymically enacts a profound non-recognition. The break between the societies involved in anthropological contact allows the denial of relativity and reciprocity through the operation of cultural translation which – as with Benjamin's *non*-ideal translator – reinforces the unchanging empire of the Same against a malleable, corruptable Other. Translation *reads* the signification (significance) of an other society within an economy of *nature* confronted with (and becoming) *culture*, or latent, unconscious experience confronted with a conscious will to knowledge. Michel de Certeau's reading of ethnology in *The Writing of History* attests to this conditional inequality, emphasising the historical necessity to keep other ('non'-) cultures strange against the rational, unchanging Self:

> The break between over here and over there is transformed into a rift between nature and culture. Finally, nature is what is other, while man stays the same.[22]

Ethnology's profound resistance to the equal relativity of human societies in de Certeau's analysis, and its consequent relegation of less powerful cultures to a position of projected dormancy, opposes itself to Benjamin's study of relativity existing alongside the intractable nature of linguistic separation. A commitment to absolute relativity, similar to Fabian's insistence on coevalness, claiming itself as a solution to this crisis of inequality, acts also as an encouragement to encounter only the self within discourses of the other. If ethnographical knowledge, conditioned by colonial histories of domination, repeatedly translates otherness into its own systems of imposed meaning, would not an insistence on interrelatedness perform a similar movement? The difficulty adheres to the problem of translation itself, where the act of re-writing, of making sense of another *differently*, performs an irreducible act of violence. Coevalness – perhaps the only immediate solution to the relegation of others to an inferior position within an imposed (a foreign) system of meaning – risks the danger of enforcing an uncritical notion of universality, without guaranteeing an equal dialogue divorced from exterior and impacting relations of power. Christopher Miller's assertion that, to relinquish even the *desire* to coincide – the commitment to recognition –

merely re-affirms the arrogance of unchallenged self-reflexivity, is a serious corrective here.[23]

This problem of relativism as an encouragement to the violent narcissism of impervious self-reflexivity can be re-thought through a re-configuration of cultural difference as the articulation, not of the *content* of opposing cultural units, but of the problematic of signifying difference itself, as the moment of enunciating cultural knowledge and meaning. Homi K. Bhabha's exploration of this issue usefully opposes the relativistic theory of 'cultural diversity' with a theory of cultural difference that emerges from the problem of interpretation:

> Cultural diversity is an epistemological object – culture as an object of empirical knowledge – whereas cultural difference is the process of the *enunciation* of culture as 'knowledge*able*', authoritative, adequate to the construction of systems of cultural identification.[24]

Encounter *between* cultures is precisely the moment at which the articulation of signs becomes apparent, caught between the ambivalence, the 'in-between space',[25] of contesting projections and linguistic negotiation. Cultural representation relies, inevitably, on this conjunction, this clash of signification on the borders and limits of cultures, which acknowledge and mediate cultural meaning always as the articulation of difference and otherness:

> Cultures come to be represented by virtue of the processes of iteration and translation through which their meanings are very vicariously addressed to – *through* – an Other.[26]

This refusal of the depth of cultural content, which can be 'known' via the 'objective' lens of anthropology, enables a further critique of Father Huismans or Migeod's confusion of the faltering of their own systems of meaning in the encounter with difference *as* the penetration into the (thus already known) 'Truth' of the Other.

Cultural translations of 'weak' by 'strong' languages take place within an ideology which insists, not on a transference, but on a *conferral* of meaning from one to another. In this way, the object of translation offers up, not a text to be *read*, but latent significance to be *written*: 'Whatever else an ethnography does, it translates experience into text.'[27] The object of ethnography becomes a possible object of knowledge through the operation of written inscription, which makes another culture *known*. This ordering of 'unconscious' cultural signs into writing is one which V.Y. Mudimbe asserts has long been practised with regard to Africa:

> The discourse which witnesses to Africa's knowledge has been for a
> long time either a geographical or an anthropological one, at any

rate a 'discourse of competence' about unknown societies without their own 'texts'.[28]

An absence of 'text' indicates an absence of self-consciousness, even of self-knowledge, which the ethnographer is then able to create and to donate to the subjects of her analysis in order for them to make sense of themselves.[29]

This system of unequal exchange has significant repercussions for a project of knowledge which is founded upon literacy. If written representation effectively erodes the chosen self-presentation of another, how can ethnographical writing allow another to speak for herself? Gayatri Spivak's analysis of this difficulty within, particularly, feminist global politics, in her essay, 'Can the Subaltern Speak?', emerges with the response that, within First World interpretrations of Third World women's lives, the meaning of these lives, radically de-contextualised, displaced and retrospectively (at a distance) reconstructed through the process of writing, is not communicated via any active dialogism. The conclusion that 'the subaltern cannot speak',[30] points to the structural inability of the written, Western text to give the Other her own voice. Spivak makes her position clearer in an interview with Walter Adamson, where she retraces her interpretation of Bhuvaneswari Bhaduri's suicide in 'Can the Subaltern Speak?':

> What I was doing with the young woman who had killed herself was really trying to analyze and represent her text. She wasn't particularly trying to speak to me. I was representing her, I was reinscribing her. To an extent, I was writing her to be read, and I certainly was not claiming to give her a voice.[31]

Rather than claiming that her interpretations provide a *prior* or a *primary* text, Spivak claims, instead, that they form only a *second* text, which merely *re-writes* that which itself has its own context and meanings. The ethical consideration that remains is, then, a *contextual* one: 'What we do toward the texts of the oppressed is very much dependent upon where we are.'[32]

This insistence upon a geo-political awareness of context helps to outline the qualitative political distinction between sociology and anthropology – the interpretive science of the 'right here' and that of the 'over there'. Sociology, the interpretation of (modern) Western societies operates at a tangent from anthropology's study of 'unknown' societies. In Miller's analysis, the divide between the status of oral and literate cultures maps out the gap between sociological and anthropological interpretation:

> The watershed between anthropology and its first-world (or urban) counterpart, sociology, seems to adhere to the distinction between oral and literate cultures; but that division is the locus of unfathom-

able myths and delusions which reinforce the barriers between 'us' and 'them'.[33]

These 'myths and delusions' coalesce particularly around ideas of time differ-ence which, in texts such as those of Lord Avebury, assign human societies to a progressive (or regressive) time-scale. Clifford's attack on ethnography's relegation of other cultures to a 'present-becoming-past'[34] has a direct rele-vance to the issue of literacy which creates historical narrative. 'Illiteracy', the lack or absence of writing, indicates a lack of time consciousness, an occupation of the blank and negative space outside or before history. The diagnosis of 'illiteracy' upon another society points directly towards a 'scrip-tocentric' world view which marks a state of 'orality' as a state of nature.[35] In a typically imperialist move, to bring literacy to another society is to impose a radically other way of being and of *seeing* the world – just as to write about another culture is to inscribe an imposed narrative order.

The vital links between writing and the visual imagination (to write is, literally, to *see*, to provide a *scopic* representation[36]) have particular signifi-cance for ethnographic practice. Oral or 'traditional' cultures offer them-selves up for visual de-coding in the drama of landscape and environment; in the visibility of bodies and faces; in the contours of masks and art forms (all of which are 'scenes' recurring in *A Bend in the River* and in *A View of Sierra Leone*). Michel de Certeau outlines the collaboration of writing and visual interpretation in his reading of Jean de Léry's ethnological text, *Histoire d'un voyage faict en la terre du Brésil* (1578). Here, it is the physical bodies of native women, devoured by the ethnographic eye, offered up to revealed 'knowl-edge', which represent the aim of ethnology's uncoverings and discoveries:

> From this labor, the women naked, seen and known designate the finished product metonymically. They indicate a new, scriptural relation with the world; they are the effect of a knowledge which 'tramples' and travels over the earth visually in order to fabricate its representation.[37]

This trampling, travelling knowledge, creating revelations through ocular penetration, effectively yokes together an ideology of space and distance with that of the violent incursion of visual representation. This mapping of the world through relentless movement has a direct relationship with the imagining of time, a significant aspect of the modernity which ethnology represents. Indar's comments, in *A Bend in the River*, provide a metaphorical reading of this link between travel and time, and the continual erosion of the specificity of other places and other times. The will to create an interchange-ability of world spaces under a unitary, literate discourse of 'homogeneous, empty time'[38] has its figurative location in the image of the aeroplane:

But the airplane is a wonderful thing. You are still in one place when you arrive at the other. . . . You can go back many times to the same place. And something strange happens if you go back often enough. You stop grieving for the past. . . . You trample on the past, you crush it. . . . In the end you are just walking on ground. That is the way we have to learn to live now.

(pp. 112–13)

This 'learning to live' within the narrative of modernity is achieved through a learning to *read* the other through the language of history. De Certeau's analysis of the writing of history is directly relevant to this objectification of an other's reality, to be absorbed as raw material into historical and ethnographic discourse:

> Modern medicine and historiography are born almost simultaneously from the rift betwen a subject that is supposedly literate, and an object that is supposedly written in an unknown language. The latter always remains to be decoded. These two 'heterologies' (discourses on the other) are built upon a division between the body of knowledge that utters a discourse and the mute body that nourishes it.[39]

Representing the other is, then, analogous to representing events and objects within time; it is a substitution of 'the obscurity of the lived body with the expression of a "will to know" or a "will to dominate" the body' (p. 6). As the past becomes a 'form of knowledge' within historiography (p. 5), so the hitherto obscured, unknown body of the other, fixed in a time and space which is neither literate nor modern, is re-inscribed within the comprehensive science of an ethnography. The written text is readable as a metaphor for the object it represents – the encoded body, the native culture, the past. However, this readability is an illusion of its own making. Historical and ethnographic writing simply re-orders the scraps and tatters of other textual references to *create* a supposedly adequate object *beyond* the text, which is retrospectively and remotely awarded an intelligible sequence and order:

> History is developed in the continuity of signs left by scriptural activities: it is satisfied with arranging them, composing a single text from the thousands of written fragments in which already expressed is that labor which constructs time, which creates consciousness of time through self-reflection.

(p. 210)

If 'consciousness of time' is a constructed fiction, born of the knowledge which it makes intelligible, the unreadability of that knowledge (its obscurity, its *mystery*) threatens the mastery of modernity's comprehensive present.

20

The constant, imperialistic activity to heal the 'rift in time' (p. 213) which an unwritten culture threatens to perpetuate, makes the expansionism of writing utterly opposed to the differential temporality of the voice. Orality lives in the local, temporal space of the moment, securely attached to the immediacy of presence and constantly subject to the creativity of change. Belonging to the tremulous nature of memory, improvisation, collective re-fashioning, the voice opposes the fixity and authority of literacy. This interpretation of the gap between writing and speech does, however, rigidify the oppressiveness of writing as an absolute intransigence, as a monologism which cannot lend itself to other readings. If this were the case, how would the witty subversion of ethnographic subjects, the knowing intertextual references of literary texts or the unconscious gestures towards other voices within historical writing be read? Close attention to writing's irreducible polyvocality allows a critical space for resistance to the surface empiricism of writing. In addition, the identity between speech and presence is not absolute. Orality contains its own structures, its own rhetorical devices. It does not provide a direct, transparent representation of a world of objects beyond itself. The break between speech and text can be more usefully read, not simply as a break between fluid transparency and recalcitrance, but as a rupture between one signifying culture and another. This rupture can become a more effective and less evaluative continuum by breaking down the primacy of voyeuristic images in ethnographic writing. Clifford, for example, argues against the dominance of the ravaging textual gaze and urges a move towards interpretations which draw their modes of representation more fervently from the oral world:

> Once cultures are no longer prefigured visually – as objects, theaters, texts – it becomes possible to think of a cultural poetics that is an interplay of voices, of positioned utterances.[40]

His question, 'But what of the ethnographic ear?', is a pertinent reminder of the familiar predominance of scopic images of other worlds, which forbids the possibility of dialogic encounter.

Competing representations: 'African' literatures

How do these analyses enhance or condition a practice of reading African texts, or texts about Africa? Reading Joyce Cary's *Mister Johnson* (1939) and Chinua Achebe's *Things Fall Apart* (1958), it is possible to analyse them as explorations of the rifts and continuities between oral and literate worlds, and as interpretations of African societies which perform contesting and contested intertextual and *intra*-textual evaluations. As figurative, fictional texts which engage with articulations of colonial structures of knowledge and confrontation, they open themselves to readings which echo the preoccupations of colonial anthropologies, the alternative realities of pre-colonial cultures, and the surplus meanings resisting the absolutism of cultural translation.

Achebe's *Things Fall Apart* performs a competing literary dialogue with Cary's *Mister Johnson* over the representation of Nigerian societies and colonial authority.[41] The haunting of the later text by Cary's novel allows *Things Fall Apart* to be read as a *counter-discourse*, or as an oppositional refiguration of the previous text's ethnographic imagination. Whereas *A Bend in the River* writes itself within the uncertain predicates of a displaced and distanced consciousness, situating its narrative voice *self-consciously* within the preoccupations of European historical understanding, Achebe's novel creates an alternative realism *outside* these predicates. The self-conscious intertextuality of *Things Fall Apart* emerges from its signification *within* an already described and interpreted African consciousness which, in turn, interprets and distantiates European colonialism. The relevance of a Western history of literacy and ethnography, and an acknowledgement of its greater representational *power*, which is a primary condition for the novel's oppositional voice, is indicated at the novel's close. The final sentence refers to an ethnographic text which will be written by the new and alien District Commissioner, whose voice in the concluding chapter takes on a sudden ironic authority. The premeditated text, *The Pacification of the Primitive Tribes of the Lower Niger*,[42] allows the preceding narrative to be read directly against colonial anthropology, whose textual authority provides an ambiguous counterpart to the novel's own literary voice. The meaning of 'Pacification' has now to be read within the alternative evidence of a narrative of colonial violence, while the obvious relevance of 'the lower Niger' to a fixed colonial mapping of African peoples has to compete with earlier, local spatial configurations.

The consistent understanding of land and space as an interpretation of time allows the novel to present an entirely self-sufficient view of oral culture. Time is measured by the demands of an agricultural environment, where seasonal weather determines the cyclical order of history. In this way, the space of the past is not fixed and disjointed from the living present of physical and moral being, but death itself exists within the time and place of the present (p. 85). The prevalence of orality within Achebe's written narrative emerges repeatedly as a telling of history, and as an interpretation of other cultures (p. 51). The complexity of oral communication and its centrality in the Ibo order of life is frequently emphasised through the abstract logic of proverbial speech (p. 5), and through the complicated sign system of the drums, which, similar to literacy, defies distance and demands advanced 'reading' skills:

> One of the things every man learned was the . . . esoteric language of the *ekwe*. . . . The wailing of the women would not be heard beyond the village, but the *ekwe* carried the news to all the nine villages and even beyond.
>
> (p. 84)

The relationship between this novel and colonial anthropology is signalled on the back cover of the novel's 1987 edition, which quotes from the journal, *African Affairs*: 'many books and anthropological treaties [sic] have told about the power of religious superstition, but here is one which forcefully but impartially gives us the reasons.' This reading of Achebe's text as a kind of insider's anthropology, or as an apology for African (religious) difference, reveals the prevalence of a certain reception of African texts as cultural information. However, the 'Glossary of Ibo Words and Phrases' at the end of the book, which explains the meaning of words left untranslated in the text, can be read, not simply as an appeal to a non-African world, but as a more local communication between African cultures, ambiguously and unevenly related through literacy and the English language.

The links between *Things Fall Apart* and the earlier *Mister Johnson* are curiously drawn attention to by the quotation from *Black Orpheus* on the back cover of the 1987 edition of *Things Fall Apart*, which positions the novel as a *continuation* of the concerns in Cary's novel rather than as an oppositional departure: 'Not since *Mister Johnson* has a novel about West Africa written in English shown such love and warmth for its subject as this first novel by a young Nigerian author.' This would seem to interpret the character of Okonkwo in direct contiguity with Mister Johnson, as both sympathetic portraits of Nigerian men in colonial times. Cary's *Mister Johnson*, however, occupies a more complicated position in regard to its African subject matter and, similar to colonial anthropology, it offers up various reading strategies and re-interpretations.

In opposition to *Things Fall Apart*, the novel presents itself as a distantiated commentary on subject matter which is both strange and *known*. The status of this knowledge is resolutely colonial, and the narrative is highly implicated in colonial constructions of Africa and racial difference, often presenting competing evaluations. William Boyd's 1985 introduction emphasises the position from which this novel presents its 'knowledge' of African material: 'It takes some genuine form of displacement – either intellectual or spatial or temporal – before one can scrutinize one's home (and its accoutrements and inhabitants) with any real curiosity or objectivity.'[43] That this objectivity is informed by the 'displacement' of colonial anthropology is evident in the way the text presents both Johnson and Nigerian communities as historically and experientially *separate*. Differing analyses of the meaning of 'Africa' compete self-consciously in a narrative which assesses African difference from the viewpoint of a spurious objectivity. The novel opens with an assessment of the appearance of the African women of the region: 'The young women of Fada, in Nigeria, are well known for beauty. They have small, neat features and their backs are not too hollow' (p. 13). The tone of generality in this statement is instantly traduced by the Eurocentricity of the aesthetic values which give it meaning. The 'pale' skin of Bamu, the Fada woman, acts as a contrast to Johnson's skin which is 'as black as a stove'. As 'almost a pure

Negro', Johnson is presented as a comic figure, whose racial characteristics underline his absurdity. Described in terms of an idea of race, where 'Negroness' can be understood on a sliding scale from 'pure' to 'pale', Johnson, as is indicated by his name, is introduced without any reference to regional, cultural or linguistic origins. The description of him as 'a stranger' to Fada, 'not only a stranger by accent, but by colour', allows him to be treated as both exceptional in the narrative *and* typical of Black Africa.

'Africa' as an idea is approached in the novel in a range of contesting ways which can be summarised in three categories: experiential, visual and historical. Each mode of Africa's representation corresponds with aspects of colonial anthropology which finally places temporal interpretation as the most significant assessment of African culture. Johnson, as a partly acculturated, partly educated Nigerian clerk, still possesses an irrepressibly *racial* way of experiencing 'Africa' – his racialised identity being repeatedly addresssed by Celia Rudbeck through his nickname, 'Mr Wog':

> To him Africa is simply perpetual experience, exciting, amusing, alarming, or delightful, which he soaks into himself through all his five senses at once, and produces again in the form of reflections, comments, songs, jokes, all in the pure Johnsonian form.
>
> (p. 103)

The possibility here of poetic or intellectual creativity is undermined by an insistent reference to natural impulse: 'Like a horse or a rose tree, he can turn the crudest and simplest form of fodder into beauty and power of his own quality' (p. 103).

This notion of 'perpetual experience' is one which informs, not only Johnson's relationship with 'Africa', but also his relationship with the idea of civilisation. For Johnson, 'civilization' is 'a feeling, more than a vision' (p. 95), which he cannot distinguish from physical sensation. His 'knowledge' of the meaning of Rudbeck's road, for example, the construction of which Johnson himself is more than intrumental in completing, is described, not as a noetic concept, but as a sensual appreciation which ties him irreducibly to the vibrancy of landscape and natural life:

> He does not need to think, 'Rudbeck's road, the great, the glorious, the wonder of the world, is about to be finished and I have helped to finish it.' He knows it in every muscle. It is there all the time, part of the music, the shouts, the shining sweaty backs and their rhythmic muscles, the yelling songs, the triumphant, intoxicating drums, the blue smoke of the fires, the trees toppling and crashing like cliffs, the suddenly exposed sky.
>
> (p. 178)

This vital connection between physicality and world view is consistently related to a differential experience of temporality. The novel is written in the present tense, a style which is defended by Joyce Cary as one which reflects Johnson's own understanding of time: 'it was chosen because Johnson lives in the present, from hour to hour' (Preface, p. 9). This inability to live within linear, historical time, allows Johnson to be characterised as unable to comprehend the link between cause and effect, or to have an intelligent sense of purpose or responsibility for his actions. This, the narrative claims, is not an exclusive quality of Johnson's character, but it is a general West African trait. The dancers at Johnson's party, for example, are described as sub-humanly merged into the frantic present of African musical time, where individuality becomes lost in the common abandonment to the rhythm of drums. They are at once aligned to inanimate, natural material and to the uncontrolled group expressiveness of animals and the supernatural world:

> A dozen or so barrack girls, who begin to scream like horses . . . the demoniac appearance of the naked dancers, grinning, shrieking, scowling, or with faces which seem entirely dislocated, senseless, and inhuman, like twisted bags of lard, or burst bladders.
>
> (p. 153)

A constitutional inability to understand the meaning of empire, patriotism and national belonging is also presented as a component of this general confusion of the immediate force and emotion of present time with spatial or racial distinctions. Johnson's musical improvisation on the theme of Englishness at a party encourages all the African guests to respond sensually to what are merely imagined desires, born out of an intense physical experience of rhythm:

> 'King', 'home', 'England', 'royal' are heard. Everybody is excited by the idea of patriotism. Every now and then, as Johnson walks among his guests, he makes a few dance steps, and sings through his nose, 'England is my country, dat King of England is my king'.

> An old Yoruba trader in the corner, very drunk, with an English cloth cap on his head, sings the chorus with Johnson, and utters loud sobs. God knows what the word 'England' means to him.
>
> (pp. 40, 41)

These sensual experiences of political and historical concepts are designated as peculiarly *African* qualities through their constant opposition to British expatriate ways of *seeing* Africa. Against Johnson's sense of Africa as continuous affect, Celia Rudbeck, the English wife of Fada's colonial administrator, 'knows Africa' (p. 102) as a distant and static *vision*. 'Africa' is something to be *seen* in its fixedness, and to be understood through a tourist imagination:

> But to Celia Africa is simply a number of disconnected events which have no meaning for her at all. . . . She doesn't really see either woman or pot, but only a scene in Africa. Even Mr Wog is to her a scene in Africa.
>
> (p. 103)

This point of view is presented as a particularly *feminine* interpretation of scenes which demand deeper political and sociological knowledge, the kind of knowledge which Celia, as a woman, cannot be expected to possess: 'Questions like these, about institutions, politics, government generally, have for Celia nothing to do with truth, but only with a set of ideas' (p. 110).

Against this 'humorously' inept form of feminine superficiality, which privileges the visual without any aid from *historical* knowledge, the text claims to present an accurate analysis of Fada village, which benefits from an entrenched sense of linear historical time *as well as* the primacy of sight. Celia's vision is presented as one which is damaged by prior information from ethnographic tourism, which interprets African scenery as *ideal* and unique, rather than depraved:

> But to Celia it is simply a native town. It has been labelled for her, in a dozen magazines and snapshots, long before she comes to it. Therefore she does not see it at all. She does not see the truth of its real being, but the romance of her ideas, and it seems to her like the house of the unspoilt primitive, the simple dwelling-place of unsophisticated virtue.
>
> (p. 111)

The home of the 'noble savage', living within a separate and self-sufficient time and space (this idea representing one ideological branch of Western anthropology), has to make way for an ideology of underdevelopment, based on an idea of galloping, accumulating time, which has to be universally applicable. In this 'superior' ethnographic analysis, Fada demands colonial intervention:

> Fada is the ordinary native town of the Western Sudan. . . . It is a dwelling-place at one stage from the rabbit warren or the badger burrow; and not so cleanly kept as the latter. . . . Poverty and ignorance, the absolute government of jealous savages, conservative as only the savage can be, have kept it at the first frontier of civilization. Its people would not know the change if time jumped back fifty thousand years.
>
> (p. 110)

This attack on Fada as a place unworthy of human consideration achieves its force from an interpretation which privileges historical time. *Things Fall Apart* directly counters this view of temporality with its own alternative vision of oral history, the cyclical time of agriculture and the influence of an ancestral past, all of which contribute to human and moral order. The role of orature as a distinct and complex cultural and intellectual activity is radically demoted, in *Mister Johnson* to another, earlier historical moment. Interestingly, orality, presented in *Things Fall Apart* in terms of the skill and dexterity of proverbs ('Among the Ibo the art of conversation is regarded very highly, and proverbs are the palm-oil with which words are eaten' (p. 5)) is, in *Mister Johnson*, related to an era which has been passed in English history, yet which is still being experienced in the colonies:

> a Fada man, like most primitives, looks upon the making of free verse as part of ordinary conversation, and, like an Elizabethan or an Irishman, uses the most poetical expression even in casual talk by the road.
>
> (p. 150)

The battle over knowledge and the meaning of civilisation takes place most significantly over the issue of literacy, and the cognitive capacities which it demands and creates. Johnson, although semi-literate, maintains a sensual relationship with writing, which responds to the written word, not as a conveyor of meaning from one time to another, but as an immediate, tactile activity. Engaged in copying an assessment report, Johnson becomes completely distracted by the letter 'S':

> He frequently practises S's alone for half an hour on end. . . . It is beautiful. The thickening of the stroke as it turns over the small loop makes a sensation. He feels it like a jump of joy inside him. But the grand sweep, the smooth, powerful broadening of the lower stroke is almost too rich to be borne. He gives a hop in his chair . . . and licks his lips as if he is tasting a good thing.
>
> (pp. 24–5)

This rapturous concentration on the intense presence of the act of writing serves to exclude any ability to read meaningfully. For Johnson, writing is creative, not intelligible, and arithmetic merely brings him repeatedly to his favourite number, five, 'because he likes writing fives' (p. 60).

As with Migeod's text describing the 'natives' of Sierra Leone, the narrative of *Mister Johnson* attests to the powerlessness of the clerk, enraptured with the domination of Empire and unable to comprehend the meaning of its domination. However, Johnson 'inadvertently' embezzles money for Rudbeck's road and for himself, stages a robbery and kills the violent White racist, Gollup. This gap between textual interpretation and narrative fact allows for another reading of Johnson, informed from the re-reading of Migeod's ethnography and Achebe's novel. Reading resistance into Johnson's motivations, rather than contingency or idiocy, it is possible to provide another form of cultural translation. Reading a moment in the novel where Johnson acts as translator between his wife, Bamu, and Celia Rudbeck, his position as mediator can be re-interpreted as one of control. If translation serves a powerful role in the interpretation of cultures, Johnson's position *between* empire and native is more ambivalent and subversive than the narrative expressly allows. Bamu, largely intransigent to psychological analysis, and presented as having no emotional connection with Johnson outside of his imagination, refuses to wear 'mission' dress for her meeting with Celia and defiantly resists Celia's invitations: 'I don't like tea. Is she going away now?' Johnson, however, by allowing Celia to hear an alternative version of Bamu's answers, 'She says to tank you mam, too much, she proud to be you frien' (p. 108), perpetuates Celia's manipulation by her own idea of 'marvellous Africa' (p. 102). The humour in the novel is, then, an unstable and uncertain narrative strategy. It cannot always be absolutely determined against whom the joke is aimed. Johnson's language throughout the novel is, however, presented as a kind of immature chatter, which is akin to a simplified form of creolised English. (This is a more advanced speech than the type of *sub*- or non-language which emanates from Sozi.) It is left unclear from which language Johnson translates when he speaks with Bamu and Celia, and his position as a stranger in Fada does not seem to limit his ability to communicate fluently with *all* African indigenous peoples.[44]

The ending of the novel with Johnson's death for the murder of Sergeant Gollup can be read as more than a defeat and an annihilation of native wit and slyness. Johnson's insistence to Rudbeck that he himself perform the execution forces a form of active recognition between Rudbeck and Johnson which is manifestly absent earlier in the text: 'Rudbeck, not very good at distinguishing one black face from another, or remembering them, stares at the boy. . . . "Why, it's thingummy-tite, aren't you?".' This non-recognition of the 'native' other as individually distinct is successfully reversed by Johnson's manipulation of Rudbeck into a personal and not an institutional killing, an act which forces Rudbeck to disobey colonial law. The weight of this confrontation between Johnson and Rudbeck, which is engineered by Johnson in an ironic reversal of colonial power relations, creates a responsibility for Rudbeck from which he is unable to escape, the threatening logic of which is contained in Johnson's ambiguous and ironic appeal:

'Ony I like you do him yousef, sah. If you no fit to shoot me. I don' 'gree for dem sergeant do it, too much. He no my frien'. But you my frien'. You my father and my mother. I tink you hang me yousef'.

(p. 247)

This reading of ambivalence into *Mister Johnson* is possible only through engagement with a range of other texts and cultural interpretations. The novel, far from existing within a fictional vacuum, makes use of cultural representations from within a colonial imaginary, which allows the text to be read in a certain way. Joyce Cary himself writes as an erstwhile colonialist where he came into contact with 'native' life.[45] Christopher Miller's insistence that, in matters African, 'representation can no longer be assumed to be transparent and monological'[46] argues for textual readings which re-examine narrative as intertextually and historically located. The challenge of reading texts which deal with African cultural material and its knowledge is caught up with the exigency of reading other anthropological, literary and historical texts which construct the codes and framework for this knowledge. Miller makes a significant point when he approaches the issue of cultural translation as a manifestly hybridised project: 'Rather my desire is to blend disciplines together in a hybrid approach befitting the complexity of cultural questions in Africa and their translation into Western understanding.'[47]

This rather sharp distinction between 'the West' and 'Africa', which has been interrogated through the reading of Naipaul's *East* Indian/African protagonist, is dramatically complicated by colonial histories of contact and contamination. 'Africa', as an object of Knowledge, is already irrevocably damaged, already entered and changed by Western influence. Johnson, far from being the unadulterated native African in confrontation with a radically other Western culture, has already received some English education, literacy and acculturation, which affords him his ambivalent and possibly subversive position. Okonkwo's mistake is his inability to recognise this change in the other villagers of Umuofia. This colonial 'interference in African systems' (p. 14) leads to the further complication that anthropology itself is an integral part of that Western interference. Miller tries to confront this 'epistemological paradox' (p. 21) quite simply by embracing it. 'Africa', already 'invented' by Western systems of control and yet resisting any total interpretation, can only be approached through 'impure' modes of analysis, which refuse both absolute self-reflexivity and a totalised notion of difference.

Henry Louis Gates' dismissal of, what he calls, the 'anthropology fallacy',[48] refers, particularly, to the repeated and long-standing habit of shunting African literatures into a space outside art and literary figuration and into sociological data. In re-applying the use of 'anthropology', certain resonances within African texts, belonging to traditions and metaphors outside the 'canon' of literary theory, may, usefully, be incorporated into more sensitive readings of *literary* signification. The danger centres around the problems of anthropology itself, and its tendency towards a holistic vision of Africa as one internally coherent and systematic – or spiritual – difference. Gates' significant contention against Black and African texts being read only as windows directly onto social reality, needing no artistic or imaginative mediation, needs to be approached at a tangent from the acceptance of Black

African literatures needing identical reading strategies to those *already formulated* by the academy. Gates' insistence that theoretical complexity should not be denied Black/African texts (p. 6), that they demand to be read on a range of levels, needs to be balanced against (and not necessarily at odds with) Anthony Appiah's statement against the grandiose authority of Western theory:

> there is surely something appealing in the notion of African theories for African texts . . . contemporary theory has often sponsored techniques of literary interpretation that yield somewhat uniform results. Our modern theories are too powerful, prove too much.[49]

Homi Bhabha provides a more precise reading of this indictment through his analysis of a tendency within critical theory to present evidence of cultural difference within a fixed picture of other, 'non-Western' cultures, which serve as secure oppositions to, and readable texts for, Western knowledge:

> However impeccably the content of an 'other' culture may be known, however anti-ethnocentrically it is represented, it is its *location* as the closure of grand theories, the demand that, in analytic terms, it be always the good object of knowledge, the docile body of difference, that reproduces a relation of domination and is the most serious indictment of the institutional powers of critical theory.[50]

Ambiguous identity: Islam and exile

Miller's idea of a 'surrender to that paradox' of African hybridity and ethnographical compromise, can be explored through a reading of Cheikh Hamidou Kane's novel, *Ambiguous Adventure* (originally published in French as *L'Aventure ambiguë* in 1962), a passage of which is discussed by Miller to illustrate the relationship between tropes within and history outside the text.[51] Miller uses a passage describing the face of the Most Royal Lady in order to confront literary criticism with anthropological knowledge. I would like to provide a reading of the novel as a whole in order to discuss, not only the location of this text within histories of French colonialism and resistance, but also the ways in which the novel dramatises difference and otherness. The novel at once seeks to entrench an idea of African difference and to demonstrate the ambivalence of this notion. Both the 'West' and 'Africa' are presented as radically encroaching on each other, in ways which disallow the simplicity of choice, the clarity of confrontation and any unsullied connection to origins.

The discourse of the novel is balanced between an authorial voice[52] and the developing consciousness of the main character, Samba Diallo. The narrative voice adds an illustrative dimension to the text, placing the psychological and spiritual aspects of Samba's consciousness within a larger historical frame-work. This context is a generalised overview of colonial conquest in Black Africa, referred to most directly in Chapter 5:

> The entire black continent had had its moment of clamor. . . . The morning of the Occident in black Africa was spangled over with smiles.[53]

This allegorical reference to colonial history in Africa serves as an ethical and interpretive background to the individual psyche of Samba Diallo.[54] In this way, Samba's specific experiences and private torments are given a symbolic status, as historically *typical* and collective African experiences of colonialism. The novel, set in colonial Senegal, providing an allegorical discussion of French colonialism within the specific 'Diallobé country' (p. 12) comes to represent the wider contextual and historical dimension of colonial Black Africa.

Ambiguous Adventure opens with a description of intense physical suffering, which is fused into a complex texture of love, spiritual exhilaration and ulti-mate subordination. The 'martyrdom' (p. 4) of Samba Diallo to the tenets of Islam is sustained, throughout the novel, as an inheritance fundamental to his identity as a member of the Diallobé and, more significantly, to his identity as an African. What are called 'the values of death' (p. 27) within Islam become the values of an African spirituality at odds with Western technologi-cal civilisation, and they create a further metaphorical link between notions of a dying civilisation, the superseded demands of dead ancestors and the exi-gencies of sacrifice in the face of colonialist destruction.

What is both curious and deeply moving about the novel is precisely this tropic collusion of Islam as Truth with the crisis that challenges this. In other words, it becomes impossible to extricate a reading of the deepest philo-sophical or theological Truths of Islam from the tragedy of Africa's colonisa-tion. Further to this, Islam itself represents a previous colonisation which forms a controlling layer over another, subdued 'Africa' beneath. What emerges within the text is a profound ambiguity around the stated fusion of African difference or Diallobé culture with Islam, and the status of 'absolute' human values or Islamic Truth in a terrain irrevocably formed and compli-cated by French philosophy and colonial culture.

The equivocation between the inheritance of aristocratic Diallobé culture and the inheritance of Islam, both dramatised as utterly non-Western, is illu-strated in the constant evocation of a pre-colonial past which is uneasily reconciled to Islam. For example, Samba Diallo's Night of the Koran is described in terms which insist on a historical and yet naturalised bond between Islam and the patriarchal descent of the Diallobé aristocracy, both united in the threat and celebration of death:

This scintillation of the heavens above his head, was it not the star-studded bolt being drawn upon an epoch that had run its course?

For a long time, in the night, his voice was that of the voiceless phantoms of his ancestors, whom he had raised up.

(pp. 72, 73)

What I have called the 'reconciliation' of the Diallobé to Islam, and yet the almost cosmic identification between the two, allows the novel to examine colonialism both as a fatal clash of two value systems, contingent upon history, and as a deeply disruptive collision between two fundamentally opposed metaphysics. The 'ambiguous adventure' which frames the novel is both physical and spiritual; individual and collective. Samba Diallo's initial exile from his father's house to the Muslim teacher's hearth is followed by his exile to the French colonial school and, later, to Paris. This journey is charted as a movement from the expansive, self-denying spirituality of Islam, described in terms of the immediacy and limitlessness of the voice, to a confrontation with objects, reflections, surfaces. From Samba's Night of the Koran, where 'In the humming sound of his voice there was being dissolved, bit by bit, a being who a few moments ago had still been Samba Diallo' (p. 72), Samba comes to recognise his new allegiance to textual signification and representation. Learning French at the colonial school, Samba begins a *written* communication with his father, which introduces a materialism fixed on the priority of sight and separated from the immediacy of thought:

This was to demonstrate my new knowledge and also, by keeping my gaze fixed on him while he was reading, to establish the fact that with my new tool I should be able to transmit my thought to him without opening my mouth.

(p. 159)

This fixing of the gaze from the son to the father in a kind of telepathic scenario emphasises the use of a new power which resists the living tremour of the voice for the intransigence and timelessness of writing. This move from oral to scopic signification indicates a new relationship to representation and the word. Samba's communion with the Word of Allah in *pre*-literate years reveals the sufficiency of the moment of 'repeating the Word' (p. 4). The accurate repetition of God's Word through speech cancels any linear apprehension of time in favour of the totalisation of the moment: 'He contained within himself the totality of the world, the visible and the invisible, its past and its future' (p. 5).

Islam's insistence on recitation and the oral performance of Koranic Truth contrasts strikingly with the silence and visual orientation of literate communication. The interpretation of 'thought' here undergoes an important transformation from instant oral improvisation to the delay incurred in writing. 'Thought' moves from immediacy to history in a way which changes the inter-action of father and son. Samba's insistence on controlling the written exchange with his father through the supervision of his gaze allows a temporal distantiation between the two which, similar to an ethnographic scene, is manipulated by the projection of watcher and writer. Writing operates as a 'tool' which separates the moment of writing from its destination. Here, before Samba's move to Paris, physical proximity and temporal dislocation are allowed to experimentally overlap. The intensity of Samba's gaze has an echo in the moment of confrontation between M. Lacroix (representing the incursion of 'the West') and the Knight of the Diallobé. Here, the Knight's sonorous voice, occupying the darkness of the space between himself and the Frenchman, is perceived as an incorporeal being, which cannot be fixed and studied (evidenced) by sight:

> He would have liked to scrutinize the shadowed face of this motion-less man who sat opposite him. In his voice he perceived a tonality which intrigued him, and which he would have liked to relate to the expression of his face.
>
> (p. 79)

Interestingly, Islam represents an intermediate stage between orality and literacy. The Word of Allah is memorised from written Arabic, understood as fixed and eternal. the Word lives in the endurance of memory, caught in the finitude of the body, a living manifestation which cannot endure beyond corporeal delivery, and yet claims its legitimacy beyond the temporality of life. Islam, in the novel, represents the temporary unity of body and spirit, conquered by the eternal spirituality of death.

The journey from spirituality to materialism, or from the infinity of death to the mechanisms of life, is also described in the Fool's discussion of his trip to Paris, where his confrontation with the terrible objectification of his own body brings on a powerfully physical revulsion:

> My legs were soft and trembling under me. I had a great desire to sit down. Around me, the stone floor was spread out like a brilliant mirror of sound that echoed the clattering of men's shoes.
>
> (p. 89)

This assault of surfaces, mirrors and echoes becomes, for the purposes of the novel, the basis of Western civilisation, which exiles human experience from what Marc, in a later chapter, calls 'the intimate heart of a thing' (p. 151). 'Western civilisation' is consistently represented in the novel as French metro-politan culture. That Paris should become a metonym for the West in this text is historically contextualised by the French colonisation of Senegal, which itself stands as a metonymic signification of 'Africa'. The concentration on the materiality of Paris becomes aligned with the onslaught of literacy in 'the West' through the issue of visibility. M. Lacroix, for example, is criticised for his 'Western' ideas by the Knight in these words: 'What you do not see does not exist' (p. 80).

Samba Diallo becomes a complex layering of identities which are ascribed to his position as an heir to the Diallobé, as a Muslim and as an African acculturated into French values and ideas. The historical accumulation of these identities, from the familial, aristocratic order of the Diallobé to French acculturation, are no longer clearly distinguishable. Just as Islam has become a fundamental aspect of the organisation of Diallobé aristocracy and its values, so Samba's understanding of himself as 'African' is crucially informed by his absorption of French colonial education. In addition, the discussion of what Lucienne, a White *parisienne*, calls 'Negroness' (p. 141) moves the ascription of difference from a historical, cultural or religious contingency to something more profound. Adèle, a Parisienne of Black Caribbean descent is immediately attuned to Samba's feeling of exile. Although born in France, her intuitive communion with Samba is allowed to be aligned to a form of racial memory or being – a *Négritude*:

> When she happened to discern in herself a feeling or a thought which seemed to her to cut in a certain fashion into the backdrop of the Occident, her reaction for a long time had been to run away from it in terror, as from a monstrosity.
>
> (p. 157)

The 'ambiguity' in the novel's title can be attributed both to Samba's colonised identity and to the impossibility of separating a critique of the West, signified through French culture, from its incorporation into and exploration of an Africa which is presented in opposition to Western influence. The existence of 'a non-Western universe' (p. 156) is, for Samba, in the country of the Diallobé, in which, however, Samba Diallo's father tells Lacroix, an occupying Frenchman, that: 'The era of separate destinies has run its course' (p. 79). Not only is the world 'becoming westernized' (p. 69) and so, in an unequal way, somehow united, its separation was itself an arbitrary, not *natural* occurrence. As Samba Diallo puts it:

> I don't think that the difference exists in nature. . . . I believe that it is artificial, accidental. Only, the artifice has grown stronger with time, covering up what is of nature.
>
> (pp. 152–3)

This emphasis on 'artifice' points to the historical problem which haunts the novel. Unable to determine the meaning or constitution of 'African difference' outside the predicates of French colonial interest, the idea of antagonism and opposition can only operate within the predicates of French modernity. This historical reference within the form of the novel reflects Miller's reading of the issue of 'otherness': ' "Africa" and "the West" ceased to be reified opposites, they entered a hall of mirrors in which cultural codes play off each other, corrupt each other, and enrich each other.'[55]

Samba increasingly analyses himself and his position in the world with reference to the *different* philosophical underpinnings of French modernity. These underpinnings rely on the profanity of a literacy which is not an eternally fixed origin (unlike the Koran) and on the materiality of science: 'Your science is the triumph of evidence, a proliferation of the surface' (p. 78). Caught as it is in what becomes a despairing equivocation between French modernity and African self-understanding, unable, in the postcolonial world, to separate itself from the French (Parisian) culture on which it is so poignantly focused, the text posits a point of no return for the African world. Resistance, as well as existence, has become, to use Edward Said's term, a contrapuntal theme.[56] As Samba Diallo claims:

> I am not a distinct country of the Diallobé facing a distinct Occident, and appreciating with a cool head what I must take from it and what I must leave with it by way of counterbalance. I have become the two. There is not a clear mind deciding between the two factors of a choice. There is a strange nature, in distress over not being two.
>
> (pp. 150–1)

The final chapter of *Ambiguous Adventure* presents what can be the only solution to Samba's exile in the form of an ultimate return to sources. In a passionate staging of the voice, which announces a continuous arrival to the 'moment which endures' (p. 177), the metaphors within the text are sustained. The move away from crushing objectivity, spiritual confinement and the time-lag between written and oral expression involves a re-entry into the values and the reality of death. Death emerges as a celebrative instance, promising the only resolution to the pain of ambiguity, but, in its reconciliation of self with the heart of Being, it is an annihilation.

I have read the novel, concentrating on its codification, both implicit and explicit, of the difference between cultures. Samba Diallo is both ethnographer and native subject, the text performing its own self-conscious interlocution between Senegal and Paris, and remaining irrevocably caught between the two, able, finally, to resolve its differences through the performance of its own dissolution.

These narratives, which explore the confrontation of colonial domination with indigenous social order, through a particular African protagonist, provide strikingly similar interpretations of the insupportability of this cultural double-bind, where a simple choice between two monoliths – 'the West' and

'Africa' – are no longer possible. The fact that the conditions for *thinking* this choice are also the very conditions which create the ambiguity and nostalgia that profoundly complicate it produce the pain and sorrow of *Things Fall Apart* and *Ambiguous Adventure*, as well as the intended comedy of *Mister Johnson*.

The politics of resistance: cultural nationalisms

The arguments of Ngũgĩ Wa Thiong'o attempt to address the nihilism in these textual conclusions, arguing insistently against what the Knight of the Diallobé envisages as the inevitable universalisation of culture through Western modernity.[57] Ngũgĩ writes within a commitment to the ongoing struggle for economic, linguistic and social self-determination by African peoples. For Ngũgĩ, literary creativity as well as literary criticism is irrevocably caught in issues of representation and power which forces any discussion of 'African literature' into an examination of colonial domination. Ngũgĩ's discussion of the problems which emerged from the Ugandan conference of 1962, 'A Conference of African Writers of English Expression', approaches the question of what constitutes African identity, and African literature. The debate about the African-ness of African literature which the conference foregrounded are summarised in this way:

> Was it literature about Africa or about the African experience? Was it literature written by Africans? What about a non-African who wrote about Africa: did his work qualify as African literature? What if an African set his work in Greenland . . . were African languages the criteria? . . . What about French and English, which had become African languages? What if an European wrote about Europe in an African language?[58]

In terms of Miller's argument – that theoretical approaches to literature may not be simply generalisable but need to be checked by other traditions echoing in or forming the text – the difficulties of finding or pinning down these other traditions becomes apparent here.

Ngũgĩ's statement, 'If . . . if . . . if . . . this or that, except the issue: the domination of our languages and cultures by those of imperialist Europe' (p. 6), focuses on what he sees as the crux of the issue for African literature. African languages and cultures are placed at the centre of African literary criticism precisely because these have been and are at the point of attack and displacement in the imperialist confrontation between Europe and Africa. In both *Decolonising the Mind* and *Moving the Centre*, Ngũgĩ associates language very closely with culture so that the two almost work on an axis of interchangeability. Both language and culture are the blueprints of identity and value for a nation or a people, leading Ngũgĩ to assert that: 'Language as culture is the collective memory bank of a people's experience in history' (p. 15).

Although conceding that culture is like a constantly moving river, 'It is like studying a river in its very movement, that is in its very being as a river',[59] it is also an organic whole – a slowly mutating but particular identity in itself: 'In this sense society is like a human body which develops as a result of the internal working out of all its cells and other biological processes' (p. xv).

In a sense, then, Ngũgĩ can accept flux and change within and communication between cultures on the basis of significant, discrete identities. The 'gift' of European languages to African cultures, because performed as an act of domination, not reciprocity, results in a non-African literature which hovers uneasily between Europe and Africa. After thrusting aside any engagement with the long quarrel over the (proper) constitution of African literature, Ngũgĩ unavoidably enters the fray. African literature written in French, English or Portuguese, for example, is *not African* literature, but 'Afro-European literature' (*Decolonising the Mind*, p. 27). What is African is located in what has become 'traditional' African culture, carried and understood through indigenous languages. This neat resolution of the problem of definition by reference to the (continuing) history of cultural imperialism does not, of course, end there. If 'Africa' is located in the (largely oral) histories of African languages, then issues of literacy, audience and the plurality of the modern world would seem to place insurmountable obstacles in the path of Ngũgĩ's protest for African literature. Ngũgĩ's struggle, however, is mounted precisely at this point of contention between what is often labelled the 'traditional' and the 'modern'. If the modern world is the technological economy of literate societies, it becomes necessary for Africa to also take its place within the structures of modernity. If there is a critical debate within and about literature, Africa has been denied an equal platform in order to participate on its own cultural, hence linguistic terms. Ngũgĩ disallows the debate to fall into a long lament for an African past *before* Europe and insists instead that Africa take its place *alongside* (rather than behind) Europe in a fair exchange of cultural gifts.

The difficulty in Ngũgĩ's argument is that this 'new', yet 'authentic' Africa becomes authentic and *different* precisely through its incorporation of European literacy (although not European *languages*) and European modernity. To make Africa 'modern' on its own terms appears to be to *create* an artificial authenticity from what are, in fact, diverse cultural materials. In this light, Africa can exist only as what is (claimed or made to be) *different* from, outside or against Europe. This concurs with the implications in Jean-Paul Sartre's statement on revolutionary action in the preface to *The Wretched of the Earth*: 'We only become what we are by the radical and deep-seated refusal of that which others have made of us.'[60] Ngũgĩ's struggle to claim a place for African literatures in a longed-for world centred on a multiplicity of different cultures is as much an argument for retaining the tension of those boundaries which create Africa's otherness – without which the refusal of Western incursion cannot take place – as it is an argument for communication.

African literary criticism has founded itself on projects of decolonisation and nationalist independence movements. Conferences, journals and books about African literature and criticism increase from the years of African independence from European colonisation. The arguments within these texts reveal a tortured relationship with and resistance to cultural imperialism in such a way that claims of equality interchange with assertions of radical difference. Chinweizu, Jemie and Madubuike's thesis in *Toward the Decolonization of African Literature* provides a self-conscious scrutiny of African identity through literary criticism in terms which both reject and mirror European critical standards. Ngũgĩ's rejection of European languages in the name of African literary decolonisation becomes replaced here with a rejection – not of the English language, nor of the values of English literary criticism per se – but of the hypocritical or ignorant *application* of these values to African literatures. Thus, the sense of reversal or counterattack is limited by and conducted within the institutional terms of English Literature.

In a characteristically direct passage, the bolekaja critics make an unflinching claim for the independence of African literature:

> But African literature *is* an autonomous entity separate and apart from all other literatures. It has its own traditions, models and norms... separate and radically different from that of the European... sometimes altogether antithetical . . . even for those portions of African literature which continue to be written in European languages.[61]

The autonomy and separateness of African literature is here celebrated within an implicit notion of organic unity. Any critical models would, from this passage, be assumed to arise from the internal coherence of the literature itself and its exclusive development. This radical developmental difference is partly explained by a description of its roots in African orature which, when recognised, must place the evaluation of African literatures outside the preoccupations of 'euromodernist criticism' and its 'mutilations' (p. 2). 'Afrocentric' criticism, which the bolekaja critics insist should take the place of the egocentric European assessment of 'the proper, the beautiful, or the well done' (p. 3), must be founded in a sensitive, well-informed interrogation of the *history* of African artistry:

> Furthermore, African orature is important to this enterprise of decolonizing African literature, for the important reason that it is the incontestable reservoir of the values, sensibilities, esthetics, and achievements of traditional African thought and imagination outside our plastic arts. Thus, it must serve as the ultimate foundation, guidepost, and point of departure for a modern liberated African literature.
>
> (p. 2)

The insistence on African orature as the 'historically indisputable core of the canon of African literature' (p. 13) is made, not simply to distance it from the linear narrative of the English literary canon, from which African literature would merely constitute a deviant 'overseas department' (p. 3), but also to assert, rhetorically, a radically different *value system* and *temporality*. What is located in the Eurocentric criticism with which Chinweizu, Jemie and Madubuike take issue is the imposition of a literary time-scale where African novels are assessed according to the traditions of late nineteenth-century European realism (p. 9), and African poetry succeeds or fails against the standards of '20th century European modernism' (p. 3).

In order to counteract and write against this Eurocentric attack on African aesthetic standards, the bolekaja critics fight the claim that African writers have *failed* European literary values and at the same moment substitute these norms and expectations with others that are *naturally in time with* African life.

> the vital nourishment of our African traditions and home soil . . . the vibrancy, gusto and absolute energy of our African oral poetry which is so firmly and deeply rooted in the African home soil.
>
> (p. 3)

This also, by an imperceptible or *natural* move, constitutes 'cultural values' and 'national ethos' (p. 12). By insisting that African literature, as an observable and qualitative object, has its distinctive origins in oral traditions, the bolekaja critics are able to circumvent the contention that African literature springs directly from its European equivalents. Notions of an essential force, occurring naturally within and belonging to Africa, which informs the particularity of African literature, would seem to push the critics' argument into a cultural or even a (racial) biological determinism. What is also significant in Chinweizu *et al.*'s argument is the problem of *time difference* which, alongside an awareness of *distance* between (distinct) cultures, is a central tenet of anthropology. This anxiety and obsession with temporality as an assessment of African culture(s) and literature in the 'ethnophilosophical' texts *about* African literature as well as *in* African literature itself rises out of the history of anthropological writing about other 'cultures' or 'races'.

The cultural essentialism haunting the arguments of the bolekaja critics, where Africa becomes a totalised vision of otherness, summarised in the phrase, 'Africa is simply not the West' (p. 30), is born of the assumptions which structure the studies of colonial anthropology. The critics work within the terms of the English literary values with which they are confronted and this leads them to claim the equal fulfillment of these values in African literatures while demanding that they be assessed by wholly other traditions and aesthetics. Their notion of 'culture' is implicitly a philosophy of racial determinism, which allows their reading of African culture to include the

39

pan-African (or Black) world. In this way, African-ness overreaches itself to become an expression of *national* identity, *racial* identity, political consciousness and heritage, which achieves its only coherence in opposition to the (White) West. The book is dedicated to 'the Black world', but in such a way that African-ness – 'one drop of Black blood' – although essential for inclusion, is subordinated to matters of personal choice and cultural commitment.

The relationship of the beliefs of either Ngũgĩ or the bolekaja critics to racial determinism is complicated. Both parties take race almost for granted in their discussions of African identity, nationalism, cultural consciousness and revolutionary thought, precisely because the 'decolonising' struggle to which the critics link the writing and criticism of African literatures has, particularly from colonial literatures and cultural anthropology, been constructed as a racial one. What are consistently conflated within these texts are 'culture' and 'race' which work together as essentialist terms while allowing a possible disconnection between culture/race and consciousness/ decolonisation; or a lamented fissure between an 'African world' and an 'African world-view'.

In the wake of Fabian's arguments on ethnography, the struggle to read the difference of Africa has repeatedly been framed as a battle between the traditional and the modern world/artist/view. It is this opposition which explicitly informs the crisis of aesthetics and values confronting critics of African texts. Emmanuel Obiechina analyses the distinction between the 'traditional artist' and 'the modern artist' in terms of a duality *within* African society,[62] which has, I would argue, become the expression of a radical confrontation between ('the true') Africa and the (encroaching, eroding) West. The deep and justifiable anxiety which emerges out of a dislocation which is starker and more threatening in contemporary Africa than it is in Britain has led to a radical difference of direction and context for African and European writing. The weight of a visibility and otherness which has been conferred in terms of race and exoticism upon African peoples and cultures has resulted in a literature which – particularly through the medium of European languages – tends towards a self-conscious representation of African people to themselves. Appiah's summary of the split between traditional collaboration and modern individualism – which acts as a tension within African literatures and for African writing – is useful here. He describes it in terms of

> a profound difference between the projects of contemporary European and African writers: a difference I shall summarise for the sake of a slogan, as the difference between the search for the self and the search for a culture.[63]

Appiah appraises the stance of the bolekaja critics in terms of 'cultural nationalism' (p. 96), or 'Nativist nostalgia' (p. 95), which can never extricate itself from its presumed enemy. Chinweizu, Jemie and Madubuike's attack on Western modernity and its assumptions falls, according to Appiah, into the trap of nativist 'culture' where 'Africa' becomes a common denominator of a spiritual, traditional and philosophical consciousness, essentially separate from the time of the West.

It must be said that African or 'Afrocentric' writers and critics have many sides to defend, due to the 'schizophrenic asymmetry' (p. 149) of prejudiced European criticism. The alternative to a call for a specifically *African* literary criticism (with tension still around the term 'Africa') has often been the call for *universal* literary values, where cultural blindness takes the place of and helps to neutralise cultural fear. The annoyance of Chinweizu (*et al.*) at calls for 'universal truths' which act merely as euphemisms for *European* truths is justified.[64]

Rand Bishop's reading of the history of African criticism under the opening question, 'By what standards is African literature to be judged?',[65] quotes a string of European critics in the 1960s whose approach to African literature swung from a defensive call for the universality of literature and humanity, to a disappointed longing for otherness and radical cultural and literary *difference*.[66] Robert P. Armstrong, in his paper for the African Studies Association in Chicago, 1964, is quoted tautologically claiming that the Africanness of African literature is that it is African (p. 1) and that this can be demonstrated, not through national languages, but through 'metaphor, symbol, situation' (p. 1). In the Conference of African Literature and the University Curriculum at Fourah Bay College, Freetown, in 1963, the perennial question, 'What is African Literature?', was again debated, with the accepted definition being voiced by the Canadian critic, T.R.M. Creighton, that 'African literature' is 'any work in which an African setting is authentically handled, or to which experiences which originate in Africa are integral' (p. 21). Cyprian Ekwensi, a year later, claims that African literature is based on African character and psychology:

> This means that the main theme may be anthropological, traditional or modern, but the traits, temperaments and reactions of the characters will be peculiarly African due to influences of tribe, culture and history.[67]

The arguments about language have ranged from Obiajunwa Wali's claim that language *defines* literature[68] to the claim made by Kane, Ezekiel Mphalele and Chinua Achebe that 'African reality' is already 'African' in complex, hybrid ways where, in fact, writing and indigenous languages do not have an equivalent relationship.[69] Given this still complicated terrain around the questions of what constitutes African culture and its connection with literature, the bolekaja critics' summary that a 'judicious exercise of commonsense is what is partly called for' (*Towards the Decolonization of African*

Literature, p. 15) in determining inclusion in 'the canon of African literature' (p. 13) has about it a ring of irony.

African cultures and literatures cannot be pushed idealistically or superstitiously into a place of spiritual isolation beyond and outside Western infiltration for evident historical reasons. The arguments surrounding Africa's 'otherness' are already formed and caught in a syncretic and conflictual struggle with the West, and Africa's over-determination as well as its invisibility is part of that struggle. Gates' resolution of the issue in terms of *Black* texts is an acceptance of their 'double heritage',[70] weaving Black and European traditions together. What is significant about this 'resolution' is that it increases, rather than diminishes, the immense demands of Black texts. By pluralising sources and influences, while not reducing the effects to a polemics of sociological observation, Gates manages to sidestep the dilemma between difference and equality. The relationship between African literatures and cultures is not a perfect mirroring. Reading literature demands a sensitivity to aesthetics and figuration *in addition to* representation. However, modes of signification and reading rely on traditions and values which are also cultural and often in contest.

Ethnophilosophy and the essential Africa

Two texts which come out of the ethnophilosophical genre of writings about Africa are Jahnheinz Jahn's *Muntu* and W.E. Abraham's *The Mind of Africa* (from 1961 and 1962). Both texts confront, in great detail, these issues of plurality within African literature(s) and culture(s). Jahn explores the clash between European influence and traditional Africa by accepting the link between 'modernization' and Europe, but not the conflation of a traditional and a 'real' Africa. For Jahn, contemporary African culture is reaching a crisis of survival whose resolution lies in the creation of 'neo-African culture', a blend of 'modern' Europe with 'traditional' Africa in order to produce 'a modern, viable *African* culture . . . out of the whole'.[71] Evading the fallacy that there ever was *one* traditional African culture, Jahn nevertheless discusses a spiritual or philosophical 'common denominator' of 'African-ness', which, through a process of *development into* history, moves from 'primitive' to 'modern' expression (p. 17). As Wole Soyinka, in *Myth, Literature and the African World*, attempts to express *the* African world-view through *Yoruba* ritual archetypes and social ideologies,[72] Jahn discusses *the* neo-African culture through the 'common denominator' of Bantu philosophy. While disclaiming the idea that culture is *innate* he discusses it as a *spiritual phenomenon* based on rational human understanding, and expressed in the world-view of Bantu tradition, which is characteristic of *all* sub-Saharan Africa. In this way, African authors and artists hold the key to neo-African culture as a unified whole. Crucially for Jahn's argument, this view is based in a dialectical relationship with colonial ethnology, and its foundation *outside* the politics of independence is irrelevant:

> The Africa presented by the ethnologist is a legend in which we used to believe. African tradition as it appears in the light of neo-African culture may also be a legend – but it is the legend in which African intelligence believes.

> (p. 17)

Abraham attacks Jahn for this reliance on spiritual/political *belief* rather than *fact* and moves the issue of authentic African literature into an engagement with 'traditional' Africa, which must be represented in African literatures in order to produce something different from and equal to English literature. For him, 'real' Africa, as a unified concept, is to be found in rural peasantry, and its paradigm is the world-view of the Akan in Ghana.[73]

It is vital to resist formulations of a holistic African world, culture or world-view which can be discovered, recovered or re-appropriated. Africa, with its plural cultures and influences has no paradigm and cannot be reduced to a single political aspiration or spiritual unity. This does not mean that African literatures should be denied their specificity, their cultural differences, the complex textures of traditions, genres and influences. African literatures pose particular and significant challenges to literary criticisms which are not sensitive to this plurality of voices. It is a relatively simple matter to attack the theoretical inadequacies of arguments which insist on Africa's independence and (cultural) difference. It is a lot more difficult to incorporate, into reading practices, an awareness of the politics of resistance, the crises of representation and the layers of reference and signification which inform and form African texts. The most difficult point to accept, for Western literary criticism, might still be that Africa is not always thinking of or speaking to the West, and that, at moments, it escapes. Even now.

Notes

1 Joseph Conrad, *Heart of Darkness*, in Morton Dauwen Zabel (ed.), *The Portable Conrad* (Harmondsworth: Penguin, and New York: Viking Press, 1987), p. 536.

2 V.S. Naipaul, *A Bend in the River* (New York: Vintage Books, 1980 [1979]), p. 146.

3 Sara Suleri, *The Rhetoric of English India* (Chicago: The University of Chicago Press, 1992), p. 161.

4 Sunday O. Anozie, *Structural Models and African Poetics: Toward a Pragmatic Theory of Literature* (London: Routledge and Kegan Paul, 1981), p. 111.

5 Talal Asad, *Anthropology and the Colonial Encounter* (London: Ithaca Press, 1973), p. 16. Further references will be cited in the text.

6 Johannes Fabian, *Time and the Other: How Anthropology Makes Its Object* (New York: Columbia University Press, 1983), p. x. Further references will be cited in the text.

7 Frederick William Hugh Migeod, *A View of Sierra Leone* (New York: Negro Universities Press, 1970 [1926]), p. xi. Further references will be cited in the text.

8 Right Hon. Lord Avebury, P.C., *On the Origin Of Civilisation and Primitive Condition of Man: Mental and Social Condition of Savages*, Sixth Edition (London, New York and Bombay: Longman, Green and Co., 1902 [1870]). References will be cited in the text. For an account of Avebury's life, work and significance, see H.W.C. Davis and J.R.H. Weaver (eds), *The Dictionary of National Biography, 1912–1921* (London: Oxford University Press, 1927).

9 James Clifford, *The Predicament of Culture: Twentieth-Century Ethnography, Literature, and Art* (Cambridge, Mass.: Harvard University Press, 1988), p. 274. Further references will be cited in the text.

10 See Homi K. Bhabha's essay 'Signs Taken For Wonders: Questions of ambivalence and authority under a tree outside Delhi, May 1817', in Homi K. Bhabha, *The Location of Culture* (London: Routledge, 1994).

11 Robert J.C. Young, *Colonial Desire: Hybridity in Theory, Culture and Race* (London: Routledge, 1995), p. 13.

12 Max Gorvie, *Our People of the Sierra Leone Protectorate*, Africa's Own Library, No. 6 (London and Redhill: United Society for Christian Literature, Lutterworth Press, 1944). Further references will be cited in the text.

13 Gorvie, p. 5. See Edward Said's discussion of the misnomer, 'Mohammedanism', as a form of Western Christian analogy and reduction – Mohammed as a kind of disfigured Christ, in Edward W. Said, *Orientalism* (Harmondsworth: Peregrine Books, 1987 [1978]), p. 59.

14 See Kenneth Little's outline of the causes and effects of the 1898 House Tax War, in 'Post-Mortem on the Mende Rising', in Kenneth Little, *The Mende of Sierra Leone: A West African People in Transition* (London: Routledge and Kegan Paul; New York: The Humanities Press, 1967 [1951]), Chapter 11. Also, see Gorvie, pp. 13–15.

15 Rev. William Vivian, *A Captive Missionary in Mendiland* (London: Andrew Crombie, 1899). Further references will be cited in the text.

16 Nicholas Thomas, *Colonialism's Culture: Anthropology, Travel and Government* (Princeton, NJ: Princeton University Press, 1994), 71. Thomas cites Johannes Fabian, *Time and the Other: How Anthropology Makes Its Object* (New York: Columbia University Press, 1983), p. 26.

17 See, for example, Vincent Crapanzano, 'Hermes' Dilemma: The Making of Subversion in Ethnographic Description', in James Clifford and George Marcus (eds), *Writing Culture: The Poetics and Politics of Ethnography* (Berkeley and Los Angeles: University of California Press, 1986).

18 Walter Benjamin, 'The Task of the Translator', *Illuminations*, ed. Hannah Arendt, trans. Harry Zohn (London: Jonathan Cape, 1970), 75. Further references will be cited in the text.

19 Crapanzano, 'Hermes' Dilemma', p. 52.

20 See James Clifford: 'Translations of culture, however subtle or inventive in textual form, take place within relations of "weak" and "strong" languages that govern the international flow of knowledge' (Introduction to *Writing Culture*, p. 22). See also, Talal Asad: 'My point is only that the process of "cultural translation" is inevitably enmeshed in conditions of power – professional, national, international', in 'The Concept of Cultural Translation in British Social Anthropology', in *Writing Culture*, p. 163.

21 Asad, ibid.

22 Michel de Certeau, 'Ethno-Graphy: Speech, or the Space of the Other: Jean de Léry', in *The Writing of History* (New York: Columbia University Press, 1988), p. 220.

23 Christopher L. Miller, *Theories of Africans: Francophone Literature and Anthropology in Africa* (Chicago: University of Chicago Press, 1990), p. 27. His statement also refers to the desire for accurate representation of 'a world of objects' which, he claims, performs a similar movement to that of a desire for knowledge of (and dialogue with) the Other.

24 Homi K. Bhabha, 'The Commitment to Theory', in *The Location of Culture* (London: Routledge, 1994), p. 34.

25 Bhabha, ibid., p. 38.

26 Bhabha, 'Interrogating Identity', in *The Location of Culture*, p. 58.

27 James Clifford, 'On Ethnographic Allegory', *Writing Culture*, p. 115.

28 V.Y. Mudimbe, *The Invention of Africa: Gnosis, Philosophy, and the Order of Knowledge* (Bloomington, IN: Indiana University Press; and London: James Currey, 1988), pp. 175–6.

29 See Clifford, 'On Ethnographic Allegory', p. 116. Here, Clifford recounts the tale of an ethnographer taking ethnographic information from a native interlocutor, after prior guidance from a known ethnographic text, only to discover that his interlocutor is also interpreting his *own* society by means of this same published text.

30 Gayatri Chakravorty Spivak, 'Can the Subaltern Speak?', in Patrick Williams and Laura Chrisman (eds), *Colonial Discourse and Post-Colonial Theory: A Reader* (Hemel Hempstead: Harvester Wheatsheaf, 1993), p. 104.

31 Interview between Spivak and Walter Adamson, 'The Problem of Self-Representation', in Spivak, *The Post-Colonial Critic: Interviews, Strategies, Dialogues*, ed. Sarah Harasym (New York: Routledge, 1990).

32 Ibid.

33 Miller, *Theories of Africans*, p. 11.

34 Clifford, 'On Ethnographic Allegory', p. 115.

35 Miller, *Theories of Africans*, p. 68. Walter Ong, however, still ascribes to the *progressive* model of writing as a maturity, as a growing out of the premature state of orality: 'both orality and the growth of literacy out of orality are necessary for the evolution of consciousness.' He also discusses the necessary, though painful move from orality to literacy: 'we have to die to continue living.' Walter J. Ong, *Orality and Literacy: The Technologizing of the Word* (London: Methuen, 1982), pp. 175 and 15.

36 See Ong, p. 123: 'Writing had reconstituted the originally oral, spoken word in visual space.'

37 De Certeau, 'Ethno-Graphy', p. 234.

38 Benjamin, 'Theses on the Philosophy of History', in *Illuminations*, p. 263.

39 De Certeau, 'Ethno-Graphy', p. 3. Further references will be cited in the text.

40 Clifford, Introduction to *Writing Culture*, p. 12.

41 C.L. Innes comments on the relationship between *Things Fall Apart* and *Mister Johnson* in her study of Achebe's novels, emphasising Achebe's decision to 'retell Joyce Cary's story . . . "from the inside"', C.L. Innes, *Chinua Achebe* (Cambridge: Cambridge University Press, 1990), p. 12.

42 Chinua Achebe, *Things Fall Apart* (London: Heinemann, 1987 [1958]), p. 148. Further references will be cited in the text.

43 William Boyd, Introduction to Joyce Cary's *Mister Johnson* (Harmondsworth: Penguin, 1985 [1939]), p. 1. Further references will be cited in the text.

44 See C.L. Innes, *Chinua Achebe*, pp. 33–4.

45 C.L. Innes points out: 'He came to Nigeria as a colonial administrator and his depiction of Nigeria and Nigerians can be understood most fully in the light of the often inconsistent policies and attitudes of the British government and of colonial

officials caught between these policies and the day-to-day realities of their work in Africa', Innes, *Chinua Achebe*, p. 13.

46 Miller, *Theories of Africans*, p. 26.

47 Ibid., p. 5. Further references will be cited in the text.

48 Henry Louis Gates Jr, 'Criticism in the Jungle', in H. L. Gates (ed.), *Black Literature and Literary Theory* (New York: Methuen, 1984), p. 5. Further references will be cited in the text.

49 Kwame Anthony Appiah, *In My Father's House: Africa in the Philosophy of Culture* (London: Methuen, 1992), p. 103.

50 Homi K. Bhabha, 'The Commitment to Theory', p. 31.

51 Christopher L. Miller, 'Theories of Africans: The Question of Literary Anthropology', in Henry Louis Gates, Jr (ed.), *'Race', Writing and Difference* (Chicago, IL: University of Chicago Press, 1986), p. 281–300.

52 Or what Simon Gikandi calls 'an implied author'; see Gikandi, *Reading the African Novel* (London: James Currey, 1987), p. 61.

53 Cheikh Hamidou Kane, *Ambiguous Adventure* (Portsmouth, NH: Heinemann, 1963), p. 48.

54 Colonialism is ethically evaluated and indicted in phrases such as that of the Most Royal Lady, with reference to the French colonists: 'we must go to learn from them the art of conquering without being in the right', Kane, *Ambiguous Adventure*, p. 37. See also, p. 152. Further references will be cited in the text.

55 Miller, *Theories of Africans*, p. 296.

56 See Edward W. Said, *Culture and Imperialism* (London: Chatto and Windus, 1993).

57 What Simon Gikandi calls 'a universal civilization', *Reading the African Novel*, p. 68.

58 Ngũgĩ Wa Thiong'o, *Decolonising the Mind: The Politics of Language in African Literature* (London: James Currey, 1987; first published 1986), p. 6. Further references will be cited in the text.

59 Ngũgĩ Wa Thiong'o, *Moving the Centre: The Struggle for Cultural Freedoms* (London: James Currey, 1993), p. 27. Further references will be cited in the text.

60 Jean-Paul Sartre, Preface to Frantz Fanon, *The Wretched of the Earth* (Harmondsworth: Penguin, 1985 [1961]), p. 15.

61 Chinweizu, Onwuchekwu Jemie, Ihechukwu Madubuike, *Toward the Decolonization of African Literature*, vol. 1, *African Fiction and Poetry and their Critics* (Washington, DC: Howard University Press, 1983), p. 4. The term, 'bolekaja' is translated as: 'Come down let's fight!', a western Nigerian term, which they use in claiming that 'we are bolekaja critics, outraged touts for the passenger lorries of African literature', p. xii. Further references will be cited in the text.

62 Emmanuel Obiechina, *Culture, Tradition and Society in the West African Novel* (Cambridge: Cambridge University Press, 1975), p. 73.

63 Appiah, *In My Father's House*, p. 118. Further references will be cited in the text.

64 Appiah's observation on the work of the bolekaja critics is useful here: 'indeed, it is characteristic of those who pose as anti-universalists to use the term "universalism" as if it meant "pseudo-universalism", and the fact is that their complaint is not with universalism at all. What they truly object to – and who would not? – is Eurocentric hegemony *posing* as universalism', Appiah, *In My Father's House*, p. 92. These debates about universal truths have a long history in criticism of African literatures. Rand Bishop quotes Dorothy Blair, a South African, speaking in Dakar, March 1963, at the Conference of African Literature and the University Curriculum, where she claims that 'understanding of suffering is universal'. In this way, cultural and historical context are rendered unimportant; Rand Bishop, *African Literature, African Critics: The Forming of Critical Standards, 1947–1966* (New York: Greenwood Press, 1988), p. 3. Chinweizu *et al.*'s fury at this attitude emerges in

such phrases as: 'imperialist motherhens. . . . They cluck: "Be Universal! Be Universal!" ', Chinweizu *et al.*, *Towards the Decolonization of African Literature*, p. 89.

65 Rand Bishop, *African Literature, African Critics*, preface, p. xi.
66 Bishop cites Blair, Stuart and Lilyan Lagneau-Kesteloot at the Berlin Conference of African Poets in 1964, where they chided Africans for being too imitative of Europeans; Bishop, ibid., p. 2.
67 Cyprian Ekwensi, 'African Literature', *Nigeria Magazine* 83 (1964), pp. 294–9; quoted in Bishop, *African Literature, African Critics*, p. 22.
68 See his article, 'The Dead End of African Literature?', *Transition* 10 (September, 1963). Ngũgĩ quotes from the article what he perceives to be its most significant message: 'that the whole uncritical acceptance of English and French as the inevitable medium for educated African writing is misdirected, and has no chance of advancing African literature and culture', *Decolonising the Mind*, p. 24.
69 Bishop, *African Literature, African Critics*, p. 31.
70 Gates, 'Criticism in the Jungle', p. 4. See also Appiah, *In My Father's House*, p. 115: 'But for us to forget Europe is to suppress the conflicts that have shaped our identities; and since it is too late for us to escape each other, we might instead seek to turn to our advantage the mutual interdependencies history has thrust upon us.'
71 Janheinz Jahn, *Muntu: An Outline of Neo-African Culture* (London: Faber & Faber, 1961 [1958]), p. 16.
72 Wole Soyinka, *Myth, Literature and the African World* (Cambridge: Cambridge University Press, 1990 [1976]).
73 W.E. Abraham, *The Mind of Africa* (Chicago, IL: University of Chicago Press, 1962), p. 42: 'I believe that there is a *type* of African culture, and that this type is essentialist in inspiration. The essentialist view of man underlying this type finds expression in the art, the ethics and morality, the literary and the religious traditions, and also the social traditions of the people.'

2

'COMING HOME'

Pan-Africanisms and national identities

Exile is predicated on the existence of, love for, and bond with, one's native place; what is true of all exile is not that home and love of home are lost, but that loss is inherent in the very existence of both.

(Edward Said, 'Reflections on Exile')

The political and literary struggles to locate and name Africa and its meanings involve a range of histories needing to be read in ways that acknowledge the various, specific textualities informing them. African identities become meaningful and politically contested within *historically located* debates and theories of race, nation, culture. The formation of postcolonial nation states, and the genesis of national consciousness in colonial African countries, are coherent within debates about pan-Africanism and within conceptions of Africa as a (heterogeneous) whole. In this chapter, I explore how African cultures become understood as *national* cultures, and how a discourse of modernity fundamentally informs constructions of African identities. The complicated relationship between colonial domination and indigenous self-understanding, the impact of Black diasporic thought on African knowledge and racial theories, and the significant gaps which frequently divide the African (coastal) capital from the rural interior in a long-standing and important ideological split between 'modernity' and 'tradition', are all factors that enable readings of African diasporic and Black identities as historically textured and politically determined constructs, contructs which rely on particular understandings of time, memory and race. In order to examine the relationship between specific national histories and pan-African consciousness, this chapter will move from a mapping of Sierra Leone as a colony and a nation, its significance in early Africanist thought and its importance as a site for exploring Creolised and diasporic Black cultures, to a reading of African-American appropriations of Africa as a focus for 'racial' memory and ideas of modernity. Sierra Leone will function as a case-study and a locus for examining how indigenous ('traditional', 'tribal') identities fit uneasily and disjunctively within a pan-Africanist framework that insists on the travelling modernity of Black cultures and on the primacy of the metropolis.

48

'Back to Africa': Sierra Leone and the African dream

Reading histories of Sierra Leone as a West African 'nation' presents a series of complications which radically unsettle any understanding of a 'people', of stable geographical boundaries, of a coherent 'time' of the nation. The gap between the naming of trading territory by Portuguese merchants in the fifteenth century[1] and the staking of colonial and, later, protectorate borders reveals the instability of narrative origins and the continual imposition of European national and colonial meaning onto other spaces. The creation of a settlers' colony in the mountainous coastal region of what was later named 'Freetown' from the 1780s frequently comes to represent the beginning of a recognisable civil state. Freetown, later becoming the capital city, is distinguished from the outer-lying towns and villages of Sierra Leone in a long and significant history of writing which repeatedly demarcates 'up-country' Sierra Leone in a differential time. The complicated and uneven approaches to Sierra Leone territory and peoples beyond Freetown involves various ideological and political responses to modernity, which gives rise to particular distinctions between 'tribal' and national cultures, understood as racial and temporal divisions.

Exploring histories of the colony of Freetown reveals a range of possible narratives that repeatedly but differently place the colony within British national imagining and economics. The botanist Henry Smeathman's expedition to West Africa during the three years between 1771 and 1774 to collect plant specimens resulted in a utopian dream of Sierra Leone as a mountain paradise perfect for British settlement (*A History of Sierra Leone*, p. 17). Smeathman's stay on the Banana Islands with the Afro-European family the Caulkers – descended from a union between an English trader and the daughter of an African chief – gave rise to his idea of a future plantation culture of free and equal Black and White citizens.[2] Smeathman's vision of agricultural enterprise runs alongside particular historical events, including the recent ending of the American Revolutionary War, the increase in anti-slavery lobbies and developments in British domestic politics. The group of free Blacks living in London, in the 1780s known as the Black Poor, became a useful focus for utopian ideas of natural equality, liberalism and democracy, necessarily located elsewhere. Targeted as the root cause of Britain's 'racial problem' in London (*A History of Sierra Leone*, p. 18), the Black Poor were urged by British philanthropists to select Sierra Leone as their future colony of 'free labour' after the British government decided against the development of the Sierra Leone coast as a prison colony along the lines of Australia (a decision due mainly to Sierra Leone's reputation as a climatic death sentence for Whites).

Smeathman's utopian dreaming was bolstered by his hope of economic gain[3] and by the image of dominion which the Caulkers represented in their government of one of the islands and much of the coast. Britain's role in the

American War, urging the active service of plantation slaves, with the promise of freedom and land (p. 20), drew freed Blacks to an England still struggling with the laws controlling slavery – a struggle greatly encouraged by the loss of British revenue and influence in the Americas. Lord Mansfield's decision in 1772 that English law did not permit the forcible removal of slaves from England (which did not recommend the abolition of slavery[4]) was prompted by the lawsuit of the slave James Somerset against his master, and sponsored by the philanthropist Granville Sharp. Sharp's success in gaining a government bursary to create the Freetown colony after Smeathman's death therefore served a range of interconnected purposes and must be situated in a network of historical contexts.

This network of historical contexts is, of course, a way into making narrative sense of the various strands which contribute to a meaningful interpretation of Sierra Leone as a colony.[5] That Sierra Leone should become the focus of British enterprise and the expected solution to domestic racial politics emerges from a significant coincidence of historical circumstance pointing retrospectively to an understanding of Sierra Leone's colonial history as a coherent beginning to British colonialism in Africa. Foucault's reading of structuralism as a way into conceptualising temporality in a spatial schema is useful here as a method of conceiving how events become intelligible as causal connections in a way which impacts on historical thinking. Structuralism's attention to synchrony encourages a systemic reading of historical events as connected symptoms of each other, writing over chaos and contingence with the violence of interpretation:

> Structuralism, or at least that which is grouped under this slightly too general name, is the effort to establish, between elements that could have been connected on a temporal axis, an ensemble of relations that make them appear as juxtaposed, set off against one another, implicated by each other – that makes them appear, in short, as a sort of configuration.[6]

This understanding of historical time not as a linear development but as a network or 'skein' (p. 22) allows geographically disparate events to become meaningful with reference to each other.

Reading Sierra Leone as a defined space with a history is also profoundly complicated by the variability of geographical boundaries. Sierra Leone's historical fluctuation from coast to hinterland, and the later distinction between colony and protectorate, is prefigured by the title of Granville Sharp's paper of 1786, 'A Short Sketch of Temporary Regulations (Until Better Shall be Proposed) for the Intended Settlement on the Grain Coast of Africa near Sierra Leone' (*A History of Sierra Leone*, p. 20), drawing attention to the fact that the modern colonial history of Sierra Leone begins *outside* its (temporary) borders. The significance of Sierra Leone as a space outside England that becomes projected as the site of a perfect multi-racial society, incorporating enlightened eighteenth-century principles of natural order, can be read through Foucault's analysis of utopian and heterotopian spaces.

Foucault's description of utopias as 'fundamentally unreal spaces', as projections of a desire for perfect or radically alternative society, contrasts with his understanding of the more concrete heterotopian space. Retaining the quality of utopian distance, being 'outside of all places' (p. 24), the heterotopian does, however, possess a recognisable location, and an insistent connection with other social spaces, its significance and meaning emerging through its function as a place of contrast, a 'counter-site', or as an idealised reflection of a culture's sense of itself. In addition, the heterotopia is not a singular or homogeneous site, but a simultaneity of multiple sites, a variety of contrasting or connected spaces whose several meanings compete and co-exist in the same place (p. 25). Sierra Leone's inauguration as a colony representing the most worthy philanthropic urges and ideological values of certain governing sections of British society in the late eighteenth century becomes necessary in direct connection with British politics and economics.

The parliamentary debates about the possibility of a Sierra Leonean colony in the 1780s present changing ideas and images of the site. Moving away from the idea of a prison colony to Granville Sharp's notion of utopian splendour (*A History of Sierra Leone*, p. 20), Sierra Leone retained its image of usefulness – either as the repository of British social ills or as the location of economic gain. Leo Spitzer's description of the colony as the 'Sierra Leone experiment',[7] whose contradictory role became symptomatic of British colonialism in Africa for 200 years, points to the importance of Sierra Leone's early history in colonial Africa and Britain. Spitzer's summary of the Sierra Leone colony as the focus of a 'curious combination of philanthropy, humanitarian idealism, economic self-interest, and cultural arrogance' (p. 54) outlines the complicated and contradictory nature of colonialism in Africa at its outset.

As a colony created and developed by various waves of immigration, the coastal settlement retained a sharp distinction from 'Africa proper', and the uneven relationship between colony and interior indicates a range of contradictory approaches to African difference and identity. The colony itself was structured by several groups of immigrants whose racial identities and cultural origins were distinct from each other. The original immigrant ships which left Portsmouth harbour for Sierra Leone in 1787 were made up not only of the Black Poor but of White and Black fortune seekers.[8]

In 1792, 1,200 freed Black slaves, exiled in Nova Scotia after fighting on the British side in the American War of Independence, left for Sierra Leone (*A History of Sierra Leone*, p. 28; *Christianity, Islam and the Negro Race*, p. 192[9]). In 1800, they were joined by 550 Maroons from Jamaica. These early waves of settlers, representing diverse motives and identifications with Africa, and being part, moreover, of a 'social experiment' (*Lives In Between*, p. 54) that continually shifted its directives and priorities, were then, in 1807, presented with the prohibition of the slave trade throughout the British Empire (*Back to Africa*, p. 75). This added significant numbers of slaves liberated from Brazilian, American and West Indian slave ships, whose inclusion within Freetown society was carefully regulated by a colonial ideology that still believed in the 'redeemable heathen' (*Lives In Between*, p. 54).

The charter of the Sierra Leone Company, formed in 1791, sought to fuse capital enterprise with the ideals of free labour, Christian doctrines and English civilisation, government and education (*Christianity*, p. 191; *Lives In Between*, p. 54; *A History of Sierra Leone*, p. 27). The declaration of Sierra Leone to be a Crown Colony at the beginning of 1808 (*A History of Sierra Leone*, p. 36; *Lives In Between*, p. 5)[10] enshrined these ideals within the colony's government and dictated the way in which West African slaves, released into the 'King's Yard' (p. 51), were apprehended as subjects. As cultural and religious undesirables they were nevertheless products for salvation through a concentrated process of conversion and assimilation into an 'English' culture modelled on enlightened principles of order, natural rights and social regularity (*A History of Sierra Leone*, p. 46). The 'Englishness' into which the 'recaptives' were expected to assimilate was a culture also firmly based on bourgeois and Protestant ethics of industry and respectability, through which Africans could become 'Christian subjects of Great Britain' (*Lives In Between*, p. 55).

The response to African subjects as redeemable raw material led to a mapping of the Sierra Leone colony that geographically distinguished Africans at various stages of 'development'. Early settlers largely occupied the commercial spaces of Freetown itself, while 'recaptives', after an initial induction to English colonial civilisation in the King's Yard, were directed into rural mountain settlements outside Freetown. In these village 'laboratories' (p. 56), recaptives would be moulded into obedient subjects of the Crown in an environment constructed to reflect the heart of England's countryside. Named after English national icons and regions, these villages – 'Leicester, Gloucester, Bathurst, Charlotte, Regent, Wellington, Hastings, and Waterloo' (pp. 55–6) – were placed between the urban centre of Freetown and the 'wild', untamed country of 'primitive' Africa. Visited by English missionaries and built for direct control by the English colonial government, these villages of conversion and education would possess a ready-made peasantry, motivated towards land cultivation and towards becoming a vanguard of civilisation which would 'penetrate the interior' (*A History of Sierra Leone*, p. 53). These distinct spaces – wild, rural and urban Africa – each present a progressive state out of a heart of darkness, where the pilgrimage by 'country' Africans to 'up-country' Africans represents the expansive and evangelical approach of nineteenth-century England to African colonialism.

This synchronic division of land into differently meaningful spaces, juxtaposing particular moments of 'progress' onto a spatial map, reveals how critical the geography of naming has been to colonial identities. Freetown itself, in the period from its original naming in 1792 (*A History of Sierra Leone*, p. 28) until the Crown Colony of 1808, continually shifts both its significance and its position, with notions of 'freedom' repeatedly changing direction and focus. Initially named by the Nova Scotia settlers to demonstrate their right to land and liberation, Freetown becomes stamped with the financial control and orientation of the Sierra Leone Company: its first twelve streets – as a form of Christian allegory – were named after the twelve directors of the Company (p. 29). The first Crown Governor of the new Colony in 1808, Thomas Thompson, seizing on the name 'Freetown' as an indication of amorality and subversion, introduces the (temporary) name of 'Georgetown', renaming the streets after the geography of Britain (p. 51). This ongoing contestation of land-ownership and naming, with the early settler colony subject to devastating attacks from Temne chiefs (from whom the land had originally been bought; see pp. 29 and 26) and from the French (as a rival colonising power; p. 31), illustrates the unstable identity of Freetown as a locus of colonial idealism. Permanently surrounded by an indigenous African population viewed as simultaneously threatening and assimilable, and vitally attached to English metropolitan control, Freetown's role as a modern African civil state in the image of enlightenment has to be endlessly reinvented.

Sharp's original dream of a distant multi-racial colony in West Africa which would become a utopia for Whites and Blacks alike was assailed by Freetown's reputation as the 'White Man's Grave', its tropical location leading to the vast majority of European deaths in that city (*Lives In Between*, p. 57). Sierra Leone's British reputation as 'White Man's Grave' is sustained into the following century. The literary account of Freetown given in Mrs Lee's novel *The African Wanderers* (1847), a 'story' which draws on information provided by travellers' tales, contrasts the regular beauty of the city's (Western) architecture and the luxuriance of its natural landscape with the deleterious effects of that environment:

> Fair was everything to the eye; Freetown, with its regular streets, steepled church, white verandahed houses, and lovely looking villas, placed on the rising ground; the whole interspersed with beautiful trees and backed by mountains: the exquisite foliage . . .; all presented a scene so attractive, that no one would have thought anything injurious could lurk underneath it. But this lovely river brought with it the most pernicious gases, from the decayed vegetable matter which floated on its surface; and the swamp beyond . . . cast its baneful influence over the lovely city, till it had become the inevitable grave of hundreds of victims.[11]

Although an ethnically diverse colony, populated by the various African peoples of the West coast (ethnicities which the colonial government attempted to override), the colony did not become racially hybrid (*Lives In Between*, p. 5), and what became 'Creole society' in Freetown paradoxically emerged from the village laboratories, which were experimenting with the production of new British colonial subjects. On the site of Sierra Leone's rural 'English' hamlets, 'primitive' African cultures thrived, retaining their originally distinct identities and at the same time developing syncretised religious, cultural, linguistic and governmental forms (see *A History of Sierra Leone*, pp. 220–6 and 286–91). The English colonial identity which the rural villages were intended to impart was already contested by Freetown's settler society, whose variegated population featured a range of dissenting Christian sects, as well as a significant Islamic presence (*Lives In Between*, p. 64). The separation of recaptives into isolated villages was part of the colonial authority's attempt to inculcate Anglicanism against the direct threat of the Nova Scotians' Methodism (*A History of Sierra Leone*, p. 232). Their history of dissent from English colonial rule (for example the 1800 settler rebellion; see p. 34) seriously challenged the production of loyal African colonial subjects; that Governor Thompson should refer to the Nova Scotian as 'a Colonial master' over the recaptives (p. 53) indicates the depth of this perceived challenge.

This radical disparity between a fixed colonial idea of Sierra Leone as an 'Africa' of distinct developmental stages – from 'primitive' to 'civilised' – and the alternative mapping of the colony as a region of multiple and contested cultural identities become more complicated on examining how colonial ideology shifted during the nineteenth century. The changing colonial idea of 'the African' was determined by mid-nineteenth-century pseudo-Darwinism impacting upon the notion of cultural revolution to produce the new idea of racial evolution (*Lives In Between*, pp. 69–70). The violence of this conceptual change is illustrated by the fact that, in 1853, the liberated Africans, or second-generation recaptives, had been officially declared British subjects. The subsequent slide from being subjects to inferior conquests contributed to the rise of pan-Africanist responses among the Creoles. These serve to indicate how cultural issues were central to nationalist concerns, and how nationalism – emerging among the Freetown Creole elite[12] – firmly negated any identification with the interior. The name reform movements and the Dress Reform Society of 1887 presupposed and hoped to create the acknowledgement of an African identity that embraced modern ideas of progress and enlightenment and also insisted on African difference. This perceived and avowed 'difference' could not be conflated with the radical 'unknowingness' of pre-enlightenment Sierra Leone. The indigenous Sierra Leonean population, at one remove from British colonial education, was also understood by nationalist Creoles to be historically removed from national consciousness. In this way, the reform movements sought to create a re-invented African within a re-invented Sierra Leonean nation. The fashion for taking Yoruba names revealed a more powerful emotional link with another area of the West coast, Nigeria,[13] and the African dress of Creole nationalism was a creative *departure* from 'bush' fashions (*Lives In Between*, p. 159).

The exclusively metropolitan character of this nationalism, powerfully influenced by the teachings of the pan-Africanist Edward Wilmot Blyden (pp. 157–8), is illustrated by the Creole writer Adelaide Casely-Hayford, born in Sierra Leone in 1868 into the Freetown Creole elite. Her short story 'Mista Courifer' expresses the cultural nationalism which began to define Creole identity. Structured as the triumph of nationalist consciousness over colonial repression, styles of fashion and architecture emerge as significant metaphors for the struggle between European and Africanist ideologies. Mr Courifer, a Creole preacher and coffin-maker, represents the anachronistic, colonial mentality of the Creole middle class, whose adulation of Englishness is made apparent by his choice of housing, furnishings and clothes. The arguments against his 'European house' and 'English' clothing raise questions of appropriateness and 'nature' that logically condemn the hot, carpeted house as 'unsanitary' and his clothing as simply 'anti-nationalist':

> So Mr Courifer wore Black. It never struck him for a single moment that red would have been more appropriate, far more becoming, far less expensive and far more national.[14]

This evocation of national appropriateness is linked directly to racial particularity. African racial difference is absolute, both physically and qualitatively. Mr Courifer's choices for his son become not only unfitting but impossible:

> From start to finish, Tomas's career had been cut out, and in spite of the fact that nature had endowed him with a Black skin and an African temperament, Tomas was to be an Englishman. He was even to be an Englishman in appearance.
>
> (p. 10)

Blyden's influence on Creole nationalism emphasised this belief in racial particularity and its relationship with occupation, social organisation and dress (see *Lives In Between*, pp. 157–8). Racial being manifested itself in terms of separate racial destinies and, in this way, race had to become the basis of African nationalism. Blyden's Sierra Leone lecture of April 1884 (in *Christianity, Islam and the Negro Race*) emphasises this passionate belief in racial determinism as the essence of nationalist development: 'It is the feeling of race – the aspiration after the development on its own line of the type of humanity to which we belong' (p. 197). The support which Blyden gained from Creole nationalists is evident in Samuel Lewis' 'Introductory Biographical Note' to Blyden's *Christianity, Islam, and the Negro Race*, in which he is at pains to advertise both his own qualifications for introducing Blyden and

Blyden's own racial qualities. Claiming his identity as 'a Negro . . . of unadulterated African blood', and pointing to Blyden's 'purest Negro parentage' (pp. vii and viii), Lewis is careful to associate himself with Blyden's understanding of African nationalism in its most dedicated and separatist form, as the continuation of an abhorrence for racial hybridity.[15]

Adelaide Casely-Hayford's narrative follows this identification of race with nationalism with a sustained concentration on dress codes. The significance of dress for the Creole middle and upper classes was directly conditioned by the desire to differentiate themselves from slaves and 'primitives' or 'up-country natives'. Richard West's analysis of this pre-nationalist approach to fashion emphasises an earlier reading of 'freedom':

> The Creoles dressed somewhat after the English fashion. Since nakedness was the badge of a slave, an abundance and even an excess of clothes was seen as the proof of freedom. The wealthier men wore jackets, waistcoats and trousers of cloth, sometimes torturing themselves with suits of wool because this was more 'English' than cotton. Top-hats and spats were often seen in the last decade of the century.
>
> (*Back to Africa*, p. 176)

West also outlines the primary importance of religion and church-going for Creole identity: 'At innumerable churches and chapels, all day and most of the night, the Lord's Word was preached, chanted, calypsoed and yelled' (p. 176).

Tomas Courifer's liberation into a man of independence and authenticity occurs via his rejection of English fashions in favour of African dress. His father's exhortation that he 'look like an Englishman' (p. 14) is exposed as absurd through Tomas' direct appeal to the natural difference of race: 'Well, sir, if I try till I die, I shall never look like an Englishman' (p. 10). Tomas' final choice to be true to his African identity by appearing in 'pantaloons and the bright loose overjacket of a Wolof from Gambia' (p. 16) reveals how Creole nationalism identified itself with tribal origins *outside* Sierra Leone, making links with a metropolitan-based pan-Africanism rather than a notion of specifically Sierra Leonean unity. The endorsement of feminist ideas within the narrative, while making concessions to 'some English customs' (p. 15), retains its reliance on 'natural' personality and inclination. The role of women within the household is judged with reference to a lifestyle perceived to be particularly English in origin, but which also has a sympathetic place within Tomas' own nature. Tomas' sympathy for women's equality is immediately revealed as an innate quality and therefore reflected in his 'feminine' style of clothing (p. 10).

Freetown Creole nationalism preserved a sharp division from the national consciousness of the village recaptive population. The British colonial policy of creating a controlled area of African British subjects whose loyalties would conflict with those of the city settlers confirmed the separation of urban from rural interests. However, the increasing migration of more successful recaptives into city spaces, and increasing British colonial activity with respect to the interior by 1876 (*The Mende of Sierra Leone*, p. 43), created a more direct antagonism between the immigrant and indigenous peoples. The declaration of the Protectorate in 1896 (p. 46) suddenly forced the hinterland into a colonial relationship with Freetown which, while it was made to contribute to state economics through the hut tax (p. 46), still retained a differential and separate territorial identity. The House Tax War, or Mende Rising, of 1898 illustrates the radical political distinction between Colony and Protectorate, and the degree to which Creole identity was tied to the colonial state. As English speakers with Western lifestyles, the Creoles were simply viewed by the indigenous Mende as English people, and as Whites (pp. 53 and 73); their fate during the House Tax War was little different from that of the British colonial administrators (p. 48). The Mende Uprising can be viewed as a form of anti-colonial nationalism which powerfully conflicted with the Creole pan-Africanism of Freetown, being intent on the protection of local autonomy.

The re-evaluation of race by the Mende as a matter of allegiance and custom, where the Creoles had lost their status as Black Africans, informed the development of a national consciousness which primarily recognised territory, language and tribal administration. The relationship between territory and narrative has been crucial to Mende collectivity, where accounts of historical origins are vital to tribal continuity. Kenneth Little argues for the idea of a Mende national consciousness by evoking 'myth, legend, and folklore' which act as accounts of a Mende 'common heritage' (p. 72). Based on similar and common narratives of hunting and migration, Mende claims to the territory of villages and towns are repeatedly attached to a story of an initial arrival from elsewhere (p. 26).[16] This mythical and historical tale of arrival became a tale of stasis and possession through the sustained accumulation of time and memory in association with place. The unbroken existence of ancestors on the land provides a seamless narrative of presence and unity, where land itself becomes the manifestation of history: 'Such land has stored up in it the memories and traditions of the past' (*The Mende of Sierra Leone* p. 87).

Mende approaches to time reveal the significance of the House (or Hut) Tax War for Mende collective self-consciousness. Traditionally, Mende history is recounted in terms of two temporalities, separating ancient from modern, mythical from remembered time. Modern or remembered time is divided from ancient or original time by the traumatic and decisive event of the Mende rebellion, which itself represents another origin. However, claims to 'authentic' Mende identity vary according to particular and carefully differentiated Mende territories.

Migeod's account of two distinct Mende 'racial' origins (see also *The Mende of Sierra Leone*, p. 28, and *Defiant Maids and Stubborn Farmers*, p. 4) is further complicated by cultural and geographical distinctions between the Kpaa, Sewa and eastern Mende (*The Mende of Sierra Leone*, p. 76), making it clear that what constitutes 'race', 'culture' or national identity relies on different narratives of origins and antagonisms.

The differential temporalities of colony and protectorate, which confronted each other with the Mende Uprising, are analysed by Bonnie J. Barthold as an essential aspect of colonial manipulations of African realities. For Barthold, the cliché of Africa's position beyond and outside Western history has resulted in two distinct conceptions of time which are significantly out of step with each other.[17] Since the colonial designation of 'tribal' or interior Africans to pre-history, what can be called a racial experience of time has come to characterise Black identities, where exclusion from the linear progress of Western time has marked a site of resistance:

> Being Black may very well imply dwelling in a perpetually contingent state of time. . . . From one point of view, the history of Black people during the past millennium has been the history of a people's rebellion against the uncertainties of time, a balancing act of circumstance and heritage.
>
> (p. 18)

The traditional Mende conception of time as a tangible synchronic space linking the seasonal materiality of the land with the presence of the ancestors conflicts with both the missionary concept of conversion and redemption into sacred time and the progressive colonial time of the civilising mission.

The links between a Mende world view and a pan-Africanist resistance, however, have been more tenuous and disjunctive than Barthold admits. Blyden's evocation of 'Negro personality', for example, was never a direct return to a traditional African world outside European modernity. The striking similarities between Blyden's call for 'African regeneration' (p. iv) and the British colonial doctrine of civilisation point to his identification with a Creole world already viewed by the Mende as White and colonial. Blyden's view of an African future is reliant on ideas of progress and development themselves dependent on the obliteration of indigenous African time. The 'primitive condition' (p. 6) of the 'superstitious inhabitants and degraded populations' (p. 123) of non-immigrant Africans needs, according to Blyden, an energetic and sustained project of commercial uplift, one which recognises the stagnation and anti-modernity of pre-capitalist societies. His discussions of Africa's condition rely consistently on the gaze of the outsider, hungry for possession:

> The modern desire for more accurate knowledge of Africa is not a mere sentiment; it is the philanthropic impulse to lift up the millions

of that continent to their proper position among the intellectual and moral forces of the world; but it is also the commercial desire to open that vast country to the enterprises of trade.

(p. 95)

This idea of opening up Africa to European markets, of mapping territory into existence and into 'knowledge' (p. 262) leads to Blyden's celebratory stance on the 1884 European 'Scramble for Africa'. As the exploratory expeditions of European travellers 'filled up the larger part of the blank spaces on maps of the "Dark Continent"' for the benefit of an 'outside world' (p. 337), so the scrambling European nations fulfil an 'admirable' task of invading, conquering and enlightening a whole continent.

Blyden's understanding of the evident cultural inferiority of traditional African peoples gains support from his absorption in religious doctrine. His dedication to the ideal of an ultimate, 'purified Christianity' (p. xiv) leads him to advocate a detour via Islam, which he eventually perceives as an excellent foundation for the inculcation of the Christian gospels. Islam, as a non-Western religion which has been historically divorced from European colonial influence (pp. 11–12), is, for Blyden, vastly superior to the beliefs of the Mende or Temne because of its adherence to literacy and the reading of the Koran:

Mohammedanism and learning to the Muslim Negro were coeval. No sooner was he converted than he was taught to read, and the importance of knowledge was pressed upon him.

(p. 188)

With their introduction into 'superior intelligence' and the 'higher processes of thought' (p. 187), Blyden views African Muslims as prime targets for eventual inculcation into Christianity:

We are persuaded that, with the book knowledge they already possess, and their love of letters, many of them would become ready converts of a religion which brings with it the recommendation of a higher culture and a nobler civilization.

(p. 188)

This inculcation of Christianity connects significantly with the American and British use of the English language, which Blyden endows with an aggressive and anthropomorphic character of its own. For Blyden, English is intrinsically active and enterprising, lending intellectual stimulus and morality to the peoples who speak it, and irrepressibly growing in influence and energy (p. 368).

This tendency to personify and circumscribe English as a unified phenom-enon is echoed in Blyden's doctrine of race, which he conceives as inclusive of innate and intransigent characteristics. Blyden's understanding of progress and development for Africans is based on an idea of distinct and divided racial destinies, designating the 'Negro race' with a particular racial deter-minism and a separate future from 'the European' (p. 276). Due to the fact that White Europeans and Black Africans are simply not 'moving in the same groove' (p. 277), the two 'races' cannot be assessed by identical stan-dards. In order to achieve the complete 'history of humanity' (p. 276) and to contribute fully to 'the music of the universe' (p. 278), each race must find its 'own race-groove' (p. 147) and develop accordingly. Blyden's appeal to bio-logical, or spiritual, determinism in his discussion of racial difference extends itself to his assessment of the appropriate African sphere of existence. Extrapo-lating from the fact of European capitalist domination, Blyden argues for a particularly African communion with the natural world. While the European continues to cultivate cerebral and scientific activities within the metropolis, the African will remain close to the land, 'in the simplicity and purity of rural enterprises' (p. 110). This division of the world into farmers and city dwellers is, for Blyden, reflective of a natural division between the vigour of masculinity and the gentleness of the feminine: 'the harsh and stern fibre of the Caucasian races needs this milder element. The African is the feminine' (p. 111).

Blyden was by no means alone in this understanding of a radical and nat-ural split between races in pan-Africanist politics. Alexander Crummell con-ceived of Black Africans as one race and, therefore, as comprising one natural political unit.[18] As an African-American pan-Africanist, Crummell's view of traditional African culture was as impatient as Blyden's, condemning the savagery of non-Christian peoples (p. 32) and pointing towards the un-avoidable links between race and psychology (p. 38). Samuel Lewis' recog-nition of the 'different but converging paths' of the Negro and Caucasian races also leads him to discuss the 'normal and natural developments' of the 'characteristics which are most distinctive of the Negro race' (*Christianity, Islam and the Negro Race*, p. vii).

The understanding of racial unity and natural African qualities in dis-courses of pan-Africanism repeatedly emerges from the standpoint of exile in the United States, and justifies notions of colonisation and conquest in the name of a return. Blyden, born on the Dutch island of St Thomas and entering Liberia in 1851 via the United States (p. xi) evokes his conception of 'the power of race instincts' (p. 100) to illustrate the racial inevitability of Black American settlement in Africa: 'the Negro is drawn to Africa by the necessities of his nature' (p. 108). Blyden's idea of race feeling is directly linked to a notion of the physical reality of race, where miscegenation presents a direct threat to the clarity of 'negro' psychology. Negro personality, determining negro psychology and spiritual desires, is profoundly tied to an idea of genetic purity:

And it is a significant fact that this impulse is coming from the Southern States. *There* is the great mass of the race; and there their instincts are less impaired by the infusion of alien blood and by hostile climatic influences. There we find the Negro in the almost unimpaired integrity of his race susceptibility, and he is by an uncontrollable impulse feeling after a congenial atmosphere which his nature tells him he can only find in Africa. *And he is going to Africa.*

(p. 125)

The idea of a race impulse which unites African-Americans with Africa is revisited by Janheinz Jahn's argument in *Muntu* for the validity of a Black cultural heritage. Jahn's celebration of Negritude and pan-Africanism depends on his implicit use of culture as a metaphor for race, while explicitly denying that race is his focus. The huge, vague, spiritual power of African-ness, taken up by Negritude writers as negro-ness, is pulled back determinedly by Jahn into a question of 'culture', so that he can claim that 'Afro-American culture belongs to African culture and . . . we may consider the two together'.[19] Jahn designates Africa as 'the true home of the exiles' (p. 191) because Africa is the 'starting point' of 'a conscious cultural heritage'. For Blyden, the return of the exiles is not in order to solidify cultural similarities but to fulfil a racial destiny which has been exclusively revealed to the liberated slaves of the Western world. Africa's ideal future is to be 'raised from the slumber of ages and rescued from a stagnant barbarism' (*Christianity, Islam and the Negro Race*, p. 129) through the timely intervention and 'inspiration' (p. 129) of 'the millions of Africans in the Western hemisphere' (p. 349).

This call for an African modernity, stimulated by Black Western subjects, is reliant not only on theories of racial determinism and character but also on a reading of geography and climate. The status of Black Americans as 'the natural and appointed agents in the regeneration of the continent' (p. 370) in place of European colonists is supported by their racial suitability to African climates. While Europeans suffer a 'pernicious miasma' (p. 263) in contact with the tropical weather, making climate the 'chief obstacle to the wholesome influence of Europeans in Africa' (p. 341), the 'Negroes' have always been repressed by temperate climes: 'Nature, instead of affording them the sympathy and shelter of her recesses, repelled them. The wintry stars, in their courses, fought against them' (p. 340). This painful sojourn in the United States under the exile of slavery has created, according to Blyden, a superior African people whose endurance of the 'baptism of slavery' (p. 282) has resulted in a modern and enlightened African subject: 'His residence in America has conferred upon him numerous advantages. It has quickened him in the direction of progress. It has predisposed him in favour of civilization' (p. 338). Blyden's task to separate modernity from Whiteness leads him to attack crude imitation and 'spurious Europeanism' (p. 352) as a false lead into the machinery of progress, as 'imitators see only results'

61

(p. 351).The liberated slave was at an advantage over the indigenous African as long as he retained the 'purity' of his race without 'mixture of his blood' (p. 15).

This reading of pan-Africanism in terms of an aggressive allegiance to Western modernity is crucial to an understanding of the African nationalism which emerged in the mid-twentieth century. Sierra Leone, as the development of a modern West African nation, incorporates significant historical narratives of territorial disjunction, 'tribal' hybridity and racial determinism that reveal the discursive and migratory connections between a notion of African autonomy and pan-African modernity. The impact of diasporic Black identities – defined within the events of slavery and (actual or desired) return – on Creole nationalism was pivotal and can be approached as paradigmatic of the development of Black African nationalisms. In fact, Blyden's colonialist politics have a precursor in the activities of a large section of the Creole merchant elite who, failing to attract government funds for the creation of a coastal colony to the west of the Niger, nevertheless returned to what is now Nigeria as businessmen.[20]

Travelling modernities: Black identities in exile

The analysis of African cultural nationalisms as pan-African, forming a travelling modernity which revisits 'Africa' as a recurring trope rather than as a static origin, instills a sense of how the slave trade created a restless re-imagining of Black specificity. Paul Gilroy's reading of the triangular trade as constitutive of pan-Africanism, with Black slaves and freemen serving as sailors on merchant and slave ships, creating a radical 'circulation of ideas and activists',[21] leads to a re-reading of enlightenment modernity as profoundly influential for, and influenced by, Black Africans. The motif of return to an African homeland was crucially affected by the longing for a freedom and justice which formed an antithesis to slavery, and which became intimately associated with national identity. Gilroy's reading of an emergent 'Black Atlantic' cultural syncretism from the late eighteenth century resonates with the records of the departure of the *Nautilus* from England for Sierra Leone in 1787, with the travels of Blyden from St Thomas to Liberia, via the United States, and with the particular character of Freetown Creole nationalism in the nineteenth century.

Structuring Gilroy's tour of major African-American intellectuals, from Blyden to Toni Morrison, is the image of the ship, 'a living, micro-cultural, micro-political system in motion' (p. 4). This image points to the recurring and still relevant memories of the Middle Passage, as well as to subsequent restless journeys, borrowings, communications and movements of ideas and allegiances. The ship becomes, literally, a floating signifier of a Black Atlantic world where a continuous circulation of Black political, philosophical and cultural identities meet in dialogue with the modern West. Gilroy's consistent punning of 'roots' with 'routes' leads to a narrative that foregrounds the transmission and transportation of identities and people against the notion of static origins and stable distinctions between Blackness and the West.

Gilroy's concentration on the (cultural and racial) 'métissage' (p. 2) of the Black Atlantic, its 'bifocal' and 'mongrel cultural forms' (p. 3), allows for an effective challenge to be made against nationalist ethnic absolutism, both in English cultural studies and in Black nationalist thinking (p. 3). His notion of a Black 'counterculture' to European modernity indicates his insistence on resisting the more restricted notions of African or African-American nationalisms, where distaste for racial mixing reflects the scientific racisms of the nineteenth century. It also places pan-Africanism very definitely within the discourses of modernity which produced African slavery (pp. 70–1) without, however, reconstituting the powerful pan-Africanist bias towards imperialist forms of progress and Christianisation that determined the prevalently evangelistic approach to Africa. Gilroy's tracing of a recognisable Black identity sensitive to intra-racial difference, social plurality and historical construction relies on a mapping of the African Diaspora as a non-essentialist unifying sensibility (p. 80), connecting Blacks in the Caribbean, Britain and the United States, particularly through popular cultural forms (such as music). His analysis of a musical 'pan-Caribbean culture' (p. 82) that has impacted on a range of more narrowly ethnic national identities – to re-invent new spaces of connection in a re-conceived Black imaginary – echoes Henry Louis Gates' theoretical approach to the creation of African-American literary traditions. Gates emphasises, not the vast racial unconscious to which Blyden refers, but a network of communication, citation, recollection and identification which has characterised the creation of Black literary genealogies:

> Literary works configure into a tradition not because of some mystical collective unconscious determined by the biology of race or gender, but because writers read other writers and ground their representations of experience in models of language provided largely by other writers to whom they feel akin.[22]

A gap opens up in Gilroy's argument, however, around the sign of Africa itself. Evoked repeatedly as the transcendental signifier of diasporic identities, patterned within a Black Atlantic tissue of memory, community, exile and distance, Africa remains as a perplexity beyond the text. Gilroy's focus on the hybrid cultures of Black modernity, the continual and passionate re-inventions of Africa outside the continent, chooses not to engage directly with the status of an African 'interior' that, repeatedly in pan-Africanist writings, is approached as so much raw material to be brought within the great capitalist present of the modern world. The insistence, in Gilroy's argument, on de-essentialising Africa's status as entrenched and pure origin encourages him to offset Africa's difference against Black Western (particularly Black

American) appropriations of the continent for pre-conceived and external agendas. This stated distance and difference of Africa proper from the projects and ideologies of a Black Enlightenment preserves the vague image of an Africa that remains beguiling, powerful and damaged.

Forced into a direct relationship with the modern West through the slave trade and its subsequent return journeys, Blacks are placed by Gilroy in a continuously agitated dialogue, both in and of the West, in a historical and political space which is at once critical of and tangential to modernity. Using W.E.B. DuBois' ascription of a painful 'double-consciousness' to Black Americans at the beginning of the twentieth century, and Richard Wright's notion of 'double vision', Gilroy is able to assess the precariousness of a consciousness which consistently perceives itself to be in exile, en route and transforming. Seemingly excluded from such self-perceptions, however, is the world beyond the borders of Freetown and the hill stations of the village laboratories, a world that retains a veiled identity, both passive before and antagonistic to the modern spaces which preoccupy early pan-Africanisms.

What constitutes 'culture', what divides the 'modern' from the 'traditional', remain hotly contested and tensely debated areas within Black politics and, according to Gilroy, may present a false dilemma. The linear model of time where tradition remains antithetical to modernity relies on a figuring of Africa as the fulfilment of (often) American ideas of cultural origins. Although Gilroy accepts that 'Africa' has continually been manipulated by particularly Western concepts of self and community, without recourse to its divergent realities, Africa remains a marginalised and troubled space in Gilroy's text. Attacking what he calls 'the provincial and the parochial' (p. 191), which he claims often galvanises Africentricity, Gilroy consistently encourages an engagement with metropolitan centres as distinct from differently localised and specific areas of the Black world. Tradition becomes aligned solely with ethnic absolutism in such a way that the restless modernity of London and New York comes to represent exclusively the fluidity and re-inventions of Black identities.

This insistent break with the local and specific relies on Gilroy's rightful reading of metropolitan appropriations as nostalgic and distanced, seeking to reify ideas of African culture from an already hybridised metropolis. Africa, however, with the brief and sweeping exception of South Africa, embraced as already modern, remains a mythologised, manipulated and distant space, subject to the frequent intellectual colonisations of successive African-Americans, with the conclusion, it seems, that attention ought to be directed elsewhere. In a book which seeks to stress the connections between Black intellectual and vernacular thought and art, Gilroy has found it necessary to play down African influences (with the exception of Nelson Mandela and Blyden, the displaced Caribbean and Americanised migrant), and has in effect compounded a problem he would deplore – the prevalent non-engagement with African reality. In a similar move, Toni Morrison's New

York is valid as a model for Black identities, whereas Zora Neale Hurston's Eatonville is merely a regional nostalgia for racial authenticity.

The conception of 'double consciousness' by DuBois as the inner 'double-aimed struggle' of the American descendant of slaves, living in terrible exile from his (not her) own body, allows a conception of the ambiguous and turbulent subjectivities from which Gilroy reads the creativities of Black Western cultures:

> One ever feels his two-ness – an American, a Negro; two souls, two thoughts, two unreconciled strivings; two warring ideals in one dark body, whose dogged strength alone keeps it from being torn asunder.[23]

The split between 'American' and 'Negro' is revealed, throughout DuBois' text, not as the confrontation between a direct and untainted manifestation of an African self with an American subjectivity, but as the clash between a racial being and a national identity which prove to be politically and socially incompatible. Reminiscent of and yet removed from C.H. Kane's presentation of Samba Diallo's confusion between an African spirituality and a European materialism, DuBois' description of African-American consciousness examines African identity through scopic images of a scrutinised racial body, an alienating visual self-awareness and evocations of 'Negro soul' and 'Negro blood'. The imagined out-cry of the American Black boy – 'Why did God make me an outcast and a stranger in mine own house?' (p. 16) – is no longer a direct mourning for an Africa in which one was once at home, but has become shifted onto the irresistible metaphor of 'Negro' visibility. Allegiance to the United States in DuBois' text further complicates identification with Africa, and he also relies on the now comforting idea of imperialist America, while desire for homeliness has become directly associated with the United States: 'He would not Africanize America, for America has too much to teach the world and Africa. . . . He simply wishes to make it possible for a man to be both a Negro and an American' (p. 17).

Identification with Africa, or with being African, presents itself repeatedly in these texts as a problem of retrospect or distance. Africa and African identity become the site of recollection, re-interpretation and literary re-inscription. The significance of this process of re-inscription is evident, not only in the writings of pan-Africanists such as Blyden and Garvey, whose meditations on Africa's urgent and inevitable modernisation are central to their immediate Caribbean origins, but also in the range of autobiographical 'slave narratives' which form an important early corpus of self-consciously 'African' literary accounts. The writing of autobiographical narrative calls on the manipulation of personal memory for purposes of wider representation, and these slave narratives, which were contemporaneous with the settlement and early development of the Freetown colony, form a powerful nexus between private recollection and racial (or 'national') identification.

The singular importance of the slave narratives for a reading of what becomes identifiable as African self-consciousness in exile lies in the specific place these texts occupy as original literatures for the Black African Diasporas. The peculiar conjunction of memory with writing creates a recognisable starting-point for a Black diasporic literary tradition – a starting-point which echoes the beginnings of pan-Africanist consciousness. Referring to the centrality of personal remembering for the history of Black people in the United States, Toni Morrison points to the slave narratives as key texts for tracing a recognisable early archive of Black self-identity:

> A very large part of my own literary heritage is the autobiography. In this country the print origins of Black literature (as distinguished from the oral origins) were slave narratives. These book-length narratives (autobiographies, recollections, memoirs), of which well over a hundred were published, are familiar texts to historians and students of Black history.[24]

The heavy emphasis placed here upon the individual act of private remembering and the weight given to these personal revelations in constructing histories of Black identity in the West point to a concept of origins which relies on reflection, imagination, iteration. Morrison's understanding of herself as a writer – with the words, 'First of all, I must trust my own recollections. I must also depend on the recollections of others' (p. 302) – is reminiscent of the way in which slave autobiographical narratives re-write memory as a site for imagining the relationship between origins and identity. Exiled from an increasingly distant African origin, through the trauma of slavery, the slave narratives increasingly and often through contradiction reconstitute the site of home from and in different places. The result is often, as is shown by Paul Gilroy, that national belonging is rethought in imaginative and complicated ways that impact on the meaning of an 'African' identity through subtle textual inflections. The operation of memory and its link with projected, constantly re-negotiated origins is described by Morrison's figurative reference to the longing of rivers, and her discussion acts as a valuable introduction to the significance of the slave narratives for pan-Africanist thought:

> It is remembering. Remembering where it used to be. All water has a perfect memory and is forever trying to get back to where it was. Writers are like that: remembering where we were, what valley we ran through, what the banks were like, the light that was there and the route back to our original place. It is emotional memory.
>
> (p. 305)

Reading the slave narratives, issues surrounding the concept of national or racial identity continually coalesce around discussions of freedom and its meaning. Freedom becomes projected backwards either as a historical or a personal memory in a way that allows a sense of future continuity only through a shifting perception of 'home'. The complicated relationship between home, origins and identity in the texts, and the peculiar set of pressures that come to bear on their meanings, have significant connections with the pan-Africanist nationalisms of nineteenth-century Freetown.

The early narrative of Olaudah Equiano, although not the first of the slave narratives,[25] can be read as a prototype of the genre, with many later texts following the formal and stylistic patterns of Equiano's story. Published in 1789, *The Interesting Narrative of the Life of Olaudah Equiano, or Gustavas Vassa, the African, written by himself* presents a chronological tale tracing the life and developing consciousness of an African, taken from Nigeria, through slavery and into exile. This developmental plot, moving progressively away from an unknowing, West African childhood to adult freedom in Europe, allows for a narrative structure which at once emphasises belonging and separation, identification and distance. By continually placing his analysis of life in Eboe, Eastern Nigeria (see p. viii) in comparison with European referents, Equiano repeatedly places himself in the contradictory position of European ethnographer and African native, using his Europeanness as the possibility of assessing an original African self. Claiming that 'we are almost a nation of dancers, musicians, and poets' (p. 3), Equiano continues to discuss 'the natives' and how 'they are totally unacquainted with strong or spirituous liquors' (p. 5). Choosing to stress the significance of retrospect and memory in his analysis of Nigerian life – 'if my recollection does not fail me' (p. 12) – Equiano nevertheless discounts this distance, conflating the present with the past in phrases like: 'As we live in a country where nature is prodigal of her favours . . .' (p. 6).

The repeated use of nation and national identity in Equiano's account is essential to the discussion of freedom that provides the motive force of the narrative. If freedom promises a return to an independent identity, and if slavery is to be viewed as the obliteration of workable societal values, then the discourse of nationhood becomes all the more significant. In Equiano's text, the language becomes the indicator of a nation and, as with Ngũgĩ, common language forms the basis of a shared national belonging which colonial slavery seeks to destroy. The narrative progression from innocence to knowledge in Equiano's text allows, in the early chapters, for a denial of relativity between European slaver and African native, where the native's home, nation and origin, unlike that of the slaver, is not in question. Equiano's bewildered questions concerning the slavers' homes – 'I asked them if these people had no country but lived in this hollow place (the ship)' (p. 27) – emphasise the home and nation which Equiano has been forced to leave behind, and the correspondingly alien displacement of the European sailors: 'I was now persuaded that I had gotten into a world of bad spirits' (p. 25).

This reversal of scrutiny from the African to the European is matched by the continual reversal of the cannibalism myth which preoccupies eighteenth- and nineteenth-century ethnographies and travelogues of Africa. In the slave's narrative, the European sailor becomes the terrible native on dangerous territory: 'I asked them if we were not to be eaten by those white men with horrible looks, red faces and loose hair' (p. 26). Equiano's obsession with being eaten by the sailors, or by the White West Indians of Bridgetown (p. 31), is actively encouraged by a European fascination with the imagined prevalence of African cannibalism, and this fascination is documented in the text as, in fact, a constant desire by Whites to imagine devouring their slaves:

> In our extremities the captain and people told me in jest they would kill and eat me, but I thought them in earnest. . . . I very much feared they would kill and eat me.
>
> (p. 36)

> He used often to tell him jocularly that he would kill me to eat. Sometimes he would ask me if the Black people were not good to eat, and would ask me if we did not eat people in my country.
>
> (p. 37)

This obsessional desire among the Whites for the existence and practice of cannibalism leans over into the kind of destructive physical lust that C.L.R. James documents as central to the nature of plantation slavery. The voyeuristic preoccupation with discovering cannibalism and with consuming their own property often became a relished activity among the West Indian planters:

> [The planters] made them [the slaves] eat their excrement, drink their urine, and lick the saliva of other slaves. One colonist was known in moments of anger to throw himself on his slaves and stick his teeth into their flesh.[26]

These documented details of cannibalistic obsession among the slavers, planters and merchant seamen of Equiano's time correspond with continual practical attempts to quell the slaves' freedom to eat. C.L.R. James' reference to 'the tri-plate mask designed to prevent the slaves eating the sugar-cane' (p. 12) recalls Equiano's horrified vision of the 'black woman slave' cooking dinner on a United States plantation in the southern states:

> The poor creature was cruelly loaded with various kinds of iron machines; she had one particularly on her head which locked her mouth so fast that she could scarcely speak, and could not eat nor

drink. I was much astonished and shocked at this contrivance, which
I afterwards learned was called the iron muzzle.

(p. 34)

The lost nationhood repeatedly evoked in the early chapters of Equiano's narrative in order to portray the meaning of freedom develops and changes in
later chapters with re-interpretations of the location of home, the understanding of exile and the significance of freedom. Equiano's powerful descriptions
of anguish at the immediacy of kidnap from Eboe, presented to underline the
'love of liberty, ever great' (p. 17), shift their focus onto England as the site
of longing and freedom. England becomes a new place of origin and return,
where anguish diminishes – 'My griefs too . . . were now wearing away'
(p. 42) – and a sense of identification with Englishness begins to emerge:

> I soon grew a stranger to terror of every kind and was, in that respect
> at least, almost an Englishman. . . . I now not only felt myself
> quite easy with these new countrymen but relished their society and
> manners.
>
> (p. 33)

This conversion to an English identity sets itself against the West Indies,
described as 'this land of bondage' (p. 62), against which 'every part of the
world I had hitherto been in seemed to me a paradise in comparison' (p. 81),
and in contrast with the loneliness of the United States plantation where
'I was constantly grieving and pining and wishing for death rather than anything else' (p. 33). The shift in the text towards England as emblem of freedom creates an understanding of exile and separation that fixes England at
the centre of the text's restless travelling. The trajectory of longing and
return becomes increasingly cathected onto England, and particularly onto
London, and the grief of slavery no longer presents the dream of a simple
reverse journey:

> I at that instant burst out a-crying and begged much of him to take
> me to England with him. . . .
>
> I determined to make every exertion to obtain my freedom and to
> return to Old England. . . .
>
> But my heart was still fixed on London.
>
> (pp. 63, 88, 97)

This presentation of England as the site of freedom is echoed in later slave narratives, where travel to England effectively acts as a path to liberation and
as a useful counterfoil to the slavery of the West Indies. For Mary Prince,

whose narrative was published in 1831, England is presented as the motive force for abolishing slavery throughout the West Indies – 'I would have all the good people in England . . . break our chains, and set us free'[27] – and English servant life becomes the measure against which Antiguan slavery is exposed:

> They have their liberty. That's just what we want. We don't mind hard work, if we had proper treatment, and proper wages like English servants.
>
> (p. 215)

Prince's journey to England as a slave, under the command of her master and mistress, and the fact of her legal freedom on English soil reveal the arbitrariness of her enslavement. The distinction between slavery as a condition and slavery as a legal and national consequence proves to be a pivotal moment in Prince's escape to freedom:

> The gentleman of the [Anti-Slavery] Society took me to a lawyer, who examined very strictly into my case; but told me that the laws of England could do nothing to make me free in Antigua.
>
> (p. 212)

The 'Narrative of Louis Asa-Asa, A Captured African', published in 1831, clearly presents the status of England in the early nineteenth century as a place of refuge beyond the violence of slavery. As a first generation Sierra Leonean captive, Asa-Asa's relationship with an African homeland is similar to Equiano's and, as a young boy who has been acculturated into English life, the desire to return has already become irrecoverable. Having been taken from Sierra Leone, two of his companions do return, whereas Asa-Asa can only reflect on the irrevocable nature of his loss: 'But poor Louis, when offered the choice of going back to Africa, replied: "Me no father, no mother now; me stay with you."' (p. 239). England becomes, of necessity, a place of divine refuge, away from the dangers of up-country Sierra Leone, itself divorced from colonial Freetown:

> I am very glad I have come to England, to know who God is. I should like much to see my friends again, but I do not now wish to go back to them: for if I go back to my own country, I might be taken as a slave again. I would rather stay here, where I am free, than go back to my country to be sold.
>
> (p. 242)

Freedom is continually described in terms of travel and escape, and rarely in terms of return to an original African ancestral home. Return to Africa presents itself as the release of death rather than as the hope of a liberated future, and the ultimate return to sources which suicide offers on the West Indian plantations is a direct expression of the impossibility of escape. C.L.R. James' descriptions of eighteenth-century Haiti illustrate this link between death and return from exile:

> Suicide was a common habit, and such was their disregard for life that they often killed themselves, not for personal reasons, but in order to spite their owner. Life was hard and death, they believed, meant not only release but a return to Africa.
>
> (pp. 15–16)

Frederick Douglass, whose narrative was published in 1845, looks to the northern states for liberty – 'Only think of it; one hundred miles straight north, and I am free!' (*The Classic Slave Narratives*, p. 294) – while, in Mattie J. Jackson's narrative of 1866, her father escapes to Chicago (*Six Women's Slave Narratives*, pp. 7–9), her stepfather to Canada (p. 11) and Mattie herself finds freedom in Indianapolis (p. 28). Annie L. Burton's later narrative, published in 1909, reveals a fully fledged North American patriotism, at last presenting the United States as the ultimate site of freedom and self-identification. The list of 'My Favourite Hymns', which serves as an appendix to her narrative, includes the patriotic song 'America', with its references to an ancestral home of belonging and liberty, and which Burton apparently envisaged to be a fitting coda to her memories of slavery:

> My country, 'tis of thee,
> Sweet land of liberty,
> Of thee I sing;
> Land where my fathers died . . .
>
> (p. 93)

Identification with 'other' homelands does not of course proscribe going 'back' to Africa. The continual assertion by Equiano of his love for and identification with England does not prevent his support for the *Nautilus* expedition to Sierra Leone in 1787, nor his appointment as Commissary of Provisions and Stores for the journey. His reaction to the planned return to Africa, even as he recognises 'some difficulties on the account of the slave dealers' (*The Classic Slave Narratives*, p. 171), is undeniably positive, and he describes the projected expedition as 'an act which redounded to the honour of all concerned in its promotion, and filled me with prayers and much rejoicing' (p. 171). His subsequent dismissal from the post, due to his concern for the conditions of the Black Poor and their lack of supplies, nonetheless indicates a genuine passion for the success of the trip and frustration at its failure:

Thus ended my part of the long-talked-of expedition to Sierra Leone; an expedition which, however unfortunate in the event, was humane and politic in its design.

(p. 174)

Equiano was significantly involved in the *Nautilus* expedition to found the Freetown colony from an early stage. His relationship with Granville Sharp began as early as 1783, where he alerted Sharp to the wholesale massacre of over 130 slaves thrown from a slave-ship off the West African coast.[28] Also, Equiano's identity as an African added considerably to his status as an authority on African slavery and to his authenticity as an insider on African issues. Paul Edwards documents the journalistic argument that erupted over the validity of Equiano's African nativity (*Equiano's Travels*, p. xii; see also *The Classic Slave Narratives*, p. 6), and the importance of Equiano's ability to 'produce evidence of his African origins' (*Equiano's Travels*, p. xii) was viewed as crucial for the anti-slavery practices of the time. In addition to this, Equiano's attempts to be ordained as a Church of England priest (despite being a Methodist)[29] in order to return to Africa as a missionary attest to his continuing sense of loyalty to the (West) 'coast of Africa'. His unsuccessful memorials to the Bishop of London contain stated proof of his identity as an African and of his yearning to return: 'Your memorialist is a native of Africa, . . . your memorialist is desirous of returning to Africa' (*The Classic Slave Narratives*, p. 168).

However, this relationship with Africa, although confirmed, is no longer presented as an unmediated identification. For Equiano, his desire to return as a missionary is also a desire to return as an acculturated and converted Englishman, seeking – like Blyden and Garvey – to remake, develop and convert his 'countrymen'. His plan to begin 'reforming his countrymen' (p. 168) clearly testifies to this newly imperialist relationship with West Africa, and his arguments for abolishing slavery, given in the final chapter of his narrative, directly concur with the colonialist aspirations of the British Empire:

It is trading upon safe grounds. A commercial intercourse with Africa opens an inexhaustible source of wealth to the manufacturing interests of Great Britain; and to all which the slave-trade is an objection.

(p. 176)

The association between travel and freedom in the slave narratives is crucial to the way in which the texts reconstitute an identity that is increasingly Western and metropolitan. Frederick Douglass' abhorrence of the countryside of plantations and fieldwork, in favour of the cities with their shipyards and cosmopolitan freedoms, is an indication of how the metropolis becomes symbolic of a new independence. Freetown's role as a harbour capital, peopled by the displaced subjects of slavery and exile, can be symbolised by such harbour cities as Douglass' Baltimore, Equiano's Falmouth and Asa-Asa's London. Douglass' eulogy on freedom, which he calls 'an apostrophe to the moving multitude of ships' (p. 293), clearly indicates the significance of travel as a symbolic and practical resistance to slavery's incarceration:

> You are loosed from your moorings, and are free. . . . You are free-dom's swift-winged angels, that fly around the world; I am confined in bands of iron! O that I were free! O, that I were on one of your gallant decks, and under your protecting wing!
>
> (p. 293)

The irony of using the image of the ship as an allegory of freedom is paramount here. From Equiano's vivid descriptions of the stench and horror of the slave-holds – about which C.L.R. James claims that 'no place on earth . . . concentrated so much misery' (*The Black Jacobins*, p. 8) – to Douglass' wistful longing for the ship's 'protecting wing' (*The Classic Slave Narratives*, p. 293) is a leap of ambiguity and contradiction that saturates the experience of slavery and displacement.

The increasing metaphorisation of Africa as a figurative and distant origin in the slave narratives affects their analysis of freedom. The meaning of liberty becomes ever more poeticised and mystical, as though the narrators are straining after a reality that has to be constantly reinvented. Released from the concrete memory of place, 'freedom' becomes a matter of the senses and the soul, continually recreated in the 'new' territories of England or the Americas. Frederick Douglass recalls the magical and tangible manifestation of freedom to him while still a slave:

> Freedom now appeared, to disappear no more forever. It was heard in every sound, and seen in every thing. It was ever present to tor-ment me with a sense of my wretched condition. I saw nothing with-out seeing it. I heard nothing without hearing it, and I felt nothing without feeling it. It looked from every star, it smiled in every calm, it breathed in every wind, and moved in every storm.
>
> (p. 279)

This heady knowledge of freedom as a distantly obtainable object is similarly described by Mattie J. Jackson in terms of sound, taste and light:

> The sound of freedom was music in our ears; the air was pure and fragrant, the genial rays of the glorious sun burst forth with a new lustre upon us. . . . Our joy that we were permitted to mingle together our earthly bliss in glorious strains of freedom was indescribable.
>
> (*Six Women's Slave Narratives*, p. 32)

Lucy A. Delaney discusses 'the light of freedom' (p. 50), while Mary Prince claims, simply, that 'to be free is very sweet' (p. 214). In the following century, Ralph Ellison's dream excursion into the past of slavery in *Invisible Man* (1952) touches on the deep and inchoate passion that the idea of 'freedom' comes to represent. Swooning in between the bars of a blues strain, an old plantation slave woman, when asked for the meaning of freedom, after having murdered to obtain it, replies:

> I done forgot, son. It's all mixed up. First I think it's one thing, then I think it's another. It gits my head to spinning. . . . Hit's like I have a fever. Ever' time I starts to walk my head gits swishing and I falls down.[30]

These representations of freedom as a welter of physical sensation and emotional passion, with self-ownership aligned with the onslaught of natural feeling, are placed alongside the significance of literacy as one of the most important paths to independent self-expression and self-knowledge. The publication of the slave narratives makes the fact of literacy a profound and pivotal issue. The moment at which Frederick Douglass overhears the forbidding tones of his master, vociferating against his learning to read and write, becomes, simultaneously, one of revelation: 'From that moment, I understood the pathway from slavery to freedom' (*The Classic Slave Narratives*, p. 275). The incompatibility of slavery and literacy for Douglass' master infiltrated the consciousness of White master and Black slave. If Blacks could read and write, they could also vote, lay claim to a human identity and defend themselves:

> Since the beginning of the sixteenth century, Europeans had wondered aloud whether or not the African 'species of men', as they were most commonly called, *could* ever create formal literature, could ever master 'the arts and sciences'. If they could, the argument ran, then the African variety of humanity was fundamentally related to the European variety.
>
> (Foreword, *Six Women's Slave Narratives*, p. ix)

The ideological and philosophical arguments against the literary abilities of Blacks during the centuries in which the slave narratives were written, including John C. Calhoun's famous statement that only a Negro 'who understood the Greek syntax' was human,[31] were arguments applied in political and legal practice: 'prior to the Civil War, the majority of Black Americans living in the United States were held in bondage. Law and practice forbade teaching them to read or write' (*Six Women's Slave Narratives*, p. xxiv).

The association between literacy and freedom develops alongside Douglass' preoccupation with ships and travel. The unlimited open spaces of ocean and horizon and the liberating promises of literacy become linked in the space of Durgin and Bailey's shipyard, where Douglass' observation of the practical work of building ships leads him to a meditation upon the constructiveness of learning:

> The idea as to how I might learn to write was suggested to me by being in Durgin and Bailey's shipyard, and frequently seeing the ship carpenters, after hewing, and getting a piece of timber ready for use, write on the timber the name of that part of the ship for which it was intended.
>
> (*The Classic Slave Narratives*, p. 280)

Equiano's enjoyment of English 'society and manners' and his desire to identify himself more closely with Englishness lead to an attraction towards reading and writing, out of 'the stronger desire to resemble them, to imbibe their spirit and imitate their manners' (*Equiano's Travels*, p. 43). These prevalent associations between literacy, freedom, travel and Englishness, linked through powerful historical contingencies, are significantly connected with Christianity. Literacy is often encouraged by relationship with Christian evangelism and with reading the Bible. Mary Prince records that her longing to read was directly responsive to her religious conversion into the Moravian church, where, 'after we had done spelling, we tried to read the Bible' (*The Classic Slave Narratives*, p. 207). Asa-Asa's expressed contentment at his stay in England is embedded in missionary rhetoric, which emphasises the significance of the Bible as a text to be read, and the knowledge of God as a fundamentally literary exercise: 'Me think what a good thing I came to England! Here, I know what God is, and read my Bible; in my country they have no God, no Bible' (p. 239).

The missionary zeal which energised Blyden's approach to Africa and its future have a precursor in Equiano's own evangelistic stance towards his native West coast. In Equiano's text, the liberating restlessness of travel and the paramount importance of literate skills for his status as an eighteenth-century English gentleman weigh powerfully on his conception of himself as a native African. The account of his childhood in Eboe, in the first chapter of his autobiographical narrative, needs to be read with reference to a later statement describing the early passion of reading:

> He taught me to shave and dress hair a little and also to read in the Bible, explaining many passages to me which I did not comprehend. I was wonderfully surprised to see the laws and rules of my country written almost exactly here, a circumstance which I believe tended to impress our manners and customs more deeply on my memory.
>
> (*Equiano's Travels*, p. 57)

This close relationship between scriptural and ethnographic text and the impact which this relationship has upon the 'memory' of his own African background give a useful insight into his missionary ambitions and into his projected understanding of himself as an African. Re-reading his childhood memories of Eboe as a comparative exercise that is clearly informed by Biblical ethnography, links Equiano very closely with the later pan-Africanists and the Freetown Creoles. The association between scripture and ethnography in Equiano's literary consciousness is made more explicit in a later chapter where Equiano remembers buying a beloved Bible on the island of 'St Kitt's' and his subsequent grief at losing his two favourite books: 'My Bible, and the Guide to the Indians, the two books I loved above all others, were left behind' (p. 81).

This represents an important departure from his earlier inhabitancy of a purely oral world, where his childhood memories were not arranged and given 'objective' meaning via the mediation of written text. Equiano's initial encounter with the peculiarity of textual knowledge is recounted in the disjunctive moment where oral and literate modes of communication collide. Equiano's secretive approach to books, as though they also occupied the universe of dialogue and exchange, presents a fascinating misunderstanding on his part of the fundamentally *historical* nature of textual discourse. In a scene reminiscent of Samba Diallo's first written communication with his father in *Ambiguous Adventure*,[32] where Diallo first learns of the specific power of literary form, Equiano asks the silent text to reveal the secret of origins:

> I had often seen my master and Dick employed in reading; and I had a great curiosity to talk to the books, as I thought they did; and so to learn how all things had a beginning. For that purpose I have often taken up a book, and talked to it, and then put my ears to it, when alone, in hopes it would answer me, and I have been very much concerned when I found it remaining silent.
>
> (*The Classic Slave Narratives*, pp. 43–4)

The publication and editing of slave narratives, usually under the auspices of anti-slavery societies and activities, have an impact on the sentiments and ideologies expressed in the texts themselves. The eulogies on the glories of English society in the narratives of Asa-Asa and Equiano, for example, are clearly appropriate for the rhetoric of English anti-slavery societies and patrons. Equiano's humble 'Dedication', at once apologising for his status as 'an unlettered African' and emphasising his consequent authenticity as a spokesperson for the abolition of slavery, contains a revealing statement on the wonders of England – an England that was, of course, dear to the hearts of abolitionist protesters. Equiano thanks 'Providence' for

the introduction I have thence obtained to the knowledge of the
Christian religion, and of a nation which, by its liberal sentiments,
its humanity, the glorious freedom of its government, and its profi-
ciency in arts and sciences, has exalted the dignity of human nature.

(*The Classic Slave Narratives*, p. 3)

This packaging of Equiano's text within the codes of English patriotism, in a
dedication dated 1792, contrasts interestingly with the American publication
of 1987, which markets Equiano's narrative, along with three others, under
the rhetoric of *American* patriotism, claiming Equiano's text to be part of 'a
uniquely American literary form that has given birth to the spirit, vitality,
and vision of America's best modern Black writers' (*The Classic Slave Narratives*, back sleeve). Similarly, the 1988 edition of *Six Women's Slave Narratives*
markets 'The History of Mary Prince, a West Indian Slave', along with five
other narratives, under the rubric of the 'African-American literary tradition'
and 'African-American women's autobiographies' (*Six Women's Slave Narratives*, back sleeve). In contrast again, the earlier 1967 edition of Equiano's
narrative markets the text in terms of its 'great literary and historical
importance in the context of African writing' (*Equiano's Travels*, back sleeve),
even though Paul Edwards chooses to edit out important sections regarding
Equiano's involvement with the *Nautilus* expedition to Sierra Leone.

These contradictory and contextual marketing impulses in the twentieth
century bear upon a reading of the editing and packaging of the slave narratives at their initial publications. The narratives typically begin with proof-
statements as to the authenticity of authorship, with original title pages
bearing claims to be 'written by himself/herself', or 'related by himself/
herself'. The strategic importance of these proof-statements relates to the
taboo on slave-literacy and self-expression. To claim authorship as a Black
ex-slave and to foreground the simultaneity of a Black identity with the ability
to write was already powerfully to refute the naturalness of Black slavery, as
Toni Morrison observes in her analysis of the slave narratives: 'these writers
knew that literacy was power' ('The Site of Memory', pp. 300–1). This forceful conjunction of Black subjectivity and authorship was difficult for Whites
to accept, even for anti-slavery supporters, and doubt is cast on the unadulterated nature of Equiano's text in a largely supportive Preface to the 1814
English edition, which quotes from *The Monthly Review* of June 1789 (see
Equiano's Travels, p. xiv):

We entertain no doubt of the general authenticity of this very intelligent African's story, though it is not improbable that some English
writer has assisted him in the compilement, or at least the correction
of his book, for it is sufficiently well-written. The narrative wears an
honest face.

(*The Classic Slave Narratives*, p. 8)

The suggestion of surprise that the conjoined words 'very intelligent African' imply and their underlying oxymoronic meaning are carefully presented through the prevailing uncertainty around Equiano's authorship and, consequently, around its accuracy. The significance of these doubts is revisited in Paul Edwards' 1967 introduction to *Equiano's Travels*, where the need is still recognised to refute any claims for large-scale textual revision: 'If the book was revised, the revisions probably consisted of little more than the working up of occasional rhetorical climaxes' (p. xiv). Edwards' lengthy investigation into Equiano's claim to authorship and his final statement that 'there is no reason at all why he should not have written the whole book' (p. xv) come long after William Lloyd Garrison's supporting statement in the Preface to Frederick Douglass' 1845 narrative, where Garrison finds it necessary to claim that

> Mr Douglass has very properly chosen to write his own Narrative, in his own style, and according to the best of his ability, rather than to employ some one else. It is, therefore, entirely his own production.
>
> (*The Classic Slave Narratives*, p. 248)

The process of editing slave narratives is often clearly accounted for in the Prefaces. Interestingly, narratives written by female ex-slaves, such as Linda Brent's 'Incidents in the Life of a Slave Girl' (1861), appear to merit quite different proof-statements from those of male authors such as Equiano or Douglass. The 'Introduction by the Editor' to Brent's tale follows the convention of upholding her ability to write and of dealing with the astonishment that this fact may engender among White readers of the era: 'It will naturally excite surprise that a woman reared in slavery should be able to write so well. But circumstances will explain this' (*Six Women's Slave Narratives*, p. 337). This statement is, however, preceded by details of the editing and revision that indeed *have* taken place in order to re-arrange, re-style and suppress sections of the narrative:

> I have revised her manuscript; but such changes as I have made have been mainly for purposes of condensation and orderly arrangement. . . . I pruned excrescences a little.
>
> (*Six Women's Slave Narratives*, p. 337)

In 1891, at last, a female author presents her work for herself, though Lucy A. Delaney's Preface to her narrative still contains an apology for her 'lack of knowledge and experience in literary achievements' (p. viii).

The relationship between oral and literate forms of the narratives is foregrounded by those that are 'related' rather than written by the autobiographers. The gaps between oral and literate styles are directly confronted in the Prefaces to these narratives and the consequent extent of editorial control can be traced through the claims made. Mary Prince's 'History', published in 1831, announces itself as the written transcript of an oral narrative, having passed through three stages: dictation, transcription and editing. The initial written version is presented as a direct transcription of the narrator's voice, 'taken down from Mary's own lips' by an anonymous 'lady', whereas the final edited version has been 'pruned into its present shape', presumably by a male editor. In addition to these changes and stages of removal from Prince's original narrative, the end-product of which is still claimed to be 'essentially her own', the editor relates the necessary process of authentication that involves him 'carefully examining her on every fact and circumstance detailed' (*The Classic Slave Narratives*, p. 185).

The 'Narrative of Louis Asa-Asa' is similarly presented as an oral narrative that has been carefully edited, although the extent and depth of the editing process is played down: 'it is given . . . as nearly as possible in the narrator's words, with only so much correction as was necessary' (p. 239). Mattie J. Jackson's narrative of 1866, which is presented 'As Given By Mattie', is 'written and arranged' by her stepmother, a Black woman doctor, whose investment in her role as editor and amanuensis is to provide a direct reproof to 'the prejudices against the natural genius and talent of our race' (*Six Women's Slave Narratives*, p. 4). The 'Memoir of Old Elizabeth, A Coloured Woman', published in 1863, allows a greater gap to open between oral and written versions by claiming only that the narrative 'was taken mainly from her own lips' (p. 3).

It should be noted that both Mary Prince and Mattie J. Jackson were themselves able to read and write, yet nevertheless had their narratives dictated, transcribed and edited. Both narratives are dated over half a century after Equiano's written text, and Jackson's was published more than eighty years later. The self-expression of the female slave appears, then, to have been subject to a more extensive process of suppression and correction, and the gendered implications of this situation may have had substantial effects on the final narrative versions. William L. Andrews, for example, draws attention to the differences of tone between Prince's and Jackson's narratives, where Prince's editor appears to have 'restrained' any declarations of 'anger and bitterness towards her persecutors' (p. xxxiv), while Jackson's Black stepmother allows expressions of triumph and justified redress to appear in the text (p. xxxv).

The coercions involved in publishing and editing the narratives extend to often radical and pertinent suppressions of what is rendered 'unspeakable'. These 'unspeakable' things were often related to the horrors of slavery, to raw and terrible experiences and sufferings deemed to be too extreme to allow into the autobiographical space of both male and female narrators. The reactions and emotions of the narrators to these disturbing memories were also rendered largely silent, and these silences, these restraints, were subsequently appraised as virtues. As lately as Paul Edwards' 1967 Introduction to *Equiano's Travels*, the *hidden* anguish and rage of the narrator's auto-biography – the very quietness at the surface of the text – is welcomed as a literary advantage:

> As a rule he puts no more emotional pressure on the reader than the situation itself contains – his language does not strain after our sympathy, but he expects it to be given naturally and at the proper time. This quiet avoidance of emotional display produces many of the best passages of the book.
>
> (p. xvii)

Equiano's text itself does, however, like many of the narratives, announce its own moments of silence, in such a way that there is no doubting the nature of these deliberate gaps and omissions. In his description of the notorious Middle Passage on a slave-ship, Equiano pauses in his account of whipping, rebellion and suicide in order to point to the bottomless pit of the unsaid: 'In this manner we continued to undergo more hardships than I can now relate, hardships which are inseparable from this accursed trade' (p. 30). The device of indicating the existence of what cannot be revealed results in what can be called a deafening silence, one that succeeds in emphasising the ideological parameters of editing and publishing. Toni Morrison's discussion of a veiled 'Afro-American presence' in American literatures furnishes an insight into the operation of silence in the slave narratives:

> We can agree, I think, that invisible things are not necessarily 'not there'; that a void may be empty, but is not a vacuum. In addition, certain absences are so stressed, so ornate, so planned, that they call attention to themselves; arrest us with intentionality and purpose, like neighborhoods that are defined by the population held away from them.[33]

What is undeniably present can be masked and camouflaged by the activity of re-naming, and the narratives are littered with accounts of lost or changed names, of forced re-identifications, hidden genealogies. Mattie Jackson bemoans the loss of a named line of ancestors, and her reflections on African origins are forced to stop short at the moment of slavery: 'By all accounts my great grandfather was captured and brought from Africa. His original name I never learned. His master's name was Jackson' (*Six Women's Slave Narratives*, p. 5). Olaudah Equiano becomes Gustavus Vassa after a violent struggle between master and slave, where Equiano fights to be recognised by his already changed name of 'Jacob' (*Equiano's Travels*, p. 35). Frederick Douglass recounts his journey to freedom via a list of pseudonyms and trace-names, where liberty depends upon strategies of disappearance and denial.

Douglass' final plea to retain his first name of 'Frederick' emerges as a last stand for self-recognition:

> I gave Mr Johnson the privilege of choosing me a name, but told him he must not take from me the name of 'Frederick'. I must hold on to that, to preserve a sense of my identity.
>
> (*The Classic Slave Narratives*, p. 322)

Attesting to the unspoken and the suppressed in what Toni Morrison calls the 'interior life' of slaves ('The Site of Memory', p. 302), Douglass refers to the 'wildsongs' of Colonel Lloyd's plantation slaves. It is in this powerful description of emotional expression and passionate utterance that the inarticulate, hidden narrative of slavery is alluded to. Douglass' insistence that in these almost unconscious displays of anguish is embedded and revealed the true meaning of slavery, the full impact of its psychological destructiveness, points away from the ability of the written autobiographical form to transmit fully the whole story. His concentration on the lack of conscious and rigid form in the songs, their flagrant improvisations and their 'apparently incoherent' structures (*The Classic Slave Narratives*, p. 263), allows the 'unspeakable' pain and violence of slavery, so frequently shadowed and hushed in the edited texts, to be more nearly intuited:

> The thought that came up, came out – if not in the word, in the sound; – and as frequently in the one and the other. . . . They told a tale of woe which was then altogether beyond my feeble incomprehension; they were tones loud, long, and deep; they breathed the prayer and complaint of souls boiling over with the bitterest anguish.
>
> (pp. 262–3)

The determination to pull the veil away and allow the 'indelicate' matters to be expressed emerges more urgently with regard to the female autobiographies. The gendered differences between the experiences of male and female slaves, and the preoccupations and losses on which each tends to focus, are crucial for reading how the texts construct racial identities and notions of liberty. L. Maria Child's editorial introduction to Linda Brent's 'Incidents in the Life of a Slave Girl' emphasises a keen resolve to break the particular traditions of repression that characterise the narratives of female ex-slaves. Referring obliquely to 'a class which some call delicate subjects' and to 'this peculiar phase of slavery [that] has generally been kept veiled' (*Six Women's Slave Narratives*, p. 337), Child succeeds in drawing attention to a range of experiences that apply particularly to the world views of women slaves. Child's evidently feminist appeal is worth noting here for its careful reference to sexuality: 'I do this for the sake of my sisters in bondage, who are suffering wrongs so foul, that our ears are too delicate to listen to them' (p. 338).

The female slave narratives are peculiar in their more sustained attention to sexual oppression and familial ties. Though Equiano does dwell on the painful loss of his sister (*Equiano's Travels*, p. 21), and Douglass remembers the sexual abuse practised upon a female plantation slave who is used as a breeder (*The Classic Slave Narratives*, p. 292), there remains a noticeable gap in conceptions of freedom and the self between the male and female narratives. For Mary Prince, Mattie Jackson and Lucy Delaney, their relationships with their mothers are of signal importance and construct their understanding of self-worth and individuality. The nurturing role that their mothers play in their lives, providing emotional and practical support, proves to be pivotal in their struggles for freedom. Jackson's conceptualisation of the sweetness of liberty is profoundly implicated in her identification with her mother, and her sense of individual happiness is inseparable from the maternal bond: 'I was overjoyed with my personal freedom, but the joy at my mother's escape was greater than anything I had ever known' (*Six Women's Slave Narratives*, p. 32). Delaney's recognition of the reality of freedom as she gazes into her mother's eyes (p. 50), and her insistent citation of her mother among 'the great ones of the earth, which are portrayed on historic pages' (p. 51), are indications of the way in which the female narratives seek to create woman-centred and familial-centred texts in order to re-instate the slave mother as a vocal and visible figure in literature and history.

The contrasting descriptions of the meaning of freedom in Equiano's and Douglass' texts emphasise the independence and restlessness of travel, of ships and oceans and, as with Douglass' physical battle with the overseer and slave-breaker (*The Classic Slave Narratives*, p. 298), the struggle to obtain individual self esteem as a *man*. Their early separation from their mothers, which Douglass claims was a deliberate practice among plantation farmers to 'hinder the development of the child's affection towards its mother' (p. 256), disallows any expression of filial identification. However, although both Equiano and Douglass marry (see *Equiano's Travels*, p. xii and *The Classic Slave Narratives*, p. 321), very little or no emphasis is placed on the significance of these alliances for their understanding of themselves as enslaved or as free individuals. Sexuality and sexual relationships are, however, given central positions in the women's texts, where sexual abuse on the part of the slave masters and the denial of sexual choices on the part of their female slaves create a severe and lasting impression of the meaning of enslavement. Mary Prince is forced to choose between a lonely freedom in England and an enslaved marriage in Antigua (*The Classic Slave Narratives*, p. 212), while Linda Brent is forced to lose a 'love-dream' (*Six Women's Slave Narratives*, p. 370) due to the sexual jealousy of her master (p. 371), forced, even, to contemplate the prospect of liberation through marriage to her free Black lover, stating hopefully: 'my lover wanted to buy me' (p. 369). Brent's argument against slavery is largely concentrated in her observation of the relationship between *mistress* and female slave, where the familial and maternal expectations of the one cancel out the human rights of the other:

> My mistress, like many others, seemed to think that slaves had no right to any family ties of their own; that they were created merely to wait upon the family of the mistress.

(p. 370)

The focus on nakedness, sexual abuse and physical violence in Prince's narrative clearly indicates her sense of the value of individual freedom. Her description of the sexual advantages taken by her master reveals the intimate relationship between violence and sexual depredation:

> He had an ugly fashion of stripping himself quite naked and ordering me then to wash him in a tub of water. This was worse to me than all the licks. Sometimes when he called me to wash him I would not come, my eyes were so full of shame.

(*The Classic Slave Narratives*, p. 202)

This reverse scenario, where it is the master's naked body that is forced into scrutiny and exhibition, reveals the power invested in the master's body, and the coercion of Prince's gaze onto his nakedness operates as a kind of violence, more threatening to her than physical abuse. This scene of scopophilic control, where the master displays his own ability to pervert familial and moral codes at the expense of the female slave, proves to be Prince's own scene of combat with her master, comparable to Douglass' battle with Mr Covey, the overseer. Whereas, however, Douglass is able to reflect on this physical fight and claim that it 'rekindled the few expiring embers of freedom, and revived within me a sense of my own manhood' (p. 298), Prince's verbal defence of herself, accusing her master of indecency and of having 'no shame for his own flesh', ends only in a temporary and abortive departure 'to a neighbouring house' (p. 203).

The impact of widespread White male abuse of female slaves on the stability and coherence of family ties is witnessed by many of the narrators as a consequent disturbance of the certainty of racial identities, and a confusion of the distinction between slave and master. Douglass, himself the offspring of a White father and a Black slave mother, recognises the steady increase in mixed-race children on southern plantations and the contradiction that this 'very different-looking class of people' (p. 257) represents for the logic of Black enslavement. If fatherhood occupies the same space as slave-mastery, racialised distinctions become blurred and familial boundaries are dangerously transgressed. Brent's observation of the presence of mulatto children on the plantations focuses on the disruptive effect this has on White family life, where southern White women notice 'children of every shade of complexion [who] play with their own fair babies' (*Six Women's Slave Narratives*, p. 368).

The ambiguities of race play an important role in the psyches of the male narrators, whose understanding of themselves in terms of Black manhood is central to their texts. Equiano's narrative, particularly, dwells on his self-understanding as an African male, and his living with the ambivalent identities of Englishman and African, or as 'the Black Christian' (*Equiano's Travels*, p. 57), leads him to painful reflections on his own racial identity. Equiano's acceptance of himself as a member of a culturally and historically defined race is preceded by the trauma of realising his visible difference from an English child. Noticing the rosy colour that characterises the face of his English child companion while washing, the young Equiano yearns to imitate her but is instead confronted with the horror of an alien self:

> I therefore tried often times myself if I could not by washing make my face of the same colour as my little playmate (Mary), but it was all in vain, and I began to be mortified at the difference in our complexions.
>
> (p. 57)

This moment of psychic self-alienation, which remains an integral part of Equiano's text through his continuing desire for cultural Anglicisation, is followed by a moment of collective self-recognition, where a Black boy, 'transported at the sight of one of his own countrymen', rushes to claim Equiano 'as if I had been a brother' (p. 50). Reading his own racialised visibility in terms of familial and national collectivities is an important part of Equiano's understanding of himself as residually African, and his constant portrayal of himself as having been externally *acted upon* in this respect – whether through the alienation of racialised difference, the sudden and perplexing embrace of a Black boy, or the literary and ethnographic ordering of his African memories – provides an insight into what it meant to live as an Anglicised African in the late eighteenth century. Equiano's preoccupation with race and its meaning re-surfaces towards the end of his narrative, where he mentions an incident that he realises to be irrelevant but which evidently excites and affects him enough to 'beg leave just to mention it' (p. 167). This 'remarkable circumstance relative to African complexion' (p. 167) involves the sight of 'a white negro woman' whose marriage to a White man produces 'three boys, and they were every one mulattoes, and yet they had fine light hair' (p. 167). The dislocation here between visible racial difference, which had so 'mortified' him as a boy, and the phenomenon of Whiteness *invisibly* producing Black offspring, evidently disturbs and disrupts the very externalised scrutiny that has ensured his existence as an African slave. The ambiguity of a 'white negro' identity, its evident internal contradiction, imaginatively offsets

Equiano's own ambiguous status as an African Englishman, a status that – as his recollection of the unpredictable and illogical biology of race makes clear – need not, in eighteenth-century England, be understood as ambiguous at all.

Cultures of resistance: nation and time

The development of Creole nationalism and its radical split from the time of the interior can be read as a useful paradigm for the creation of African post-colonial nation states. The relationship between the Freetown capital and pan-Africanist modernity is vital to the construction of a Sierra Leonean nation state that, in the late nineteenth century, begins to understand itself in racial and generic terms. The gaps between the bourgeoisie of Freetown society and the peasantry of up-country Sierra Leone, which became manifest during the nineteenth century, as well as the ideologies of race and nation, are readable through the significations of time. The impact of modern and Western pan-Africanist thinking on Freetown Black nationalism and the ensuing restlessness to convert, develop, dominate and modernise an 'inert' tribal interior have deep repercussions for twentieth-century nationalisms of decolonisation. From reading Frantz Fanon's examination of anti-colonial resistance within African nationalisms, and probing his conceptualisations of culture, modernity and time, this section of the chapter will move to a closer reading of African cultural nationalisms, which are further explored in relation to African literatures in the next section of this chapter.

Frantz Fanon's discussion of African colonisation presents a typology or generic pattern for the organisation of colonial states. His reading of the rigid demarcation of colonies as Manichaean divisions between settler and native, in which anti-colonial resistance has to follow the radical process of direct antagonism and necessary violence, relies on a reading of time and dependence that consistently places nationalist resistance within a logic of paradox and temporality. Fanon's repeated acknowledgement of the 'truth' in the forces of decolonisation in turn relies on his formulation of colonialism as intolerable precisely because of domination by the settler, and its resolution requires nothing less than a total reversal of terms. His invocation of the Messianic hope of the New Testament, 'The last shall be first and the first last',[34] expresses what B. Marie Perinbam names 'holy violence',[35] which can only operate within the already paradoxical terms of colonial power. These terms are described by Fanon as located within the White colonial desire to destroy everything native and assert once and for all, and without the fear, an absolute supremacy. This move would, in actuality, take away the role of dominant settler, of colonialist. It would destroy the principle and possibility of colonialism altogether: 'It is evident that this vacuum cleaning destroys the very thing that they want to preserve' (*Wretched of the Earth*, p. 67).

Abdul R. JanMohamed elaborates upon the inherent paradoxes of colonialism in his *Manichean Aesthetics*, and illuminates the foundations of colonial
Manicheism as a complicated play of contradictions. In his introduction he
traces three main conflicts inherent in the colonial situation. A Manichean
theory demands the utter negation of the native as an evil contamination
from which the settler is absolutely separate. This exists hand in hand with
the absolute necessity of the native as foil to European splendour and civilisation, as the means to White privilege. JanMohamed highlights a clear contradiction in colonial terms: 'the colonial system simultaneously wills the
annihilation and the multiplication of the natives'.[36] Similarly, the resolution
of one theoretical dilemma creates another in the realms of colonial paradox.
Having dispossessed the natives of land and political self-determination, the
European settler speaks self-consciously of humanism, fraternity, liberty and
democracy.[37] However, according to JanMohamed, if the coloniser pursues
these theories to their ultimate conclusion through a civilising mission, colonial authority is inevitably destroyed:

> This creates another contradiction for him: if he genuinely pursues
> his manifest destiny and 'civilizes' the native, then he undermines
> his own position of social privilege; if the democracy from his home
> country is extended to the dominated country, then the colonizer
> can no longer retain his superior status.
>
> (*Manichean Aesthetics*, p. 5)

If colonialism is fundamentally paradoxical, a contradiction in its very
nature, then its elimination depends upon an engagement with paradox. For
Fanon, the reality of unconscious life determines the new forces of identification that create nationalist decolonisation. The paradox of colonialism is not
to be found merely in external conditions, in the politics of appearance and
strategy; it permeates the natives' dream-world, constructing and affecting
the nature of desire and sexual identity. Colonialism changes, creates human
experience and subjectivity, rearranges the terms of being for both settler
and native. The confusion between hatred and desire, where resistance is
complicated by yearning and imitation, is, for Fanon, a central dynamic
within anti-colonial struggle.

The difficulties of decolonisation and the problems of Manichaeism can be
explored at the locus of violence. Fanon's investment in violence as a necessary cleansing force, the glorious secret of decolonisation, is joined with his
recognition of the ambiguities of violent action, its perjured origins and dangerous conclusions. The demands which are followed up with violence have
been furnished by colonisation, demands such as land ownership, the concept
of nation or a national economy, and such counter-claims contain a host of
contradictions. Violence is a 'cleansing force', release from the agonising
stalemate of native 'inferiority'; it pushes unconscious repression out into the

open, so it can be acted upon. Since 'the settler's work is to make even dreams of liberty impossible for the native' (*Wretched of the Earth*, p. 74), violence represents a triumph of inner creative life over attempts at its suffocation. The imagination is fed into wild activity by violence, and dream-work is thrown into recreation.[38] It is a cathartic remoulding and strengthening activity, the creation of a new identity, on an individual and a collective level:

> For the colonized people this violence, because it constitutes their only work, invests their characters with positive and creative qualities. The practice of violence binds them together as a whole, since each individual forms a violent link in the great chain, a part of the great organism of violence which has surged upwards in reaction to the settlers' violence in the beginning.[39]
>
> (*Wretched of the Earth*, p. 73)

These readings of violence and contradiction in Fanon's text are applicable to analyses of the plantation slave system in the slave narratives. Douglass' physical battle with his overseer for self-recognition is presented in terms similar to Fanon's treatment of violence as the path to self-determination, and the scenes of savage murder conflicting with the owner's desire for procreation reported in the narratives, support Fanon's and JanMohamed's theories of colonial paradox. The paradox of violence in Fanon's text is bound up with the phenomenon of utopian dreaming. The conflation of desire with envy, and of violent passion with the temptation to imitate, creates a complex pattern of dependence and mutual reliance. Longing for a world beyond colonialism is necessarily implicated in new and fixed patterns of struggle. Emotional groping after the meaning of freedom in the slave narratives is a useful complement to Fanon's ideas of an inevitably compromised notion of revolutionary liberation. Equiano's self-fashioning as an Englishman, and his understanding of literacy as a peculiarly English form of liberty, along with the saturation of north American patriotism in the African-American slave narratives, function as reminders of historical paradox.

The ambiguities of the colonial system itself are foregrounded by Fanon's discussion of colonial interlocutors and those who occupy the ambivalent spaces of collaborator or acculturated native. The deliberate fragmentation of a colonised people into separate spaces – as in the uneven divisions of nineteenth-century Freetown – results in a 'native' collectivity which is radically diverse, culturally and mutually antagonistic. Fanon's conclusion that colonial policy 'does not simply state the existence of tribes; it also reinforces it and separates them' (p. 74) is illustrated by Albert Memmi's examination of the Jewish people under French colonialism in Tunisia who occupy the ambiguous space *in-between* coloniser and colonised. Resolutely 'not Black' by decree of the Tunisian French authorities, and less colonised by a law which bestows quasi-Frenchness, the Jews are nonetheless unable to be totally assimilated. Writing from within this ambiguous territory, on the shifting ground between coloniser and colonised, Memmi bears witness to the splintering of antagonisms which is a necessary characteristic of colonialist policy. The Tunisian Jew's masquerade of coloniser-impersonation, while remaining chained to a colonised identity, is a signal presentation of colonial complexity. Memmi's assertion that his Jewishness led him to 'know the colonizer from the inside almost as well as I know the colonized' gestures towards the significance of this liminal space.[40]

Fanon's approach to time relies on his sense of the particular temporality of unconscious life, where desire and dreaming introduce a temporal plane that, while vital in encouraging anti-colonial sentiment, is dangerously elusive. The 'permanent confrontation on the phantasmic plane' (*Wretched of the Earth*, p. 43) must be translated into an acute awareness of the material present. This realm of transcendence or escape belongs to the imagined time of a pre-colonial past or utopian future, which subverts any active revolutionary engagement. Fanon's appraisal of unconscious activity as the key to notions of freedom, where, as with Douglass' meditation on the restlessness of ships, 'the dreams of the native . . . are of action and aggression. I dream I am jumping, swimming, running, climbing' (p. 40), is aligned with his refusal to continue living in a system that has lost its relevance and provides courage only to tilt at ghosts:

> By entangling myself in this inextricable network where actions are repeated with crystalline inevitability, I find the everlasting world which belongs to me, and the perenniality which is thereby affirmed of the world belonging to us.
>
> (p. 43)

This insistence on the meaning of temporality, with his simultaneous acknowledgement of contradictory times of struggle, is central to his argument. The continued attention to paradox and to the temporary contingencies of nationalist struggle is eloquently outlined at the beginning of *Black Skin, White Masks*:

> The architecture of this work is rooted in the temporal. Every human problem must be considered from the standpoint of time. Ideally, the present will always contribute to the building of the future.
>
> And this future is not the future of the cosmos but rather the future of my century, my country, my existence. In no fashion should I undertake to prepare the world that will come later. I belong irreducibly to my time.[41]

Fanon's intense concentration on the temporality of logic and strategy, which invest his argument with a restless fluidity and attention to contradiction, follows a Hegelian phenomenological schema. The *Phenomenology of Spirit* was described by Marx (in his 'Critique of Hegel's Dialectic and General Philosophy') as 'the true birthplace and secret of Hegel's philosophy'.[42] Irene Gendzier draws attention to Hegel's influence on Fanon's writings, centring particularly on Hegel's account of the master/slave dialectic: 'Three elements dominated Fanon's discussion of Hegel, which was limited to an analysis of the section in *Phenomenology* on "Lordship and Bondage": recognition, reciprocity and struggle' (*Frantz Fanon: A Critical Study*, p. 23).

Fanon's reading of Hegel's 'Lordship and Bondage' powerfully influences his conceptualisation of violent decolonisation, identity and history. His understanding of violence as the route to self-knowledge, and his focus on oppression as leading to a superior understanding of the self *and* the Other, are deeply marked by Hegel's construction of the master/slave dialectic. However, Fanon's reading of Marxist ideologies, particularly the impact of dialectical materialism on the concept of historical time and political identities, conditions his views on national culture and national consciousness and qualify any determination of his thinking as purely or uncritically 'Hegelian'.

Marx's criticisms of Hegel's writing call into question the very basis of the philosopher's logical progression and, in his 'Critique of Hegel's Dialectic and General Philosophy', he describes what he understands to be 'the one-sidedness and limitations of Hegel'. This 'one-sidedness' is, according to Marx, Hegel's reliance on 'abstract thought' as the central pivot of his philosophy, and not on objective, empirical reality. Hegel's 'uncritical idealism' ('Critique of Hegel's Dialectic', p. 100) is sewn into the *Phenomenology*, preventing any opportunity for genuine political engagement, for an appreciation of the actual, real 'spheres like religion, the state, civil life, etc.'. For Marx, Hegel's human being is a self-consciousness and consequently a being whose medium is essentially and only an abstraction: 'the self, abstracted and fixed for itself, is man as abstract egoist, egoism raised to its pure abstraction in thought' (p. 102). In this way, the external world is only a conception of the human self-consciousness, each object is merely a 'mirage' or an 'objectified essence' of the human mind. The very senses which have contact with what is outside of the immediate self are viewed by Hegel as belonging to the Self, that is, as being a part of the operations of self-consciousness: 'his eye, his ear, etc., take their nature from his self.' From this point, Marx begins his quest for the objective world.

Marx's analysis of labour is crucial: history is the reappropriation of labour by the worker, bringing about a positive relation between self and product. History is the path to true self-externalisation through creativity, the arriving at the point of Hegel's concept of the bondsman who progressively realises his own powers by working on the object.

Marx's views on the progression of History and state unification have notable consequences for his assessment of colonialist economics. His article on 'The Future Results of British Rule in India' (1853),[43] while it champions the cause of history as a positive progression that, through revolution, restores true human power to the unjustly powerless, has equally to be supportive of imperialism. Describing the British colonisation of India, Marx details some of the vast and sweeping changes forced onto Indian life. He outlines what he believes to be the role of the British Empire in India:

> England has to fulfil a double mission in India: one destructive, the other regenerating – the annihiliation of old Asiatic society, and the laying of the material foundations of Western society in Asia.
>
> (p. 332)

This 'double mission' is based on the analysis that 'Indian society has no history at all, at least no known history' (p. 332), and, therefore, industrialisation marks the beginning of a conscious History which will change the relationship between the worker and the product – a necessary precondition for the progress of humankind. Hailing British colonial rule as the advent of History, Marx dismisses pre-colonial Asia as a blank, prehistorical wasteland in 'the isolated position which was the prime law of its stagnation' (p. 333).

Reading Hegel and Marx offers inroads into Fanon's writing on national culture and the creation of African nation states. His use of Marx's concept of History in constructing a theory of anti-colonial revolution leads Fanon to push continually for new forms of cultural organisation and cultural expression. His acknowledgement of a 'time-lag, or a difference of rhythm' (*Wretched of the Earth*, p. 85) between nationalist leaders and the city proletariat, and of the further temporal rift between city and country regions, recognises the uneven narratives of history and cultural allegiance that characterise various sections of colonial society. Identifying the nationalist party leaders in the city capitals as inevitably isolated from the 'medieval' time of rural societies, Fanon emphasises the interested role of colonial administration in maintaining these rifts and in ensuring the 'petrification' (p. 87) and 'obscurantist traditions' (p. 86) of the rural areas. The eventual and inevitable anti-colonial uprisings of the outlying districts are directly out of time with the Europeanised proletariat of the capital city, who have merely become associated with a minority elite. A reading of the difference between Marx's account of proletarian revolution in highly industrialised societies and the rise of independent nation states in colonial Africa, while focusing on the revolutionary potential of the peasantry, still keeps in play the impatient desire for a dynamic approach to time and the historicisation of culture. Colonial repression of indigenous societies becomes analysed by Fanon in terms of the anti-historical rigidification of time: 'down there at the bottom [is] an undivided mass, still living in the Middle Ages, endlessly marking time' (p. 118).

Fanon's pinpointing of the rural peasantry as the locus for a radical and definitive anti-colonial uprising might facilitate an analysis of the 1898 Hut

Tax War in Sierra Leone: 'As for the people, they join in the new rhythm of the nation in their mud huts and in their dreams' (p. 101). However, his immediate invocation here of *nationalism* would need to be questioned. The Hut Tax rising (discussed in more detail above) mobilised the Mende, as a specific group, against the Freetown colony, possibly spurred by a sympathetic identification with the Temne chief, Bai Bureh.[44] Relating a culturally defined indigenous collectivity's violent resistance to colonial enemies – which included Creole nationalists – to Fanon's definitively nationalist organisation is difficult to justify.

Fanon's discussion of national culture in Africa makes various distinctions between nationalism, national consciousness and African consciousness. For Fanon, national consciousness in Africa is inevitably linked to African consciousness through the nature of European colonialism as a pan-African phenomenon. To understand African consciousness as a racialised collectivity that coalesces around a concept of 'Negro culture' (*Wretched of the Earth*, p. 170) is, for Fanon, a matter of historical logic, which determines that collective resistance be located on the site of attack: 'Colonialism's condemnation is continental in scope' (p. 170). However, the historical necessity and inevitability of a pan-Africanist consciousness under the racial concept of Negro-ism has, for Fanon, a separate time that is both preceded and succeeded by national consciousness: 'every culture is first and foremost national' (p. 174).

This insistence that collective resistance and identity in colonial and post-colonial societies be theorised as *national* is placed within a curious narrative sequence. Fanon attacks any tendency for racial and tribal unities to become paramount over national unity by claiming these identifications as part of the 'process of retrogression' (p. 119). Insistently mapping the nation in a progressive time scheme leaves a lingering uncertainty around the question of the nation's beginning. Fanon discusses the impact of colonial domination as the onset of a 'cultural obliteration [which] is made possible by the negation of national identity' (p. 190) and he claims that colonialism's effect on African countries is to call 'a halt to national culture' (p. 191). This would seem to locate national consciousness as a *pre-existent* aspect of pre-colonial societies, where culture was already 'first the expression of a nation' (p. 196). However, Fanon's discussions of anti-colonial nationalisms regularly emphasise the notion of 'continuous renewal' (p. 197), of new departures and novel formations, pointing towards the inauguration of original group identities and expressions. The existence of this phase of Fanon's argument alongside his recognition of anti-colonial struggle as an attempt to '*re-establish* the sovereignty of the nation' (p. 197; my emphasis) leaves unclear the precise meaning of nation and culture in Fanon's text.

Fanon's reading of History is, however, constantly re-working and re-arranging the relationship between past and present, and insisting that present contingencies and new departures condition and dominate the past.

Paradoxically, the past, in Fanon's argument, is rescued wholesale from colonial rhetoric and 'given back its value' (p. 170) and, in continental and holistic terms, 'culture' is 'directly extracted from the past' (p. 170). Equally, 'culture' is an expression of changing and dynamic social realities that is relentlessly opposed to the 'desire to attach oneself to tradition' (p. 180).

This temporal balancing act in Fanon's text, where he seeks to follow a range of strategic responses to various historical moments in African nationalisms, can be analysed via Partha Chatterjee's reading of the difficulties and contradictions which are inherent in any expression of colonial nationalisms:

> Where nations are inexact, and have political value precisely because they are inexact and hence capable of suggesting a range of possible interpretations; where intentions themselves are contradictory and consequences very often unintended; where movements follow winding and unpredictable paths; where choices are strategic and relative, not univocal and absolute.[45]

Chatterjee's analysis of the differences between Western and Eastern nation states underlines the role of 'culture' as an important component in national self-consciousness. For 'Western nations', cultural organisation is presented as highly advanced technologically and capable of translation into sophisticated national unities, whereas 'Eastern nations', constantly in a comparative position vis-à-vis the West, were faced with the need to re-equip themselves culturally: 'the search therefore was for a regeneration of the national culture, adapted to the requirements of progress, but retaining at the same time its distinctiveness' (pp. 1–2). Referring this to Fanon's presentation of national cultures in African colonies, the sense of dislocation between the nation and its *need for* a suitable collective cultural self-understanding illuminates the disjunctive nature of Fanon's time scheme.

The problems in Fanon's positing of a *generic* African nation state emerging from a *typified* African colony also create particular conceptual difficulties around his analysis of national culture and revolution. His refusal to countenance the role of differential ethnic identities within the totality of the nation, or to call for the unification of the state *within the same time*, is reminiscent of Blyden's treatises on the urgent modernisation of indigenous cultural unities under the mantle of metropolitan values, and Fanon's identity as a Caribbean migrant to a part of colonial Africa (Algeria) may also be pertinent. Christopher Miller comments on Fanon's use of generalised critical patterns, indicating precisely how his generic terms have specific geographical locations: 'when Fanon says "nation", I think he means Algeria. When he says "Africa", he also seems to mean Algeria.'[46] This use of Algerian particularities as paradigmatic for all African nations, in an overshadowing relation between North and South, can be read as a coercion analogous to the coercion Chatterjee questions in relation to European colonial narratives:

Why is it that non-European colonial countries have no historical alternative but to try to approximate the given attributes of modernity when that very process of approximation means their continued subjection under a world order which only sets their tasks for them and over which they have no control?

(*Nationalist Thought and the Colonial World*, p. 10)

Possible futures: modernity and tradition

This section of the chapter will re-visit the issues of African national cultures and resistance through novels by Ngũgĩ Wa Thiong'o, Sembene Ousmane and Wole Soyinka. These modern African novels engage with the questions discussed in this chapter and reveal their continuing relevance for modern African self-consciousness. The role of national identity, the meaning of independence, the problem of modernity and the place of women in these problematics are significantly refigured in these works. Focusing on the parameters of historical thinking and the interpretation of land, space and territory within the literary texts, the meanings of nationhood, culture and race as political and social imaginaries can be determined. Connections between African anti-colonial cultural nationalisms and modern African-American appropriations of Africa for re-readings of history and origins will be traced through an examination of African-American feminisms and women's writings in the following chapter.

The novels of Ngũgĩ attempt to use political ideas and analyses of colonial and postcolonial Africa as artistic form, and his use of mimesis and imaginative creativity as an assessment of colonised and independent Kenyan society allows his novels to function on various levels, simultaneously didactic, political, historical and predictive. The differences between political and literary texts and the uneasy disjunctions between the two are focused onto the relationship between imaginary character and political vision, where it is the connections *between* elements that provide political and social meaning. Simon Gikandi's analysis of Ngũgĩ's role as both artist and ideologue leads him to read the novels as an attempt to 'strike a balance between consciousness and characters as modes of mediating reality'.[47]

Ngũgĩ's textured narrative form, where characters are vitally connected in a tissue of historical and political contingencies, and individual destinies are powerfully affected by group activities, leads to a continual foregrounding of collective consciousness as the central interpretative locus of the novels. In *Petals of Blood* (1977),[48] the presentation of characters as irrevocably connected by the historical and social forces determining their lives – characters who, beyond these connections, are condemned to an absence of meaning – emphasises the creation and role of culture – or group – expression as an essential factor of individual identities. This notion of collective consciousness is used in a range of different ways to denote a transcendent or inclusive narrative voice, providing objective or subjective interpretations of character or situation, or as a force located in the interweaving personal narratives of the characters themselves. The use of a communal 'we' to represent the group consciousness of Ilmorog village occurs at moments where the narrative collapses back on itself to project the subjective, intimate voice of a living community: 'Still the question remained: why Ilmorog? Maybe now all our children will come back to us, for what's a village without young blood?' (p. 31). At other moments, a contrasting narrative voice provides an objective scrutiny of Ilmorog and its life, with the more distant use of 'they'. The ethnographic perspective provided by phrases such as: 'Peasants emerged from the fields of maize and grouped in twos or threes in the open paths' (p. 33), and its alternation with the more directly subjective passages, is similar in structure to Olaudah Equiano's narrative of African childhood in Eboe. The need at once to identify with and analyse Ilmorog village society intersects with the continual representations and mutual self-definitions which operate in the intimate conversations and revelations of the central characters. Both an increasingly interconnected and related group of people and also separate, distantiated and heterogeneous individuals with repressed and private pasts, these central personalities – Wanja, Munira, Karega, Nyakinyua and Abdulla – present the complicated and negotiated interplay between individual and group, community interaction and cultural expression.

Representing the dispersed and yet mutually significant lives of these key characters relies on Ngũgĩ's use of narrative time. Flashback, belated revelation, the alternating relation of fragmented individual recollection are used to present a past that is constantly reinterpreted, constantly in flux. Narrative time continually circles back on itself, recapitulating individual past events in the illuminating totality of collective signification, and relentlessly overlapping one life onto another. The importance of past history for the novel's presentation of culture is revealed in Munira's expression of his need for lonely isolation: 'he was not one to want to tear the veils round another's past' (p. 33). The multiple yet mutual histories of independent Kenya are signified by this group of characters, whose relationships with each other are conditioned by the operation of political and institutional power. Each damaged by the anguish of the past and connected by the magical dreaming of Theng'eta, the apparently discontinuous threads of Kenyan history gain an important political unity. The structure of empathy upon which these several threads rely is a consequence of love, recognition and self-knowledge: 'she had somehow drawn Abdulla and Munira into her world and they seemed also to experience this wound, or maybe it reminded them of their own wounds' (p. 41). The mapping of one story onto another to create a complex singular narrative is never allowed to imply the closure of the past in a quiet and distant resolution. Karega, for example, reflects on Nyakinyua's revelations of Ilmorog's past to find himself caught in a web of discontinuities and open-ended uncertainties:

Karega glanced at her figure, bent so, and repeated to himself: no longer the same. He turned the phrase over and over again in his mind as if this alone explained all the agony, all the hidden meanings in her unfinished – well, in their unfinished – story.

(p. 214)

This meditation on personal memory leads to a tortured interrogation of the narrative of African history, and the interweaving of mythical time with economic history, missionary education with pan-Africanist unity, is preceded by the question: 'Which past was one talking about?' (p. 214). Africa, conceived as a totality with a shared imperialist history is nevertheless subject to a war of historical interpretation, the translation and selection of which is placed at the centre of the novel's political vision: 'Africa, after all, did not have one but several pasts which were in perpetual struggle. Images pressed on images' (p. 214).

The dependence of historical interpretation on the dynamics of art and culture builds a powerful symbolic connection between the living reality of the land and the energy of cultural exchange. The novel's obsessive revisiting of the seasonal, changing and enduring presence of the natural landscape is illustrative of how Ngũgĩ envisages the foundation of historical and cultural life in the eternal flux of native environment. Discussing the origin of Kenyan peoples in an ancient and passionate communion with the land, Ngũgĩ is able to provide a defence of *national* consciousness:

The story of the heroic resistance: who will sing it? Their struggles to defend their land, their wealth, their lives: who'll tell of it? . . . Just now we can only depend on legends passed from generation to generation by the poets and players.

(p. 67)

That national consciousness should take its cue from the dramatic beauty and climatic shifts of the land, where rural farmers develop an intense knowledge of self and community survival through their struggle with nature's unpredictability, emphasises the *unnatural* inroads of an artificially imposed metropolitan national culture. In close agreement with Fanon, the novel demonstrates the importance of culture as the expression of a people in their own developing sense of community and continuity. The advent of KCO as an instrument of coercion from the Kenyan capital to organise rural populations into an artificial bond of 'cultural authenticity' and 'ethnic unity' (p. 186) merely presents static and rigidified ideas of African culture from a pre-colonial past to *suppress* the rural interior into the restraining force of the capital. In opposition to the structure of repression and false petrifications of culture, Ngũgĩ recalls a pre-colonial past whose values were directly tied to notions of community, communication and respect for the independence of nature, the living majesty of the land:

> Yes: the native was still afraid of nature. But he revered man's life as much as he revered nature. Man's life was God's sacred fire that had to remain lit all the way from the ancestor to the child and the generations yet unborn.

The gap between village and metropolis is presented in terms of a temporal imbalance, where Ilmorog's vital connection with its past and the land occupies a 'traditional' space which is far removed from the disconnected temporality of the modern city. The dramatisation of this distantiation between 'traditional' and 'modern' is given in the central narrative of the epic journey that the main characters undertake from Ilmorog to the capital. This central image of migration, which acts as a pivotal movement of change in the novel, echoes the centrepoint of *Things Fall Apart*, where Okonkwo endures a seven-year exile in the dislocated and separate time of his mother's village. This pilgrimage of appeal from country to city cannot succeed precisely because of the dominating stance of metropolitan authority and the combined forces of a corrupt and unchecked modernity. Munira's assessment of Ilmorog's place as a peripheral and deprived rural landscape, cut off from the concentration of power and wealth in the former colonial centres, emphasises the role of geographical distance as a way of conceptualising power:

> Our erstwhile masters had left us a very unevenly cultivated land: the centre was swollen with fruit and water sucked from the rest, while the outer parts were progressively weaker and scraggier as one moved away from the centre.
>
> (p. 49)

Significantly, the change brought about by the long pilgrimage is described in terms of the infiltration and disturbance of time, spilling the influence of past actions and distant places onto Ilmorog's own time: 'We did not then know that within a year the journey . . . would send its emissaries from the past, to transform Ilmorog and change our lives utterly, Ilmorog and us utterly changed' (p. 242).

The dramatic and sudden disruptions of industrialisation in Ilmorog, presaged by the coming of aeroplane, road and the division of land into several private ownerships, allows disjunctive times to exist side by side in an unhealable rift between Old and New Ilmorog. The commercialisation of Theng'eta's mythical power to re-invoke the memories of Mau Mau, ancient settlement and cultural unity occurs alongside the re-interpretation of land into property, and the former harmony of independent histories into coherent narratives becomes a series of splintered and discontinuous times and spaces:

'It was New Kenya. It was New Ilmorog. Nothing was free. . . . There were several Ilmorogs' (p. 280).

However disjointed the time of New and Old Ilmorog may be, the novel reveals an intricate pattern of connections in the play of colonial and imperialist power. Ngũgĩ's description of the operations of power in colonial Africa, reminiscent of the issues presented in *Ambiguous Adventure*, relies on a conception of three dependent and mutually supportive faces of colonialism, and he seeks to uncover the oppressive ideological force which Christianity has become in independent African nation states:

> We can imagine the fatal meeting between the native and the alien. The missionary . . . carried the Bible; the soldier carried the gun; the administrator and the settler carried the coin. Christianity, Commerce, Civilisation: the Bible, the Coin, the Gun: Holy Trinity.
>
> (p. 88)

These three forces, religion, economic domination and military oppression, become actualised in the three central figures of power, Mzigo, Chui and Kimeria, and it is this symbolic centralisation of power that allows the novel to create its powerful denouement, tying together the strands of the past in order to usher in an analysis of the future. Gikandi reads African political novels as attempts to place African peoples 'on a specific time scale, to understand the meaning and dimension of history' (*Reading the African Novel*, p. 111). This illustrates Ngũgĩ's use of History as a narrative force, holding the secrets of its own conclusions in the seeds of the past. This reading of history as a teleology, which progressively draws meaning and significance from disordered fragments into intelligible wholes, leads the novel to a demonstration of the activities of fate and destiny. The murder of Chui, Mzigo and Kimeria in Wanja's bordello is repeatedly foreshadowed in earlier sections of the novel where, for example, Munira accidentally sets fire to the curtains in Wanja's hut (p. 62), leading Wanja to recall the terror of death by fire (p. 65), and, preceding this, Munira recalls a childhood memory of ritualistically burning the effigy of a house: 'He watched the flames and he felt truly purified by fire' (p. 14).

The vision of a peasant and proletarian revolution at the end of the novel – 'Tomorrow it would be the workers and the peasants leading the struggle and seizing power' (p. 344) – which is conceived in class and internationalist, rather than racial, terms (p. 165), is based on a utopian dreaming of the future, which is simply gestured towards at the novel's close: '"Tomorrow . . . tomorrow . . ." he murmured to himself' (p. 345). Miller analyses this projective move in Ngũgĩ's text as an important part of revolutionary thought, which seeks to create the belief and desire for another possible world: 'The ability to think oneself out of reality, into an *irreal* but *possible* sphere, is the trademark of authors like Ngũgĩ' (*Theories of Africans*, p. 297).

The link between the Mau Mau uprisings in colonial Kenya between 1952 and 1957 and the anticipation of a worker and peasant revolution is presented as a vital historical continuity. The sacrifices of the Mau Mau, still lingering in the memory of the land, and in Abdulla's personal recollections, have not been entirely superseded by the industrial modernity of New Ilmorog. Wanja's conception of a child by Abdulla, presented as the force of a prophesied destiny, tied inexorably to natural forces, creates a sense of the Mau Mau's future continuation though the new generations. The novel's title can be read as the poetic expression of the indelibility of past sacrifice in the national imaginary, and the text foregrounds the relationship between the Mau Mau and the earth on and for which it fought:

> 'Look. A flower with petals of blood.'
> It was a solitary red beanflower in a field dominated by white, blue and violet flowers. No matter how you looked at it, it gave you the impression of a flow of blood.
>
> (p. 21)

Ngũgĩ's *Petals of Blood* moves towards its close with Joseph, a young adult in the poor section of modern Ilmorog, holding a copy of Sembene Ousmane's novel *God's Bits of Wood* (p. 338). Between *Petals of Blood*, a novel from post-colonial East Africa, and *God's Bits of Wood*, set in French colonial Senegal, the connections are salient, each text presenting the same international perspective of class and capitalism. Between Sembene's novel, first published in French as *Les Bouts de bois de Dieu* in 1960, and Kane's *Ambiguous Adventure*, first published as *L'Aventure ambiguë* in 1961, though both explore the consequences of French colonialism in Senegal, the differences can be located in the diverging political worlds each novel represents.[49] Whereas *Ambiguous Adventure* examines colonialism as a spiritual trauma resulting in individual psychic alienation, *God's Bits of Wood* founds itself in the material universe of labour relations, anti-colonial trade unionism and the struggles of a newly defined and self-defining West African community.

In concordance with *Petals of Blood*, Ousmane's novel presents the inter-relationship of history and community as of singular importance, with the stability and continuance of communal life being subject to the forces of industrialisation and change. The novel, based on a strike by Senegalese railway workers in 1947,[50] opens with a description of nature, of season and landscape: 'The last rays of the sun filtered through a shredded lacework of clouds. . . . It was an afternoon in mid-October' (p. 1). This description of natural forces as the opening drama of the novel, introducing the territory of a regional village, is placed in stark contrast with the cityscape of industrial waste and decaying, discarded objects that introduces the following chapter. This bleak modernist wasteland of inanimate and animal detritus, 'where all the rot of the city has gathered' (p. 13), becomes symbolic of an alienated world of products against which the drama of climate and earth illustrates a world of human passion and ancient forces: 'Indeed, all human activities in the novel take place against a background of the earth and the sky, two stable frames for an otherwise dislocated universe' (*Reading the African Novel*, p. 119).

The 'dislocation' of the novel's universe results from the domination of industrial labour, and a pitched battle for control of and recognition from this world of mechanical production gives rise to a series of dramatic revelations. The role of industrial labour in forming self-consciousness and identity becomes manifest at the moment of industrial seizure, and the inactivity produced by strike action allows a sustained and central transformation of the railway worker's self-understanding.

The realisation that 'the machine ruled over the lands' (p. 32) leads to a new concentration on their human condition:

> They began to understand that the machine was making of them a whole new breed of men. It did not belong to them; it was they who belonged to it. When it stopped, it taught them that lesson.
>
> (p. 32)

This description of the central importance of labour for human identity and self-knowledge forces the recognition, not that a more 'truthful' subjectivity lies in the pre-colonial past where 'Africa was just a garden for food' (p. 32), but that a changing industrialised future, which is, in turn, recreating humankind and determining human allegiances, is now the primary cultural destination:

> Something was being born inside them, as if the past and the future were coupling to breed a new kind of man, and it seemed to them that the wind was whispering a phrase they had often heard from Bakayoko: 'The kind of man we were is dead, and our only hope for a new life lies in the machine, which knows neither a language nor a race.'
>
> (p. 76)

The new culture of class, increasingly erasing older nationalist identifications, also determines the relationship between coloniser and colonised, so that a striking worker is able to claim to the French director of railways: 'You do not represent a nation or a people here, but simply a class. We represent another class, whose interests are not the same as yours' (p. 182). In this way, the 'freedom' which is so painfully striven for in the slave narratives becomes re-articulated here as indissoluble from the dynamism of industrial life. Bakayoko's declaration of his own relationship with his physical and spiritual self is directly mediated by the power of his relationship with machine and labour:

> I take on a sense of absolute identity with everything that is in the train, no matter whether it is passengers or just freight. I experience everything that happens along its whole length . . . once the engine is on its way, I forget everything else . . . I don't even know any longer whether it is my heart that is beating to the rhythm of the engine, or the engine to the rhythm of my heart.
>
> (p. 208)

This total sexualised and spiritualised identification with the mechanical object of labour determines the meaning of the strike as a constructive re-affirmation of equality between worker and train, and not as a destructive denial of the sublimation and projection of self onto machine which characterises what has become the passion of labour. Ownership and control of self in modern industrialised Africa is here shown to lie in control of the means of production, which in itself becomes an anti-colonial strategy.

National identity and a relationship with the nation of Senegal, although redefined in internationalist and communal terms, remains a critical foundation for the novel. Each chapter, named after a town or city in Senegal, creates a sense of geographical reality, and asserts the importance of place, distance and national mapping in the new connections and exchanges that are made. The role of space and place in determining communal or familial identity and change is paramount, and the 'cinematic' focus of the opening chapter, descending from sky to earth onto the courtyard life of the women in Bakayako's household, establishes the separateness of men's and women's landscapes. Women's place at the hearth, with family and children, is resolutely linked with the dispersal of space, with walls and enclosures. The solidity of past generations and their role in familial life is figured in Niakoro's grandmotherly position against the 'hard, clay wall' (p. 1) that provides the backbone of house and courtyard. The family's construction out of 'God's bits of wood' (p. 40) emphasises the importance of people's communal interconnections, which, equally, converge to create solid, societal constructions. In this way, communal change affects the intimate and vital exchanges between people: 'these characters are always presented as members of a community, or in relation to a social group that holds certain distinctive values, so that their growth as individuals indicates significant changes in the nature of this society' (*Reading the African Novel*, p. 115).

Alienation from this community of women, which forms a central component of village life, is analysed as a situation of isolation and false consciousness. For N'Deye, her separation from the life and value of Bamako's society is a result of her absorption in European literatures, centring her vision on alien geographical and cultural landscapes: 'Real life was there; not here, in this wretched corner' (p. 57). Ignorance of one's own environment, signified antithetically by N'Deye's excellent knowledge of European geography – 'she had won the prize in geography several times' (p. 58) – results in her acute inability to understand the Africa in which she lives: 'But she had never read a book by an African author – she was quite sure that they could teach her nothing' (p. 58). Thus, Niakoro's grandmotherly advice to Ad'ji-bid'ji is shown to have a certain validity, upholding the value of exchange between generations: 'Among my people, who are your father's people, too, no one speaks the white man's language and no one has died of it!' (p. 4).

Once the foundational role of women and their habitually circumscribed domain has been presented, the industrial changes brought about by the strike are made to reveal the patterns of reliance which pertain between each member of the community. Radical disturbances between men and labour become profound disruptions in female subjectivity: 'And the men began to understand that if the times were bringing forth a new breed of men, they were also bringing forth a new breed of women' (p. 34). This transformation, figured in geographical terms, leads women beyond the circumscriptions of courtyard enclosures in a march across the national landscape of Senegal, and uncovers the links between female domesticity in the villages and the city world of men and machines. Breaking away from the hearth, the transformation of women is figured in images of physical violence, energetic travel and passionate expression. From emerging as 'a band of Amazons . . . armed with clubs, with iron bars, and bottles' (p. 22), the women cross the boundaries of regional districts in order to create a powerful feminist identity, articulated in the visceral power of song:

> The women had not stopped singing. As soon as one group allowed the refrain to die, another picked it up, and new verses were born at the hazard of chance or inspiration, one word leading to another and each finding, in its turn, its rhythm and its place.
>
> (p. 190)

Allowing the women to represent continuity and exchange and using them as the expressive core of the community, Ousmane is able to reveal the extent of the revolution which the strike entails. Gikandi's analysis of Ousmane's approach to women as 'the real preservers of African culture' (*Reading the African Novel*, p. 122) illuminates the vision that ends the novel. Concluding his narrative with the image of a blind woman singing a revolutionary song, Ousmane, in a vein similar to Ngũgĩ, presents the future of African culture in terms of industrial modernity and proletarian struggle:

> From one sun to another,
> The combat lasted,
> And fighting together, blood-covered,

They transfixed their enemies.
But happy is the man who does battle without hatred.

(p. 245)

A discussion of modernity in Ngũgĩ's *Petals of Blood* and Ousmane's *God's Bits of Wood*, and of their analyses of history, nation and culture, can be furthered by looking here at Wole Soyinka's novel *The Interpreters*.[51] Published in 1965 and set in independent Nigeria, Soyinka's text can be read as an examination of the parameters of modern West African life, and of the relevance of traditional African cultures in modern African cities. The movement between the coastal life and value of Lagos and the ancient familial continuities of the interior – a paradigmatic structure that informs many of the texts discussed in this book – allows the novel to discuss how African identities are mediated by Western currencies. The constant invasion of demands, spiritual disturbances and memories from up-country Nigeria into the fragmented space of the city reveals how complex are the mediations of modern African identities with an indigenous past.

The modernity explored in *The Interpreters* is one which simultaneously and uneasily juxtaposes the chaos of the city and the certainty of family and dynasty; secular Lagos and communion with the gods; life and the reign of the dead. Egbo's struggle with the destiny of his own past leads to constant but unsuccessful attempts to place death outside and beyond the individual and the present. Asked by Bandele what the past means to him, Egbo answers:

> It should be dead. . . . When people die, in one sense or the other, it should not matter what they were to us. They owe the living a duty to be forgotten quickly, usefully. Believe me, the dead should have no faces.

(p. 120)

The value of this attempt to 'become ruthless with the fabric of the past' (p. 120) is counteracted both by the corruption and cynicism of modern, educated life and by Egbo's own spiritual communion with the gods or with the haunting meaning of his familial past, where he recognises: 'Knowledge . . . a power for beauty often, an awareness that led him dangerously towards a rocksalt psyche, a predator on Nature' (p. 127).

His sorrowful and frustrated question about the power of family and dynasty rests on a genuine dilemma about the relevance of continuing traditions to the bourgeois sway of individualism. As he says:

> Over there is a blind old man and a people, waiting on some mythical omniscience of my generation. But what on earth can such an existence hold out for me?

(p. 12)

Egbo's references to 'blood skeins and their . . . tyrannous energies' (p. 12) and Dehinwa's confrontation with 'blood cruelty' (p. 39) initiate an interrogation of individual and collective identifications with modern Africa and complicate what might be meant by family, race, history or culture.

Caught in the ambiguities of a modern (Nigerian) nation, the characters are faced with multiple interpretations of the meaning of national identity. Egbo's statement that 'there is also my pride of race . . . I am after all, an Egbo' (p. 12) refers to family and tribal identity, as well as to a religious devotion, a kingdom and a village culture. Implicit in these contradictions between urban and agrarian life are dichotomies such as Nature and Culture, Past and Present, Living and Dead, Collectivity and Individuality, dichotomies that become restlessly confused, interrogated and dissolved.

The character Sekoni's idea of the 'dome of continuity' insists, through the cracked and splintered difficulties of his speech (which frustrates the fluidity of its own message), on the Yoruba notion expounded in Soyinka's *Myth, Literature and the African World*[52] of the *plurality* of life in the unity of religious experience:

> In the d-d-dome of the cosmos, th-there is com . . . plete unity of lllife. Llife is like the g-g-godhead, the p-p-plurality of its mmmani-fest . . . ations is only an illusion. Th-the g-g-godhead is one. So is life, or d-d-death, b-b-both are c-c-contained in the single d-d-dome of ex . . . istence . . .
>
> (p. 122)

Sekoni's stutter expresses the alienation both of himself and of the unity of which he speaks from the competing value of modern Nigerian life.

Egbo's use of 'race' as a family identity is taken up by Joe Golder as a 'negro' or pan-African identity tied inexorably to the physical and visual body. Conceiving Blackness to be his cheated birthright, buried deep within his body, Joe Golder, as an American in Nigeria, perceives his own hidden African-ness in a similar way to his own non-visual sexuality; it is something which needs to be declared, to come out. His references to Blackness are pathologically linked to ideas of sentimental homecoming, longing to belong, which serve to personify and reify Blackness into stereotypes:

> I like black people, I really do. Black people are exciting, their colour has such vitality, I mean it is something really beautiful, distinctive. . . . Black is something I like to be, that I have every right to be. There is no reason at all why I shouldn't have been born jet black.
>
> (p. 195)

Sagoe's retort that Golder is 'mentally white' (p. 195) contrasts with the references to the albinos, Lazarus and Usaye, whose 'mental blackness' contradicts the Whiteness of their skin. The horror of Lazarus' body, which seemed 'not to share with him a normal physical consistency' (p. 119), and Usaye's almost magical non-humanity, whose 'miracle' is her two Black parents (p. 48), serve to question the discourses of race and heritage which are implicitly relied upon in writing on African identity. The physical perversion of the albinos' appearance is presented, in fact, as no more a perversion than Joe Golder's 'slavering over blackness' (p. 217), as the repository of all that is valuable and able to be recaptured in Africa.

'Nigeria' and African values are translated or 'interpreted', and the idea of 'Africa' itself as a spurious or unexamined unity is explored, for example, in the performance of fire-eaters in a cabaret show in the bar, through which can be envisaged the unified image of the 'Africa' which lives in world exports:

> The drumming had turned brisk for the floorshow, it was the familiar beat that announced the guttural entry of the witch doctor in foreign films on Africa.

> (p. 157)

The movement of this chapter from an exploration of the founding of the Freetown colony on Africa's West Coast to a reading of certain twentieth-century African novels, is intended to uncover the relationship between colonial and early nationalist constructions of Africa and African identities. The impact of pan-Africanist re-articulations of the meaning of Africa, which introduce and perpetuate cultural exchanges between the Americas, Europe and the African West Coast, is of lasting significance for twentieth-century attempts at redefining the place of African cultural specificities and African nationalisms in the modern world. The restless travels and forced migrations of enslaved African peoples, and the later struggles to demonstrate the meanings of freedom and independence, have continuing reverberations within movements for decolonisation and the creation of African nation states, as well as in the theoretical and imaginative literatures that interpret, metaphorise and reconstruct the histories and futures of Africa.

Focusing on Sierra Leone as a place of historical reference usefully demonstrates the close relationships and exchanges between the Caribbean, African-America and Britain. The crucial historical contingencies that connect diasporic thought, politics and culture with West African coastal capitals continue to determine the parameters within which 'Africa' is imagined and through which political movements are organised. After tracing links between nation and race in Sierra Leone's history, and in the writings of slaves and pan-Africanists, analogous constructions and complexities have been located in twentieth-century African 'political' literatures. The difficult connections and disconnections of race, gender and nation, and the reconstructions of African and Black identities that emerge in twentieth-century women's writing, will perform a vital re-visitation of the historical issues and debates figured in this chapter.

Notes

1 See John Peterson, *A History of Sierra Leone, 1787–1870* (London: Faber & Faber, 1969), p. 19. Further references will be cited in the text.

2 Richard West points out that Smeathman's motives were certainly unclear, and probably suspect. His 'main ambition of winning a fortune' makes Smeathman's plan, for West, a dishonest one; see Richard West, *Back to Africa* (London: Jonathan Cape, 1970), p. 22. Further references will be cited in the text.

3 This included his wish to be paid the sum of £4 for every settler; see Peterson, *A History of Sierra Leone*, p. 18.

4 See Edward Wilmot Blyden, *Christianity, Islam and the Negro Race* (Edinburgh: Edinburgh University Press, 1967 [1887]), p. 191: 'Through the efforts of Sharp, a decision was obtained from Chief Justice Mansfield in 1772, laying down the principle that "as soon as any slave sets foot on English ground he becomes free".' Further references will be cited in the text. See also West, *Back to Africa*, p. 14.

5 See Hayden White, *Tropics of Discourse: Essays in Cultural Criticism* (Baltimore, MD: Johns Hopkins University Press, 1978), p. 51: 'A historical narrative is thus necessarily a mixture of adequately and inadequately explained events, a congeries of established and inferred facts, at once a representation that is an interpretation and an interpretation that passes for an explanation of the whole process mirrored in the narrative.'

6 Michel Foucault, 'Of Other Spaces' (originally 'Des Espaces autres', lecture, March 1967), Diacritics 16(1) (1986), p. 22. Further references will be cited in the text.

7 Leo Spitzer, *Lives In Between: Assimilation and Marginality in Austria, Brazil, West Africa, 1780–1945* (Cambridge: Cambridge University Press, 1989), p. 31. Further references will be cited in the text.

8 Richard West adds that 'a few white artisans and officials with their families, and a group of white women of doubtful number and character' were among the passengers. He mentions that 'most history books' state that these women numbered 'seventy London prostitutes' (*Back to Africa*, p. 24).

9 Blyden also mentions the transportation from the United States in 1815 of thirty emigrants by the Negro Paul Cuffee (*Christianity, Islam and the Negro Race*, p. 198).

10 See Kenneth Little, *The Mende of Sierra Leone: A West African People in Transition* (London: Routledge and Kegan Paul; New York: The Humanities Press, 1967 [1951]), p. 43, where Little dates the Colony from 1806. Further references will be cited in the text.

11 Mrs R. Lee, *The African Wanderers: or, the Adventures of Carlos and Antonio, embracing interesting descriptions of the manners and customs of the western tribes, and the natural productions of the country* (London: Grant and Griffith, 1850 [1847]), pp. 60-1.

12 See West, *Back to Africa*, p. 161: 'the Black ruling class in Sierra Leone during the nineteenth century was formed from the recaptured slaves. . . . Although the first recaptives had to fight for a place in society, they soon outnumbered and later absorbed the descendants of the original settlers, the Nova Scotians and the Maroons.'

13 See West, ibid., on the 'tribes or peoples from which the recaptives had come. The most numerous of these two peoples were the Yorubas, nicknamed Akos, from what is now western Nigeria, and the Ibos from what was recently Biafra.'

105

14 Adelaide Smith Casely-Hayford, 'Mista Courifer', in Charlotte H. Bruner (ed.), *Unwinding Threads: Writing by Women in Africa* (London: Heinemann, 1983), p. 10.

15 Sir Samuel Lewis was a key member of the Creole upper classes, being the first Creole to be knighted and a powerful lawyer and mayor; see West, *Back to Africa*, pp. 172 and 173.

16 See also Donald Cosentino, *Defiant Maids and Stubborn Farmers: Tradition and Invention in Mende Story Performance* (Cambridge: Cambridge University Press, 1982), pp. 2–4. Further references will be cited in the text.

17 Bonnie J. Barthold, *Black Time: Fiction of Africa, The Caribbean, and the United States* (New Haven, CN: Yale University Press, 1981), p. 5. Further references will be cited in the text.

18 On Crummell see Kwame Anthony Appiah, *In My Father's House: Africa in the Philosophy of Culture* (London: Methuen, 1992), pp. 4–5. Further references will be cited in the text.

19 Janheinz Jahn, *Muntu: An Outline of Neo-Colonial Culture* (London: Faber & Faber, 1961 [1958], p. 191. Further references will be cited in the text.

20 See West *Back to Africa*, p. 165: 'By 1842, as many as five hundred recaptives had gone back as businessmen to the land of their origin.'

21 Paul Gilroy, *The Black Atlantic: Modernity and Double Consciousness* (London: Verso, 1993), p. 4. Further references will be cited in the text.

22 Henry Louis Gates, Jr, Foreword to *Six Women's Slave Narratives*, the Schomberg Library of Nineteenth-Century Black Women Writers (New York: Oxford University Press, 1988), p. xviii. Further references will be cited in the text.

23 W.E.B. DuBois, *The Souls of Black Folk* (New York: Bantam Books, 1989 [1903]), p. 3. Further references will be cited in the text.

24 Toni Morrison, 'The Site of Memory', in Russell Ferguson *et al.* (eds), *Out There: Marginalization and Contemporary Culture* (Cambridge, MA: MIT Press, 1990), p. 299. Further references will be cited in the text.

25 See Olaudah Equiano, *Equiano's Travels*, ed. Paul Edwards (London: Heinemann, 1967 [1789]), p. vii. Further references will be cited in the text. However, reference will also be made to the more complete version of this narrative featured in Henry Louis Gates' collection *The Classic Slave Narratives* (see note 27). I am obliged to use both of these editions because although Edwards' has the more useful critical introduction, it excludes certain key passages relating to the Sierra Leone expedition which are essential to my argument.

26 C.L.R. James, *The Black Jacobins: Toussaint L'Ouverture and the San Domingo Revolution* (London: Virgin Publishing, 1991 [1938]), p. 13. Further references will be cited in the text.

27 Henry Louis Gates, Jr (ed.), *The Classic Slave Narratives* (New York: Mentor, 1987), p. 200. Further references will be cited in the text.

28 See reference to this in Paul Edwards (ed.), *Equiano's Travels*, p. xi.

29 For a reference to this, see Gates' Preface, *The Classic Slave Narratives*, p. 8.

30 Ralph Ellison, *Invisible Man* (Harmondsworth: Penguin, 1987 [1952]), pp. 13–14.

31 P. Thomas Stanford, 'The Race Question in America', in *Six Women's Slave Narratives*, incorporated into Annie L. Burton's 'Memories of Childhood's Slavery Days', p. 62.

32 See my analysis of this scene in Chapter 1, p. 33.

33 Toni Morrison, 'Unspeakable Things Unspoken: The Afro-American Presence in American Literature', *Michigan Quarterly Review* 28(1) (1989), p. 22. Further references will be cited in the text.

34 Frantz Fanon, *The Wretched of the Earth* (Harmondsworth: Penguin, 1985; first

published in 1961 as *Les Damnées de la terre*), p. 28. Further references will be cited in the text.

35 B. Marie Perinbam, *Holy Violence* (Washington, DC: Three Continents Press, 1982).

36 Abdul R. JanMohamed, *Manichean Aesthetics: The Politics of Literature in Colonial Africa* (Amherst, MA: University of Massachusetts Press, 1983), p. 4. Further references will be cited in the text.

37 Sartre's Preface to *The Wretched of the Earth* (pp. 7–8) outlines this infamous paradox:

> Then, indeed, Europe will believe in her mission; she had hellenized the Asians; she had created a new breed, the Graeco-Latin Negroes. . . . By and large, what they were saying was this: 'You are making us into monstrosities; your human-ism claims we are at one with the rest of humanity but your racist methods set us apart.'

38 Irene L. Gendzier (*Frantz Fanon: A Critical Study* (New York: Grove Press, 1973), p. 27 characterises the nature of violence in Fanon's writing as a release, an oppor-tunity for active change and self-fashioning:

> He longed for the declaration of war that would justify his doing battle. Then at least the lines would be clear, and the struggle would provide an opportunity to work out externally what had built up internally in the form of this private knowledge. This man sought confrontations, for he saw them as providing him with the means of becoming who he was.

39 See B. Marie Perinbam, *Holy Violence*, pp. 6–8, where she outlines Fanon's schematic understanding of violence, which moves between the psychic and the physical. See also *Holy Violence*, pp. 9–10:

> If it seems that Fanon was working with a paradox, it is because he was. . . . Of all his paradoxical concepts, holy violence was by far the most stunning. . . . Containing two contradictory ideas in the same concept which remained in con-flict with each other, both parts of the paradox belonged together, and repre-sented the whole. . . . Hence, by using contradictory ideas that make nonsense to commonsense, Fanon was not only using a figure of speech proven tried and true, but he was also capturing readers by assaulting their imagination.

40 Albert Memmi, *The Colonizer and the Colonized* (Boston, MA: Beacon Press, 1967), pp. xii–xiv.

41 Frantz Fanon, *Black Skin, White Masks* (London: Pluto Press, 1986; first published as *Peau noire masques blancs*, 1952), pp. 14–15. Further references will be cited in the text.

42 Karl Marx, 'Critique of Hegel's Dialectic and General Philosophy', in David McLellan (ed.), *Karl Marx: Selected Writings* (Oxford: Oxford University Press, 1977), p. 98. Further references will be cited in the text.

43 Karl Marx, 'The Future Results of British Rule in India' in *Karl Marx: Selected Writings*. References will be cited in text.

44 See Little, *The Mende of Sierra Leone*, p. 47: 'Possibly, the successful resistance of Bai Bureh in the north was the decisive factor in prompting the Mende to open revolt.'

45 Partha Chatterjee, *Nationalist Thought and the Colonial World: A Derivative Discourse* (London: Zed Books, 1986), p. vii. Further references will be cited in the text.

46 Christopher L. Miller, *Theories of Africans: Francophone Literature and Anthropology in Africa* (Chicago, IL: University of Chicago Press, 1990), p. 48.

47 Simon Gikandi, *Reading the African Novel* (London: James Currey, 1987), p. 134.

48 Ngũgĩ Wa Thiong'o, *Petals of Blood* (Portsmouth, NH: Heinemann, 1988 [1977]). Further references will be cited in the text.

49 Cheikh Hamidou Kane, *Ambiguous Adventure* (Portsmouth, NH: Heinemann, 1963); Sembene Ousmane, *God's Bits of Wood* (Portsmouth, NH: Heinemann, 1962). Further references will be cited in the text.

50 See Wole Soyinka, *Myth, Literature and the African World* (Cambridge: Cambridge University Press, 1990 [1976]), p. 117.

51 Wole Soyinka, *The Interpreters* (London: Heinimann, 1987 [1965]). Further references will be cited in the text.

52 Soyinka's discussion of the continuity and unity that a Yoruba or African world view or religious existence creates is exemplified in his statements: 'In Asian and European antiquity . . . man did, like the African, exist within a cosmic totality, did possess a consciousness in which his own earth being, his gravity-bound apprehension of self, was inseparable from the entire cosmic phenomenon'; 'Continuity for the Yoruba operates both through the cyclic concept of time and the animist interfusion of all matter and consciousness', Wole Soyinka, *Myth, Literature and the African World*, pp. 3, 145.

3

REMEMBERED LANDSCAPES

African-American appropriations of Africa

> Did I mention my first sight of the African coast? Something
> struck in me, in my soul, Celie, like a large bell, and I just
> vibrated.
>
> (Alice Walker, *The Color Purple*)

This chapter continues the analyses of African and diasporic identities under-
taken in Chapter 2, in order to explore African-American appropriations
and interpretations of Africa in twentieth-century literatures. Reading
African-American Black identities in terms of their historical and imaginative
connections with Africa and African origins, this chapter re-visits the topol-
ogy of geographical space, of memory and time, to examine how the United
States, as a national territory, has been explored as a place of contesting and
differential histories in Black texts. The intersections of historical time and
geographical place, through strategies of memory and migration, lead to particular constructions of race and racial identity. The imbrications of race
with sexuality and the place of feminist analysis and female identity are interrogated here through textual readings. The focus on the United States and
on imaginative literatures serves to expose the role of historical contingency
and African self-understanding discussed in the preceding chapter as it is
manifested in the metaphorical and political texts of Black America.

Beginning with a reading of Alice Walker's *Possessing the Secret of Joy*, the
chapter explores how Black American feminisms and women's narratives
can become implicated in oppressive forms of American nationalism, where
a pan-Africanist feminism selects African women as objects for cultural
reform. Having examined alternative representations of women as cultural
visionaries, rather than victims, in African texts, the chapter will focus on
analyses of African-American women's literatures to read how memories of
Africa and migration surge into the imaginary of Black America, creating
representations of American nationality as a multi-layered and contested
concept, challenged and redefined by urgent historical remembering. From
an interrogation of racial memory and mourning, it will be argued that
the literary histories of the slave narratives, with their motifs of migration,
their preoccupation with naming, race and nation, and their complicated

relationships with Africa, have a significant impact on twentieth-century African-American literatures. Finally, the chapter will examine how race has been imagined in both White political journalism and White popular fiction in the United States to show how these representations of racial borders, through the metaphorics of race and time, are confronted with the irrepressible colonial histories and ethnographies of the first two chapters.

'In the flesh': gender, sexuality and sisterhood

Representations of Africa in African-American texts are conditioned by the histories of exile that have been discussed in the preceding chapters, and also by the location of African-Americans in the United States – a nation whose cultural and political dominance has reached global proportions. The position of Black Americans *within* the nation, although as a dispossessed and marginalised people, is nevertheless a position which confers United States citizenship, structures national identifications and conditions, in ways which are explored in this chapter, the relationship between Black Americans and other diasporic Blacks.

I shall begin with a discussion of Alice Walker's *Possessing the Secret of Joy* (1992)[1] as an introduction to the conceptual problematics involved in African-American identifications with Africa and, in particular, as an interrogation of the political difficulties of Black feminist organisation *across* the boundaries of nation and continent. Walker's novel is a recent exposition of the variant cultural practices of 'female circumcisions', or 'female genital mutilation', among particular African peoples. Walker's text presents a framework for presenting the consciousness of a 'circumcised' African woman to the scrutiny of Western feminisms.

Taking as main character an African woman, Tashi, from Walker's earlier novel, *The Color Purple*, *Possessing the Secret of Joy* ostensibly presents a dialogue between the West and Africa through the interaction of American, African and European characters. Tashi, from an imaginary African people, the Olinka, who are never given a location (though Walker mentions that the actress who played Tashi in the film of *The Color Purple* was Kenyan (p. 267)), allows herself to be excised and infibulated as part of her expression of cultural independence from British colonialism. What follows is an intimate description of physical and emotional pain expressed through the corresponding frames of European and American culture. The text insists on a collective female experience, possible through empathy, and given coherence through the wider and supposedly universal lens of anthropology and psychoanalysis. This collective female experience is proposed to exist within the identical and extra-cultural frame of the sentient female body, through which sexual identities and psychologies are assumed to subsist in a (spiritually) communal space of transparent femininity, beyond the artificial barriers of medical and familial cultures. In fact, Walker herself reveals a mystical and *physical* link with her character Tashi through the direct mediation of the body, presented in Walker's epilogue as the most tangible and truthful area of female bonding and sympathy: 'she also appeared to me in the flesh' (p. 267).

What results is an attempt to represent the practices of female circumcision as, not only specific cultural practices, but as a metaphor for women's subordination and oppression on a global scale. In this way, the various operations of female circumcision can be culturally aligned with the Marquis de Sade (p. 132), or Western 'slash' movies, as when Lisette, a French woman, is reported as saying: 'It's in all the movies that terrorize women . . . only masked. The man who breaks in. The man with the knife' (p. 131). The presence of Jung, the Old Wise Man of Europe, as Tashi's analyst, to heal her of the psychological scars of her excision, allows for a communion between European and African cultures in such a way that the novel can resist difference. Jung, named in the novel as simply 'the doctor' (p. 17), or 'uncle Carl' (p. 81), is described being surrounded by what are called 'tribal' furnishings (p. 10). He is likened, by Tashi, to 'an old African grandmother', and he describes his relationship with Tashi and Adam (an African-American) in terms which form the basis of the narrative's insistence on absolute relativism and the possibility of a universal frame of cultural reference. 'Uncle Carl' says:

> I am finding myself in them. A self I have often felt was only halfway at home on the European continent. In my European skin. An ancient self that thirsts for knowledge of the experiences of its ancient kin. Needs this knowledge, and the feelings that come with it, to be whole. . . . A truly universal self.
>
> (p. 81)

The novel's celebration of the value of anthropology for understanding African culture, taken as a whole, and a human collective Unconscious, recoverable through sympathy, leads the narrative, in fact, to incorporate a vision of Africa within rigidly North American terms. 'Africa' emerges as a dying culture; both *victim* – through the ravages of AIDS (pp. 233–6) and the suffering of circumcised girls – and as its own destroyer – due to the tyrannous collusion of female circumcisers with male sadism. The description of the AIDS floor in Tashi's African prison illustrates the novel's presentation of Africans, and particularly of African women, as passive victims of a continent which ravages its own people. Olivia, watching the crowds of emaciated and dying African sufferers from AIDS, comments on the lack of control, the lack of knowledge, from which they are also dying. From the assumed position of an informed observer, Olivia reports the reflexes of Tashi's liberated consciousness, freed and strengthened by the self-knowledge uncovered and narrativised by Jung's analysis, which encourage her to draw a contrast between her new self-awareness and that of the dying Africans:

No one has any idea why he or she is sick. That's the most difficult thing. Witnessing their incomprehension. Their dumb patience, as they wait for death. It is their animal-like ignorance and acceptance that most angers Tashi, perhaps because she is reminded of herself. She calls it, scornfully, the assigned role of the African: to suffer, to die, and not know why.

(pp. 233–4)

This image of inarticulate and bestial death is one which Simon Watney carefully uncovers in his reading of Western journalistic reporting of AIDS in Africa. Likening the metaphors and images of this journalism with Conrad's *Heart of Darkness* (p. 90), Watney unravels the textual relationship between AIDS and Africa:

> It is as if HIV were a disease of 'African-ness', the viral embodiment of a long legacy of colonial imagery which naturalises the devastating economic and social effects of European colonialism in the likeness of starvation.[2]

Walker's imaginary Olinkan state – a supposed paradigm, or microcosm, of the essential attributes of Africa as a whole – is close to Watney's reading of 'the language of metaphor that informs so much African AIDS commentary' (p. 92), being deeply saturated with ideas of a 'heart' of Africa. Tashi's idea in *Possessing the Secret of Joy* that AIDS has become a women's disease in Africa through the transmission of HIV by 'the unwashed, unsterilized sharp stones, tin tops, bits of glass, rusty razors and grungy knives used by the *tsunga*' (p. 235), and that it has created a situation, peculiar to African countries, where 'there are as many women dying as men' (p. 234), leads to the sustained image of African women as sexually mutilated, sexually truncated victims of a sexuality to which they can get no access:

> A sweet-faced, woeful-eyed young woman has died. Her husband . . . explained to Adam that although they had been married three years they had no children because he had been unable to sleep with her as a man does normally with his wife. She had cried so, and bled.

(p. 236)

Watney analyses the conflation in Western journalism of African women with AIDS by focusing on the contradictory reporting of women as dangerously and actively sexual, 'the author of her own destruction' (p. 90), and as the *targets* of White/Western male 'fascination' (p. 90). Watney's interpretation of the commentary about Africa and AIDS targets precisely the generalising and totalising categories which Walker uses to discuss 'African culture' and cultural practices. As with the variant practices of excision, clitoridectomy and infibulation in various countries and among different peoples, AIDS also has a cultural diversity that needs attention in the struggle against its spread:

> In this respect the notion of 'African AIDS' already obscures the specific characteristics of the different AIDS epidemics in these countries, constructing them in the spurious unity of an 'Africa' which is immediately denied any of the cultural, social, economic and ethnic diversity which are taken for granted in Europe and North or South America.
>
> (*Out There*, p. 94)

Tashi's agony makes her turn against both the Olinkan nation state (p. 100) and the Olinkan woman, M'Lissa – both victim and sadist – who circumcised Tashi at her request. Tashi's pain and what is called her 'resistance' is seen to be contained within the logic of Olinkan culture (p. 196), whereas her affection, strength and salvation lie within Europe and the United States. Tashi's recurring expressions of her love for the United States (pp. 53, 158) leads to a vision of the United States as a microcosm of global empathy, representing and substituting itself for a damaged Africa. Tashi, as an African woman, is ultimately moved to see herself in an American reflection:

> An American, I said, sighing, but understanding my love of my adopted country perhaps for the first time: an American looks like a wounded person whose wound is hidden from others, and sometimes from herself. An American looks like me.
>
> (p. 200)

Tashi's voluntary circumcision, brought about by the fervour of nationalist decolonisation and the need to be 'completely woman. Completely African. Completely Olinkan' (p. 61), allows the novel to reinscribe colonialism as the possibility of correspondence and unity between the West and Africa. Lisette's Paris becomes saturated with a paternalist or maternalist love of Algeria, symbolised by her son Pierre, whose mixed race origins can be substituted for Algerian identity, and the novel's moral frame, concurring with the title – 'Black people are natural . . . they possess the secret of joy' – is attributed to the wisdom of 'a white colonialist author' (p. 255).

Tashi's names, oscillating between, or being hyphenated by, European alternatives – Evelyn and Mrs Johnson – are clearly intended to allow her to represent – and be represented by – women of different cultures. She becomes the voice of Everywoman, articulated within the idealised terms of African-American womanhood, who, against the 'sliding gait' (p. 144) of broken African women, become icons of strength and power (p. 111). The repeated use of 'Evelyn' and 'Mrs Johnson' as substitute names for Tashi and, in the final section, as progressive points on the road to salvation – 'Tashi Evelyn Johnson Soul' (p. 263) – works to obliterate Tashi's allegiance to Africa and, indeed, the validity or value of her African identity.

Walker's epilogue 'To The Reader' is particularly significant for reading the structure and meaning of the novel. Discussing her use of fabricated 'African' words, the author claims: 'Perhaps it, and other words I use, are from an African language I used to know, now tossed up by my unconscious. I do not know from what part of Africa my African ancestors came, and so I claim the continent' (pp. 267–8). This claiming or appropriation of a whole continent for Walker's American literary anthropology exposes the difficulties and dangers of a relativism that would seek to deny, not just the significance of cultural difference on a grand scale, but the validity of con-textualising and locating where one is speaking from, about whom and with what egotism. The novel is narrated by a range of characters who interpret Tashi's experiences and their relationship with her. They form part of a historical and psychological jigsaw of Tashi as a circumcised African woman – a kind of case history from the viewpoints of participant observers. In this way, Tashi's identity is owned, explained and transmitted by the people who *claim* her, and any discordances or disagreements between the observers and Tashi about her own role and meaning are erased, to the extent that the observers *control* Tashi's self-understanding *for* her.

Possessing the Secret of Joy performs a simultaneous double move by insisting on the alien and deviant principles that dominate and construct African cultural practices, while also claiming the *universality* of patriarchy and female consciousness. Walker's use of Jungian psychoanalysis to ground her loosely ethnographic study of Africa allows her to recognise African cultural difference while at the same time denying the psychological implications of this difference. By upholding American feminist consciousness as the ultimate destination for 'freed' African women, Walker presents an alternative slave narrative, with the United States as the territory of 'Northern' freedom. This use of slavery as the iconography of the text is made explicit in the words of Lisette, who aligns the oppression of women in general terms with the twin motifs of slavery and sexual violence: 'I recognised the connection between mutilation and enslavement that is at the root of the domination of women in the world' (p. 131).

The novel's intent to prove the existence of a universal feminine Uncon-scious, indivisible by racial, cultural or historical differences, is expressed in its ultimate refutation of the American doctor's claim that 'Negro women . . . are considered the most difficult of all people to be effectively analysed' (p. 17). Tashi's indignation at this point, at being so dismissively collapsed into the same category as Black Americans, seems to fit uneasily into the wider aim of the novel, which is to diminish the depth of the separation between African and African-American women:

Since I was not a Negro woman I hesitated before hazarding an answer. I felt negated by the realization that even my psychiatrist could not see I was African. That to him all black people were Negroes.

(p. 17)

Re-reading Tashi's answer, however, her refusal of and anger at the doctor's dismissive generalisation that 'all black people' are Negroes rests more clearly on an irritation at the doctor's implicit denial that all Black people are *Africans*. The latent use of 'Negro' here as a racial category that slides over the geographical and historical origins of Black Americans, and which is used by the doctor as a racial slur – 'Your people like lots of kids, he allowed' (p. 17) – is presented as the problematic which the narrative tries to refute. This underlying message, that all Black Americans are Africans, is clearly supported by Walker's epilogue, where she claims a *familial* relationship with Tashi:

I suppose I have created Olinka as my village and the Olinkans as one of my ancient, ancestral tribal peoples. Certainly I recognise Tashi as my sister.

(p. 268)

Possessing the Secret of Joy recognises the significance of colonial histories in per-verting or creating cultural narratives and instigating grand battles between a supposedly coherent West and a holistic Africa. However, Walker's novel moves impatiently towards a modernity that can unproblematically include all peoples, all women, within a humanist framework that, via Jungian psychoanalysis, promises a terrain free of difference. Her claim on an Africa that is inherent to Black Americans manages to dismiss the dominating stance of the United States over Africa, and the social and imaginative inclu-sion of African-Americans in Western narratives of Africa.

The simplistic and one-dimensional representations of African women in Walker's text contrast sharply with the revolutionary women of Ousmane's novel *God's Bits of Wood* and with Ngũgĩ's character Wanja in *Petals of Blood*. These female characters are represented as powerful women who, rather than become sexually and psychologically flattened by the African cultures in which they live, choose to redefine their roles in supportive and mutual relations with African men and families. The character of Wanja, although the survivor of a society that forces her into contradictory roles with conflict-ing expectations and values, many of which are oppressive and sexually exploitative, is allowed to emerge as that of an autonomous, decision-making being. Balancing the many images of her womanhood, as grand-daughter of Nyakinyua, echoing the history of a clan, as the daughter of Christians, as an exploited city barmaid, a powerful woman in love, a fighter and mother, Wanja interprets and re-interprets her position as a woman in a rent and changing society, discovering that, like the different, twining, contradictory and repeating narratives around her, it consists of multiple masquerades, suffering and *choices*:

> She had carried dreams in a broken vessel. Looking back now she could not even see a trail of the vanished dreams and expectations. . . . She had chosen. Everybody chose to accept or not to accept. The choice put one on this or that side of the line-up in the battlefield.[3]

Walker's representation of Africa, fundamentally a Black American appropriation of Africa to highlight 'liberated' American cultural ideals, fails to acknowledge the infusion of American cultural patterns and self-understanding that has inevitably occurred amongst diasporic Blacks living in the United States. Walker's seamless and uncomplicated 'remembering' of her African origins in a mystical form of 'racial memory' does not take account of the dividing and transforming effects of diasporic movement on a people, the new allegiances that are formed and cherished, alongside the old and prior loyalties that remain to be dreamed. *Possessing the Secret of Joy*, while intent on dissolving the political barriers between women of different nations and cultures, does not analyse the poeticisation and narrativisation of a history which has continuously reinvented Black Americans from the time of slavery onwards. It is these necessary and radical reinventions, fused with the literary, political and practical energies involved with new approaches to and re-creations of the meaning of freedom, of national identity and of 'home', which have re-conditioned the role of Africa as trope, origin and destination for Black Americans. Walker's easeful crossing of oceans and time to embrace her imaginary African 'sister', ready to convert and re-model her into an image of American femininity, shows no awareness of these political realities.

Space has a feeling: the geographies of racial memory

Moving beyond Walker's framework of 'empathy', this section of the chapter discusses other articulations of African-American identities with reference to African origins and racial difference. In recognising the inclusion of African-Americans in United States national history, and the specific allegiances which are a result of this inclusion, more politically sensitive and incisive representations of Africa are possible. Three African-American women's texts that do engage with such complex and multi-layered histories of Black America, remaining attentive to the continuities between and divergences from an African past and an African identity, are Toni Morrison's *Beloved*[4] and *Song of Solomon*,[5] and Gloria Naylor's *Mama Day*.[6]

Henry Louis Gates, while discussing the place of the slave narratives in an African-American literary tradition, reflects on the role played by African-Americans as members of the United States. Quoting from an 1886 essay entitled 'The Coming American Novelist', written by an anonymous Philadelphia 'lady', Gates lets her argument speak for itself:

> When we come to formulate our demands of the Coming American Novelist, we will agree that he must be native-born. His ancestors may come from where they will, but we must give him a birthplace and have the raising of him. . . . In a word, suppose the coming novelist is of African origin?[7]

This anticipation of an African-American writer – who can be imagined to be a woman – becoming representative of a *national* literary tradition, and being hailed as one of *the* American Novelists, announces the arrival of writers such as Toni Morrison. Morrison's statement[8] that her books attempt to show that the meaning of United States' national identity is inextricably bound up with and created by African-American culture makes two significant claims: the first is that something as distinct and definable as 'African-American culture' has been created out of the experience of Diaspora and displacement; the second suggests that the United States – though it is predicated on notions of Western hegemony, of economic, military and cultural imperialism – is, as a *nation*, inherently *defined* by its own politically marginalised peoples.

Partha Chatterjee's appraisal of nationalism in independent ex-colonies emphasises the contradictory site of the nation as both primordial and modern, borrowed and fiercely autonomous, presenting a unified culture and wracked with internal cultural divisions. Like Fanon's insistence on culture as national ideology (as explored in Chapter 2), Homi Bhabha's analysis of the time of the nation illustrates the tension between narrative representation and poetic amnesia in the national longing for a unified cultural past:

> Fanon writes against that form of national historicism that assumes that there is a moment when the differential temporalities of cultural histories coalesce in an immediately readable present.[9]

Reading Bhabha's discussion of the multiple narratives which coexist and compete to construct the idea of the nation, it is possible to analyse the United States in which *Beloved* is situated as a place where the present is disrupted by the traumatic incompatibilities of variant cultural pasts. It is these incompatible national narratives which *Beloved* is engaged in exposing as a challenge to the seamless and 'innocent' constructions of an 'American type' (the Philadelphia 'Lady', cited by Gates, *Six Women's Slave Narratives*, p. xii). Bhabha formulates the several possible threads of these vexed and vexing

117

national texts in terms of a series of territorial and historical referents that foreground the salience of migrant identities:

> It is from this *instability* of cultural signification that the national culture comes to be articulated as a dialectic of various temporalities – modern, colonial, postcolonial, 'native' – that cannot be a knowledge that is stabilised in its enunciation.
>
> (*The Location of Culture*, p. 152)

Such a disjunctive and contradictory time schema in national imagining is explored in depth in *Beloved*, where time is theorised as a phenomenon tied irreducibly to space. The physical and emotional character of time when conceived as a racial imaginary or a personal 'rememory' transgresses a sequential logic and locks experience into immovable and tangible manifestations. The character of time as constantly translatable according to trauma and historical positioning emerges in personal accounts of racial oppression, love and suffering. Sethe links time to the narrative and the visual, to movement and stasis. The eternal is the unforgettable; land both holds and cancels the tie between past and present:

> I was talking about time. It's so hard for me to believe in it. Some things go. Pass on. Some things just stay. Places, places are still there . . . even if I die, the picture of what I did, or knew, or saw is still out there. Right in the place where it happened.
>
> (pp. 35–6)

Personal and collective histories survive mortality and repeat, through the aegis of geography and descent, a returning of unspent emotion. An intense focusing on spatial metaphor enacts a poetry of place where suffering and desire continually delineate physical space. The notion of home in *Beloved* holds a powerful concentration of racial and familial history and the structure of home is threatened and shaken by a returning of death and grief. Baby Suggs' conviction that 'not a house in the country ain't packed to its rafters with some dead Negro's grief' (p. 5) speaks of a racial legacy that prioritises the body and the anxieties of ownership and place. The past resurges in a binding together of the natural, the emotional and the biological. Racial violence follows Sethe in her flesh as a 'chokecherry tree' while the trees of Sweet Home hold the swinging Black dead, and Paul D lives the agony of unbelonging through a directly sexualised communion of body and land:

> The beauty of this land that was not his. He hid in its breast, fingered its earth for food, clung to its banks to lap water and tried not to love it.
>
> (p. 268)

The physical drenching of sorrow in the red light at the entrance to 124 lends itself to a personification of inanimate space, represented by convulsion, mental illness and the familial:

> Denver approached the house, regarding it, as she always did, as a person rather than a structure. A person that wept, sighed, trembled and fell into fits. . . . A nervous, idle relative.
>
> (p. 29)

The female body that emerges from the water in *Beloved* is a body formed by death, violence and mourning, which has rocked the foundations of home, which forms and channels desire, disturbs the unities of love and revisits dead rages upon the living. Her name a metaphor for the gathering at the grave, her death a necessity of love, her resurgence reconstitutes the past as incarnation and female experience as an embodiment of histories within the present. It is suffering that lives on, that forces itself into physical reality, inhabiting tangible places through the agonising creativity and destructiveness of love. *Beloved* theorises a Black conception of the body and of home as realities formed in the shape of past experiences, which insist upon their place in the present through the exigencies of grief and anger.

This notion of past energies and events erupting onto the scene of the present is discussed by Peter Nicholls in terms of the traumatic disjunction of physical reality with a memory that cannot be controlled:

> That idea of recovering an occluded or 'buried' past derives from a traditional association of knowledge with recollection and depends on a thoroughly metaphysical 'presencing' of what is absent.[10]

This movement of past events into the temporal space of the modern is not a one-way signification. Nicholls' observation of 'a related tendency to conceive the past as a phantasmic space to be reinhabited and repossessed' (p. 199) draws attention to the place of Morrison's text in deliberately re-visiting and re-occupying the historical time of the slave narratives, a movement that forms as intense a desire for modern African-American self-understanding as was apparent in the passionate appeals in the slave autobiographies *to be remembered*.

History as multiply conceptual, layering land with both White and Black stories, creates circularity and ellipsis; produces an understanding of narrative as collective, broken, sequential and repeating. Edward Bodwin, the White owner of 124 and its land, perceives time as a splitting of the personal and the collective, readable in two spheres of land-ownership – the individual and the patriotic:

As he drew closer to the old homestead, the place that continued to
surface in his dreams, he was even more aware of the way time
moved. Measured by the wars he had lived through but not fought
in (against the Miami, the Spaniards, the Secessionists), it was slow.
But measured by the burial of his private things it was the blink of
an eye.

(Beloved, p. 260)

For Bodwin, space has a feeling: home encourages 'sweeter and deeper' emotion. The past remains containable and stable. For Sethe, living is a steady
realisation that 'time didn't stay put' (p. 272), that such imminent treachery
must be dealt with daily: 'Nothing better than that [working dough] to start
the day's serious work of beating back the past' (p. 73). The notion of continuity is a question of communication, of balancing and blending narrative to
dream a liveable future: 'He wants to put his story next to hers. . . . We need
some kind of tomorrow' (p. 273).

Time as a physical monstrosity emerges via the Black body in the White
nightmarish image of the jungle. Human nature is conceived in marriage
with its 'origin', drawn by the racialisation of environment. The immutability
of the past through a dreaming of geography and environment becomes a
racial fantasy:

Whitepeople believed that whatever the manners, under every dark
skin was a jungle. Swift unnavigable waters, swinging screaming
baboons, sleeping snakes, red gums ready for their sweet white blood.

(p. 198)

The metaphor of the dead, Black body returning through the claustrophobia
of the familial space, transgressing death through incarnation, splits time
into a war of temporal zones. Desire forms the leaking-point between past
and present in the charged intensity of infantile sensual need. Coming
through the cracks, the interstices of language, the splintered dreams and
sense, it is grief and suffering that survive the separation and leave traces in
the unconscious of a generation. As Beloved collapses the difference between
the living and the dead, the conscious and the 'insane', the shadows and
ghosts of past racial violence insist upon priority in the place called 'home':

He kept on through the voices. . . . This time, although he couldn't
cipher but one word, he believed he knew who spoke them. The
people of the broken necks, of fire-cooked blood and black girls who
had lost their ribbons.

(p. 181)

The notion of 'home', through Minnie Bruce Pratt's topographical approach to her everyday encounters with other cultures and histories in modern Washington DC, suggests a way into reading and living these confusing, changing cultural spaces, where people do not stay put. What emerges from this seemingly other perspective is a personal orientation that is always rigorously aware of the juxtapositions, the overlappings, the mutualities of racial histories. Hers is a constant ethnographic working-through of personal and collective responsibilities, offering another alternative to Alice Walker's cultural monologism.

Pratt's essay 'Identity: Skin Blood Heart'[11] introduces the geographical features of the cities and towns in which she – as White, female and Protestant – lives and has lived. What emerges is a mapping of streets, buildings, distance which recognises the dividing lines of racial and communal identifications. For Pratt, 'home' is a question of imagined dimensions, meanings, limits; it is a particular interpretation of the times in which one lives. Yearning to transgress a conventional visual/spatial *fixing* of the Other and the Self, Pratt seeks to practise new ways of seeing. The panorama of her point of view does not reveal the spread of free space, the expansion of her being-at-home, but exposes division, concealments, hidden narratives of identity and heritage – overlapping, coinciding, contradicting.

Learning to see ghosts, Pratt's reappraisal of place and time recreates her vision of 'home'. Surging onto her sweet, private memories of 'a place of mutuality, companionship, creativity, sensuousness, easiness in the body . . . safety and love' (p. 24) moves a war of conflicting pasts, denied histories, boundaries imagined and forgotten. The new visibility, to her, of Black and Jewish communities, of White and male violence, of sorrows and celebrations once hidden from view, is made possible precisely through the sense of crisis caused by love. This catastrophe of communication, of seeing other narratives, other stories colliding with the singular, homogeneous vision of homeliness, is forced into immediacy, a time of dialogue. Voice, tone, gesture, accent – the clash of dialogues – illustrate the vital nature of racial and sexual difference as it is lived, as it is played out on the territories of nationality and history. The calling of her name by a Black woman using the tone and lilt that mark the words of her childhood, her region of 'original' belonging, emphasises, for Pratt, the grief of historical and cultural separations:

> Yet I knew enough of her history and mine to know how much separated us: the chasm of murders, rapes, lynchings, the years of daily humiliation done by my people to hers. I went and stood in the hallway and cried, thinking of how she said my name like home, and how divided our lives were.
>
> (p. 19)

Pratt's Lesbian identity, in pushing her beyond the horizons of community, family, safety, is never allowed to enclose her in another bounded space of cultural blindness, 'because it is how I love that has brought me to change' (p. 20). Pratt's new way of seeing geography and time refuses the notion of a singular, monolithic identity that exists in its own, privileged, exclusive space. The cultural borders of Carolina and Washington DC are mapped onto distance as well as layered onto the temporal:

> I learn a way of looking at the world that is more accurate, complex, multi-layered, multi-dimensional, more truthful: to see a world of overlapping circles . . . instead of the courthouse square with me at the middle.
>
> (p. 17)

Pratt's reading of diverse racial histories becomes a matter of excavation. Cultural geographies demand a reading of imagined and emotional limits, offering different possibilities and levels of narrative. This discovery opens up the world, which shatters light into hidden places, and threatens identity with the loss of stasis and certainty: 'Instead I felt that I had no place, that, as I moved through my days, I was falling through space' (p. 27). The loss of self and meaning illustrated by this sense of space's collapse *into* time is a risk that comes of another disavowal of history. This is the anarchy of freefall, of acknowledging the multiple heritages of the southern states without recognising one's own specificity, one's own placing by the tyrannies of time, love, family, memory, gender and race. Beginning to understand others' claims on history and land, Pratt refuses the weightless vertigo of 'falling through space' and learns to accept the political and cultural responsibilities of her own identifications:

> And yet it is mine. I am my father's daughter in the present, living in a world he and my folks helped to create.
>
> (p. 53)

Pratt's concentration on the present as a site of hidden and differential histories and allegiances, and her choice to use feminist analysis as a way into acknowledging these different conceptions of nation, of town and neighbourhood, acts as a useful political complement to the ideas that structure *Beloved*. The attention paid by both Pratt and Morrison to the realities of US national histories must be placed in relation to the figuring of origins that lies behind these investigations. The representation of African-American histories in *Beloved* through the re-imagining of particularly female slave autobiographies allows an attention to histories of migration and arrival, without allowing the *idea* of an African origin to spill over into the appropriation of African realities. 'Africa', as an original home, exists at the limits of the imagination. It belongs to, and is allowed to remain as, a point of departure, with no conscious remembering of place, territory and landscape. 'Africa', in *Beloved*, has already been metaphorised into the floating space *in between* Africa and America, where its *absence* comes to represent a homelessness and restlessness out of which new identifications are formed.

The coming of Beloved into the enclosed space of family and home results in a breakdown of representational language into the fragmented poetic breaks of first-person speech. It is here that time becomes eternalised into the continuous present, without the shifts into and collisions with other times and spaces. This section of the novel implicates the time of 'In the beginning' (p. 211) with an idea of the ever present, inescapable self:

> All of it is now   it is always now   there will never be a time when I am not   crouching and watching others who are crouching too   I am always crouching   the man on my face is dead   his face is not mine   his mouth smells sweet and his eyes are locked   some who eat nasty themselves   I do not eat.
>
> (p. 210)

This dreaming of the Middle Passage as the unfixed yet eternal space from which an African-American origin can be traced makes the wide and uncertain journey *away* from shore, rather than the reality of Africa's shore *itself*, into the founding moment of Black American consciousness. The lack of punctuation in this section, with empty and open gaps between phrases, allows each phrase to be read as if in a *timeless* series, where words signify *at the same time*. This layering of simultaneous and unnarrativised experience evokes Ralph Ellison's descriptions of the act of hearing music in *Invisible Man*. Listening to Louis Armstrong, the nameless protagonist proclaims:

> Instead of the swift and imperceptible flowing of time, you are aware of its nodes, those points where time stands still or from which it leaps ahead. And you slip into the breaks and look around. That's what you hear vaguely in Louis' music.[12]

This slipping between the interstices of notes and sounds to discover depth and stillness offers a way into *hearing* Morrison's text. The separation of each broken phrase into an unpunctuated spatial series throughout this section of *Beloved* can be read *backwards*, as it were, into Ellison's descriptions of musical time:

> The unheard sounds came through, and each melodic line existed of itself, stood out clearly from all the rest, said its piece, and waited patiently for the other voices to speak. That night I found myself hearing not only in time, but in space as well. I not only entered the music but descended, like Dante, into its depths.
>
> (p. 11)

The 'invisible' man's analytic listening to the simultaneity and speed of musical notes as the distribution of elements in space invites a re-reading of Morrison's text as a representation of the simultaneous, harmonised 'beam of lyrical sound' (*Invisible Man*, p. 11) of Ellison's text. In this way, the separate identities of the unnamed slaves in the slaveholds are imagined in their forced and necessary moment of becoming mutually identified and communally emergent.

Morrison takes up Ellison's explicit reference to the music of Armstrong in her more academic text, *Playing in the Dark*.[13] Discussing Marie Cardinal's autobiographical *The Words to Say It*, Morrison fixes on a moment in that text where, having listened to Armstrong playing jazz, Cardinal is struck with unbearable ecstasy, pain and torment and she runs 'into the street like someone possessed' (p. vii). This experience of 'possession' by the agony and sublimity of jazz is analysed by Morrison as Cardinal's 'conceptual response to a black, that is, non white figuration' (p. viii). Locating Armstrong for a peculiarly Black heritage and imaginary, the metaphoric connections between his music, where 'each note would be important and would contain within itself the essence of the whole' (*Playing in the Dark*, p. vi), and Morrison's own literary rendering of the 'possession' of the past in *Beloved* are not accidental. Morrison's claim that she read Cardinal's text 'some years ago, in 1983 I believe' (p. v) places her discovery of 'the Louis Armstrong catalyst' (p. viii) before the publication of *Beloved* (in 1987), and her discussion of the impact of this discovery is notable:

> The Louis Armstrong catalyst . . . encouraged me to reflect on the consequences of jazz – its visceral, emotional and intellectual impact on the listener.
>
> (p. vii)

The idea of an aesthetics of music which refuses to discard the primacy of any separate note fits well with the textual aesthetics of *Beloved*, where each 'I' in this vision of the Middle Passage becomes representative of a group, a culture and a history that own, and are owned by, all Black Americans: 'I am Beloved and she is mine' (p. 210). This is also illustrative of the importance of the slave narratives as *autobiography*, where each personal witness to the meaning of slavery comes to 'speak for' the group.

The movement which the text encourages between oral (or aural, musical) and visual (literate) scenes, which is readable through the engagement with a jazz aesthetic, is also present in Morrison's representation of history and definitions as a conflict between oral and literate languages. The contrast staged between oral memories and traditions and the written histories of White America – figured in Bodwin's approach to 'the old homestead' – is also evident in the historical journey from plantation to free state, echoing the narratives of 'freedom' that characterise the slave autobiographies.

The bond with an African past is figured in Sethe's memories of plantation life, where the woman who nurtures her in childhood is remembered speaking to her in 'different words':

> Words Sethe understood then but could neither recall nor repeat now. She believed that must be why she remembered so little before Sweet Home except singing and dancing and how crowded it was. What Nan told her she had forgotten, along with the language she told it in. The same language her ma'am spoke, and which would never come back.
>
> (p. 62)

The elision of direct remembering into the memory of song and movement reveals the way in which 'Africa' remains in formal, emotional and transformed shades and shadows of meaning, the *feeling* of which can be violently experienced: 'But the message – that was and had been there all along' (p. 62). Recognising the reality of this gap, this distance, and embracing the aestheticisation of African memories into the physical expressiveness of music, avoids Walker's more literal, simple slide into the modern political territory of Africa.

In *Beloved*, Sixo's refusal to allow the progressive distantiation of himself from the 'different words' of his African past, with his turning away from the English language of the US plantations 'because there was no future in it' (p. 25), links the passionate nature of his night dances, 'to keep his bloodlines open' (p. 25), to the physical and emotional expressiveness of chain gang songs:

> They sang it out and beat it up, garbling the words so they could not be understood; tricking the words so their syllables yielded up other meanings.
>
> (p. 108)

This separation of surface meaning, or meaninglessness, from the deep channels of pain, longing and past knowledges that energise the songs answers the call of Frederick Douglass' description of slaves singing 'The Great House Farm' (see Chapter 2, p. x).

In a move typical of the slave narratives, Morrison presents Denver's escape from the confines of 124 into the classroom as a move towards self-determinism and an objectification of herself in the world:

> The effort to handle chalk expertly and avoid the scream it would make; the capital *w*, the little *i*, the beauty of the letters in her name, the deeply mournful sentences from the Bible Lady Jones used as a text book. . . . She was so happy.
>
> (p. 102)

Emphasis on the writing of her name, and Denver's physical response to writing, underline that sense of literacy as self-presentation and self-definition which the slave narratives symbolise. The aesthetic, even emotional joy which writing brings recalls the powerful reaction experienced by Mr Johnson to the letter 'S' (see Chapter 1, p. x), and Morrison's description of the meaning of this joy acts as a significant re-reading of Cary's images of a childlike and 'primitive' Johnson.

This description of the role of literacy for a sense of personal liberty, emphasised by Denver's ability to *pay* for the labour of her teacher and therefore to *earn* her services without debt – 'the nickel, tied to a handkerchief knot, tied to her belt, that she carried to Lady Jones, thrilled her' (p. 102) – is set alongside other images of personal freedom and other images of the role of religion in expressing and understanding the power of independence. Baby Suggs' sudden recognition of the existence and autonomy of her own body when she obtains her freedom, and the realisation that she is her own property, 'these hands belong to me. These my hands' (p. 141), leads to a celebration of spirituality that is not reliant on scriptural text: 'uncalled, unrobed, unanointed, she let her great heart beat in their presence' (p. 87).

Reading *Beloved* into the tradition of the slave narratives facilitates a close attention to the issues which preoccupied those narratives and that linked them so closely to the pan-Africanist nationalisms of Freetown. The historical connections between the 'enlightened' imaginings of Africa prevalent in Caribbean, African-American and Creole writers of the nineteenth century and the twentieth-century literary texts of African-American writers such as Morrison, Walker, Ellison and Naylor allow us to read how the slave narratives still haunt, shape and define twentieth-century Black identities. The geographies of space and time which self-consciously structure *Possessing the Secret of Joy* and *Beloved* represent the continuing need to interrogate the meaning of territory and land, the significance of borders and crossings, the weight of national belonging. Examining three further novels – Toni Morrison's *Song of Solomon*, Ralph Ellison's *Invisible Man* and Gloria Naylor's *Mama Day* – these questions become serious and urgent, not only for seizing the relevance of Africa as origin or identity, but also the meaning of the United States as 'home'.

Morrison's *Song of Solomon* explores how land and territory are invested with meanings drawn from personal and collective histories, memories and desires, determining how natural landscape, or the small and local corners of a city, come to reflect the cultural energies of a people. Land in the novel is fought over, murdered for, named, loved and sung, and its interpretation as national space, as property, or as the terror of alien regions, occurs through the political and emotional vocabularies of the narrative. Describing the northern city, with its officially named streets and zones, Milkman meditates on American naming:

He read the road signs with interest now, wondering what lay beneath the names. The Algonquins had named the territory he lived in Great Water, *michi gami*. How many dead lives and fading memories were buried in and beneath the names of the places in this country. Under the recorded names were other names . . . names that had meaning.

(p. 328)

This recognition of earlier and more *meaningful* landscapes beneath the named territories of the modern city is closely aligned with the naming of people. The memories and meanings which linger in the creative or forced naming of Black people – 'Names that bore witness' (p. 328) – attest to the subordination of the individual to the claims and recognitions of community life. This horizontal, relational bearing witness to the character, childhood, habits and tastes of individuals, through the power of naming, acts also as a way of reclaiming territory from the governmental imposition of official maps. In this way, territory is mapped and lived through an active aesthetics of naming:

Like the street he lived on, recorded as Mains Avenue but called Not Doctor Street by the Negroes in memory of his grandfather, who was the first colored man of consequence in that city. . . . So they named a street after him.

(p. 328)

This creative communal reclamation of city territory as a witness to the lives, triumphs and realities of particular cultural histories competes with other territorial reclamations. Macon Dead's fear of exile, of homelessness, activates his response to the demonstration of personal liberty as a matter of the ability to possess:

Let me tell you right now the one important thing you'll ever need to know: Own things. And let the things you own own other things. And then you'll own yourself and other people too.

(p. 59)

This longing to be in possession leads to Macon's own possession by what he perceives to be the malevolent exclusionary sentiments of the house he owns. While the daylight dies, Macon's encounter with his own property reminds him of the impossibility of projecting one's own sense of self onto the ownership of external things. Desiring to be in control of objects, which are assessed only in terms of profit, and not in relation to the human histories around or located within them, Macon realises the extent of their separation from himself:

> Scattered here and there, his houses stretched up beyond him like squat ghosts with hooded eyes . . . now they did not seem to belong to him at all – in fact he felt as though the houses were in league with one another to make him feel like the outsider, the propertyless, landless wanderer.
>
> (p. 32)

Likening the houses to 'ghosts' draws attention to past and present habitations that invest them with creative energies and meanings unknown to and unsought by him.

In contrast to Macon's avaricious need for autonomy through the subordination of city territory into personal property, Pilate's wanderings through the states of North America arrives at a communion with the land that heralds a different vision of national belonging. Having crossed the borders of states and countries, Pilate counteracts the homelessness of migratory movement by physically making the land a part of herself, by laying claim to it as a symbol of the reality of her own and her family's lives, by carrying it with her as the burden of her own inheritance:

> Pilate had taken a rock from every state she had lived in – because she *had* lived there. And having lived there, it was hers – and his, and his father's, his grandfather's, his grandmother's.
>
> (p. 328)

Macon and Pilate's separate reactions to the singular importance of land for the children of slaves who did not own or officially name the land on which they worked are both expressed in the remembered exhortations of ex-slaves in the Georgia of Macon's father: 'We live here. On this planet, in this nation, in this country right here. *N*owhere else!' (p. 237). The lesson here, missed or mis-interpreted by Macon's lust for the empty symbolism of ownership, is a lesson on the *labour* involved in laying roots, in claiming a valid identification with the land, in *investing* the land with the physical, loving and sensual aggression of being *there*:

> Grab this land! Take it, hold it, my brothers, make it, my brothers, shake it, squeeze it, turn it, twist it, beat it, kick it, kiss it, whip it, stomp it, dig it, plow it, seed it, reap it, rent it, buy it, sell it, own it, build it, multiply it, and pass it on.
>
> (p. 237)

This idea of loving the land aggressively is taken up by Guitar's rendition of the activities of the Seven Days Black nationalist organisation, which reinterprets love as an act of violence. Grieved and tormented by the sacrificing of slaves and indigenous peoples in the name of national territory – 'the earth is soggy with black people's blood. And before us Indian blood' (p. 159) – the Seven Days express their claims on the earth as being in direct and murderous conflict with White Americans: 'if it keeps on there won't be any of us left and there won't be any land for those who are left' (p. 159). As a contrast to this, other kinds of loving are explored that relate the work of land cultivation, expressed as a passion in Macon Dead's Georgia, to the labour of human love, its longing for reciprocity, its active and creative desire for mutual recognition, its intimate attentions. The loving of Milkman and Sweet is a persistent and joyful *task*: 'She put salve on his face. He washed her hair. She sprinkled talcum on his feet. He straddled her behind and massaged her back' (p. 286).

The sustained concentration on land and its meanings, exploring the concepts of love, freedom, nation and identity through the iconographies of earth and place, also encompasses an examination of the uneasy relationship between water and land. Whereas land represents the possibility of home, of roots, water transmits ideas of migration, of movement and wandering. Water's ability to gesture towards the release of departure and landing is explored in comparisons between rivers, lakes and oceans, and through a concentrated re-visiting of the nature of borders. The text focuses on the Canadian/United States frontier, for example, and its signifying of the limits of nation and state, by using the presence of the Great Lakes as a locus for the mixed and misplaced metaphors of complete departure:

> But those five Great Lakes which the St Lawrence feeds with memories of the sea are themselves landlocked, in spite of the wandering river that connects them to the Atlantic.
>
> (p. 164)

Seascape as the memory of leaving is an idea used as an alternative or sister metaphor to flight and the final freedom of being airborne. Opening with Robert Smith's promise to fly over Lake Superior, the novel unites the images of water and flight with those of death and departure, and the dead body of Pilate and Macon's father, after floating down the river, is deposited on its banks, in a representation of *untimely* and violent death. In comparison with this, the framing image of Solomon's flight from a southern plantation to Africa, representing the slave celebration of death, is the triumph of a chosen return to origins:

> He just took off: got fed up. *All the way up!* No more cotton! No more bales! No more orders!. . . He left everybody down on the ground and he sailed on off like a black eagle.
>
> (p. 327)

The novel leaves Solomon's flight in its mythical frame of *American* imagining, without seeking to investigate other lands and landings, and this allows the 'return' to remain suspended in the half-remembered songs, place names and personal names that make up the landscapes of Black America. The reverse journey of Milkman from northern city to the site of southern plantations, in a refiguring of the slave narrative genre, seeks to demonstrate the urgency of the past, the need for its pilgrimage and the indelibility of its traces.

Morrison's *Song of Solomon* elaborates on concepts of racial identity and resistance, revisiting slavery, migration and the slaves' longing for Africa as a way into reading the relationship between familial and cultural myths, and individual identities. The framing image of Solomon flying back to Africa from the southern plantations lives in a garbled song that underpins the freedom-fighting, the money-making and the familial battles of Milkman Dead. 'Africa' remains as a symbol of origins that has more to do with slavery and the South, with discovering the roots of a specifically Black American consciousness, than with a pan-African vision. *Beloved* is also haunted by an already mediated African identity, born from the Middle Passage and plantation labour, and united in a multivocal collective memory. Both novels emphasise the ambiguous place of Africa as 'racial memory', and a cultural origin which is placed *in between* the United States and Africa, and caught in that contradiction. That Pilate buries the bones of her father on Solomon's Leap, the southern site that was Solomon's point of departure for Africa, figures precisely this double claim.

These territorialised explorations of American Black identities in the late twentieth-century can be read against and alongside analogous figurations in Ralph Ellison's *Invisible Man*, from 1952. The multiple sites of the novel's dizzying opening are responses to, and creative of, widely different politics. As an exploration of history and identity, it continually repositions the possibility of origins, symbolic beginnings, aims, goals and definition for African-Americans. Whether United States Black identity draws its validity from Dr Bledsoe's leg shackle of slavery, or Ras the Exhorter's longing for Africa, from class struggle, or from radical, bitter separatism, the results force a continual reorientation of meaning.

The need to speak from a stable place comes up sharply against the shifting ground of hidden agendas, other histories, the difference within 'us': The 'Keep this Nigger Boy Running' motif becomes a theme of the novel, referring to the impossibility even of a direct oppositional stance. The positive empowering claim by the narrator that 'my world has become one of infinite possibilities' (p. 464) encounters its immediate underside in the phrase: 'None of us seems to know who he is or where he is going.' The claim that 'America is woven of many strands' would seem to indicate that the politics of each definition inevitably rests in that timeless, temporary moment of the White founder's statue holding the metallic veil above the eyes of the kneeling slave:

And I am standing puzzled, unable to decide whether the veil is really being lifted, or lowered more firmly in place; whether I am witnessing a revelation or a more efficient blinding.

(p. 34)

Ellison is here re-figuring DuBois' rendition of the 'veil' that separates Black from White Americans and provides Black Americans with an acute angle of vision, allowing them at once greater perceptions of the reality of racism and the US nation, and shutting them out from a range of freedoms:

Then it dawned upon me with a certain suddenness that I was different from the others; or like, mayhap, in heart and life and longing, but shut out from their world by a vast veil.[14]

These oblique and imagistic references to the literary histories and political writings of Black America allow the text to be read as an alternative narrative of American national history. The scene in the Prologue where the protagonist listens to Louis Armstrong lets the music emerge as a range of levels and foundations, with a multiplicity of voices building a deepening, widening picture of different times. Glimpses from slavery, from Black Protestantism, questions of freedom and its meaning, co-exist spatially with an urge for action and an intense yearning for tranquillity, crystallising in the lonely statement: 'I too have become acquainted with ambivalence' (p. 13).

The novel becomes a meditation on identity, forming an uneasy alliance between collective consciousness and individual subjectivity, beginning and ending in a temporary moment of despairing, private inauthenticity. Claiming that 'the world moves: not like an arrow, but a boomerang' (p. 9), the novel ends with a cry about 'coming out' and an unsubstantiated move towards having 'a socially responsible role to play'.

Invisible Man probes a history of Black politics in the United States and, in so doing, outlines contemporary options for Black resistance. Different and often conflicting constructs of race, culture and origins are explored, until notions of home, belonging and ultimate goals become confused.

Having rejected Dr Bledsoe's vision of interaction and advancement along Western capitalist lines, the narrator's cry that 'I have come home . . . I've found my true family! My true people! My true country!' (p. 279) becomes based on a non-racial alliance with communism. Just as Bledsoe's obsession with slavery masks a *reliance* on inferiority, so the communist non-racial brotherhood masks endemic racism and the exploitation of 'the race'.

The repeated violent images of Ras the Exhorter, with his constant claims for identification with Africa, insist on a specifically *racial* form of brotherhood (p. 299), becoming dangerously coercive as Ras the Destroyer. 'Africa' becomes an image of war, of power and destruction (pp. 447–9), caught in a moment of absolute opposition and violence, which the narrator sees as part

131

of a wider, more sinister operation on behalf of someone else's propaganda. The novel spirals into a meditation on 'the beautiful absurdity of . . . American identity' (p. 480) that continually deals in images and symbols from questionable cultural origins, making Black politics and African-American identifications with Africa, slavery or economics difficult and challenging.

The tension in the novel seems to be between a notion of the individual, as an authentic and equal self, and of a collective politics that seems to be inevitably caught in a dialectical relationship between Black and White nationalist ideals. As he says: 'Weren't we *part of them* as well as apart from them and subject to die when they died?' (p. 463).

In this way, 'Africa' operates as a blurred vision of freedom, loss, unity, racism and violence.

Gloria Naylor's *Mama Day* continues the interrogation into the meaning of time and space that was traced in the novels already discussed above. An immediate difference, however, is the placing of the narrative in the future, bringing the engagement with Black histories and memories to the cusp of the twenty-first century. The voice of the text, speaking from within the insular Black community of Willow Springs, employs a structure of address that stresses the separation of the narrative from a present outside of the text, in a reversal of *Beloved*'s position within the past of United States history:

> We're sitting here in Willow Springs, and you're God knows where. It's August 1999 – ain't but a slim chance it's the same season where you are.
>
> (p. 10)

This voice from within the community, later shifting between the various first person narratives of particular characters, and reminiscent of the address of *Petals of Blood*, enforces the idea of interpretative control and self-definition as the prerogative of Willow Springs society. The opposition between Willow Springs and 'God knows where' creates for Willow Springs a primary stability of place and space in a time that is resolutely *more modern*.

These parameters are further developed through the divisions between country and city, or North and South, which operate as illustrations of a theorisation of modernity and nation. Cutting between the scenes of New York, reported in the past tense, and Willow Springs, which remains in a continuous present, and future, tense, Naylor examines and reverses the ways in which city and country signify the 'opposites' of modernity and tradition. The pattern of the metropolis interpreting and defining its rural margins, an ethnographic scene that, as we have seen, haunts colonialist, pan-Africanist and certain American feminist texts, is repeated in the description of 'Reema's boy', a migrant to the city, whose 'mainside' education informs an anthropological visitation of Willow Springs, in order to 'put Willow Springs on the map' (p. 7). The colonialist echoes here, of 'mapping' the area, lead to the enthnographer's spurious translation of a key historical date and time, 1823, into the spatialised terms of national and global mapping:

> He done still made it to the conclusion that 18 + 23 wasn't 18 + 23 at all – was really 81 + 32, which just so happened to be the lines of longitude and latitude marking where Willow Springs sits on the map.
>
> (pp. 7–8)

This imposition of other sources and theories of knowledge onto rural spaces from the (migrant) ethnographies of the national mainland (an echo of Freetown's understanding of indigenous cultures) is countered by the superior, more informed understanding of the narrative's communal voice: 'Reema's boy couldn't listen . . . or he woulda left here with quite a story' (p. 10).

The separation of Willow Springs from the United States by an unstable bridge over turbulent water and its position *outside* the geography and regulation of nation and state – 'And the way we saw it, America ain't entered the question at all when it come to our land' (p. 5) – allows the community to be predicated in the subsistent space of its own historical imagining, in the Black community of Willow Springs. Owning the land which is beyond United States' control and placing it in possession of the *future* exists in the autonomous narrative of its own memories and definitions: 'it's always owned two generations down' (p. 219).

As in Morrison's novels, time is continually made meaningful with reference to space, and is constantly subject to the laws of memory. The annual ritual of Candle Walk night enacts the collective history of Willow Springs through an active trek over land to the edges of the sea. This re-enactment of historical events by means of the metaphoric mapping of present to past, from the land to the sea, follows the significance of Sapphira Wade's mythic journey. The slave myth of flying back to Africa over the blank and homeless spaces of the sea is presented here as a simultaneous retracing of history from present to past realities:

> But she got away from him and headed over here towards the east bluff on her way back to Africa. And she made that trip – some say in body, others in mind.
>
> (p. 206)

Sapphira's African and slave identities create her into the founding vision of Willow Springs itself which, neither American nor African, exists in the in-between, liminal spaces between the two. The idea that it is precisely within these margins, at the cusp of past and present, that an opening to the future can be traced, is an important one for a refiguring of Black narratives in the modern world. Mama Day's presentiments of the future, between 'two ticks of the clock' (p. 138), are linked with her communion with the past and her relationship with the land. The magical power of her conjuring, tied closely to the memory of Sapphira Wade's 'witchcraft', bonds these elements together in an image of the fundamental power of female knowledge or 'the workings of Woman' (p. 251). That this knowledge has a forceful understanding of the future and that Mama Day herself is given a place in the twenty-first century brings the relevance of myth and magic into a modernity that has already given dignity to science fiction:

> She's always liked things neat, and when she's tied up the twentieth century, she'll take a little peek into the other side – for pure devilment and curiosity.
>
> (p. 312)

The texts explored in this chapter create a mapping of African-American identities as specific, historically situated and nationally located imaginaries. Reading *Possessing the Secret of Joy* against Morrison and Naylor, the difficulties and responsibilities of (American) feminist theorising become apparent. The implicit role of American structures of femininity in creating the conditions of cross-border unity in Walker's text is foregrounded and more rigorously analysed in the African-American novels here. The connections between the slave narratives of the preceding chapter and the issues which emerge in the literary texts analysed here are clear and attest to the historical continuities between nineteenth- and twentieth-century subjectivities.

Notes

1. Alice Walker, *Possessing the Secret of Joy* (London: Jonathan Cape, 1992). References will be cited in the text.
2. Simon Watney, 'Missionary Positions: AIDS, Africa and Race', in Russell Ferguson, Martha Gever, Trinn T. Minh-ha and Cornel West (eds) *Out There: Marginalisation and Contemporary Cultures* (New York: The New Museum of Contemporary Art and Cambridge, MA: MIT Press, 1990), p. 91.
3. Ngũgĩ Wa Thiong'o, *Petals of Blood* (Portsmouth, NH: Heinemann, 1988 [1977]), p. 328.
4. Toni Morrison, *Beloved* (London: Picador, 1987). References will be cited in the text.
5. Toni Morrison, *Song of Solomon* (London: Triad Grafton, 1980). References will be cited in the text.
6. Gloria Naylor, *Mama Day* (London: Vintage, 1990 [1988]). References will be cited in the text.
7. Henry Louis Gates, Jr, Preface to *Six Women's Slave Narratives*, The Schomberg Library of Nineteenth-Century Black Women Writers (New York: Oxford University Press, 1988), pp. xii–xiii. Further references will be cited in the text.
8. See interview with Salman Rushdie for Channel Four Television, June 1992.

9 Homi K. Bhabha, *The Location of Culture* (London: Routledge, 1994), p. 152. Further references will be cited in the text.

10 Peter Nicholls, 'The Belated Postmodern: History, Phantoms, and Toni Morrison', *Borderlines: Studies in American Culture*, 1(3) (March 1994). Further references will be cited in the text.

11 Minnie Bruce Pratt, 'Identity: Skin Blood Heart', in Elly Bulkin, Minnie Bruce Pratt and Barbara Smith, *Yours in Struggle* (New York: Long Haul Press, 1984). References will be cited in the text.

12 Ralph Ellison, *Invisible Man* (Harmondsworth: Penguin, 1987 [1952]), p. 11. Further references will be cited in the text.

13 Toni Morrison, *Playing in the Dark: Whiteness and the Literary Imagination* (Cambridge, MA: Harvard University Press, 1992). References will be cited in the text.

14 W.E.B. DuBois, *The Souls of Black Folk* (Greenwich, CT: Fawcett publications, 1961 [1903]), p. 16.

4

CROSSING BORDERS

Race, sexuality and the body

> A dozen shades slid by. There was sooty black, shiny black,
> taupe, mahogany, bronze, copper, gold, orange, yellow, peach,
> ivory, pinky white, pastry white. There was yellow hair, brown
> hair, black hair; straight hair, straightened hair, curly hair,
> woolly hair. She saw black eyes in white faces, brown eyes in
> yellow faces, gray eyes in brown faces, blue eyes in tan faces.
>
> (Nella Larsen, *Quicksand*)

This chapter continues the discussions of time which informed the previous
chapter by exploring the roles of postmodernist theories and debates about
racial identities and migration. The argument focuses more particularly on
British contexts in order to revisit the journeys invoked in the slave narratives
and to examine the impact of 'new' Caribbean migrations to Britain.

The chapter develops the analyses of Black migrant identities from the
previous chapters by exploring how race is figured in representations of the
body and sexuality. Each of the preceding chapters has inquired into constructions of race as ethnographic, cultural and nationalist discourses, placing
narratives of Black identity within or against conceptions of history and
geography that are continually re-visited and re-articulated.

I analyse two texts that return to the territories of *Heart of Darkness* and
A Bend in the River (discussed in Chapter 1), and I attend to the way in which
the images and metaphors of colonial narratives are redeployed in African
texts. These images of Africa and racial difference, which are exploited in
the symbiotic texts of Conrad and Naipaul, reappear in the textual ironies of
Tayeb Salih's *Season of Migration to the North* and Ama Ata Aidoo's *Our Sister
Killjoy*. The migrations figured in these novels *from* Africa *to* the West also act
as an ironic commentary on the enlightenment narratives of pan-Africanist
exiles, which are discussed in Chapter 2, and on their investigative, evangelist
journeys 'back' to Africa. The playful and more serious interrogations into
the links between sexuality and race in these texts are taken up and read
through two texts by White authors that, through the novel form and through
journalistic autobiography, investigate the meanings of race and sexuality
approached by Salih and Aidoo.

Moving from these comparative inquiries into sexuality and race, which use images of travel, of crossing borders, in various and related ways, the chapter will provide readings of African and African-American texts that explore motifs of cultural hybridity through analyses of the sexual and racial body. The chapter will include discussions of the related problematics of mixed-race identities in African, African-American and Black British literary texts, tracing the connections between popular cultural perceptions of race and feminist political analysis. The chapter argues, in particular, that representations of race, sexuality and the body are textually and historically connected to the ethnographic, colonialist and nationalist discourses of 'African' cultures and races that have framed the preceding chapters.

Postmodernism and the Diaspora

The theorisation of the past and of history that structures Ellison's investigation into Black American identities in *Invisible Man*, and which is revisited in *Mama Day*, is a way into thinking a role for African-Americans in the future. The fin-de-siècle framework of Naylor's text opens a space for presentiments of the future beyond the year 2000 and places Naylor's novel firmly within debates around the postmodern and its relation to Black consciousness. The place of Black texts within postmodernist aesthetics, and the relationship between Black feminisms and the politics of postmodernism, is often perceived as fraught and uncertain. How useful postmodernist theories are in conceptualising the histories and subjectivities of Blacks and of women becomes an important question for the literary texts discussed in Chapter 3 because of the central place each reserves for thinking about history. The energies devoted to the invocation of hidden, forgotten, marginalised narratives of the past in these texts can be approached in postmodernist terms as the dissolution of the Grand Narratives of 'the' American culture and nation. Postmodernist emphases on dismantling the master tales of dominant cultures, narratives which seek to foreground a transcendental Truth, in favour of more local, 'little' narratives of contingent, temporary truths, allow attention to what has been made marginal or silent. The grand universal Human Subject is displaced for a recognition of multiple and fractured subjectivities. Any overarching Narrative is revealed to be bound to terror and exclusion.

In her essay on 'Postmodern Blackness', bell hooks takes such departures for postmodernist analysis as a basis for inquiry into the politics of Black identity, and writes: 'It has become necessary to find new avenues to transmit the messages of Black liberation struggle, new ways to talk about racism and other politics of domination.'[1] This need to find 'new avenues' for expression that are sensitive to the *changing* racisms and nationalisms of modernity can, according to hooks, be sought in the radical interpretations of identity and history that exist within postmodernist arguments:

When Black folks critique essentialism, we are empowered to recognize multiple experiences of Black identity that are the lived conditions which make diverse cultural productions possible.

(p. 29)

It is, however, a corrective to any uncritical embrace of the pertinence of postmodernist thought to witness the cultural dominance of postmodernist forms in the capitalist centres of the world. Fredric Jameson observes that postmodernism 'is no longer at all oppositional in that sense; indeed it constitutes the very dominant or hegemonic aesthetic of consumer society itself and significantly serves the latter's commodity production as a virtual laboratory of new forms and fashions'.[2] This invites an uncertainty around the continued usefulness of an 'oppositional' strategy once it has become centred. Patricia Waugh's interrogation of the helpfulness of postmodernist theories for feminist politics and analysis asks how an attention to the splintered relativities of cultural and historical narratives can yield a space for stable and cross-cultural appeals to ethics, morality and value. Her central question is formulated as: 'Is it possible for feminists to draw on the aesthetics of Postmodernism as strategies for narrative disruption without embracing its nihilist pragmatism?'[3] The answer would seem to lie in an awareness of feminism's double and simultaneous claim: for female autonomy and for the critique of female essentialisms. Rescuing the categorisation of subjects from totalising enlightenment discourses and *at the same time* struggling for recognition and justice *within* the discourses of humanism and law has already been a strategy employed within Black politics (for the last two centuries at least). Waugh's claim that feminism, on its own terms, can be viewed as being already 'intrinsically post-modern' (p. 343) solicits a reminder that the critically dominant terms of postmodernist theory have in part emerged out of the passionate claims and perceptive interrogations of Black *as well as* female subjects.

The importance of identity politics, of laying claim to an autonomous self that, in its radical and stable subjectivity as Black and/or female, can be displayed on the frontispiece of slave narratives and autobiographies, or clearly attested to in the forewords to texts on pan-Africanism or on the sleeves of novels, is discussed in Toni Morrison's essay 'Unspeakable Things Unspoken'.[4] Tracing the shifting debates between Black politics and central state institutions such as academe (law and government could be included), Morrison pin-points the way in which Black analyses of race and specific collectivity have been systematically marginalised:

When Blacks discovered they had shaped or become a culturally formed race, and that it had specific and revered difference, suddenly they were told there is no such thing as 'race', biological or cultural, that matters and that genuinely intellectual exchange cannot accommodate it.

(p. 3)

This consistent marginalisation of claims on identity that have been historically formed and narrativised, and which highlight the significant connections between colonial histories and the present, is one which has alarmed certain areas of Black political thought. bell hooks' description of 'yearning' as a common modern psychological state – a 'longing for critical voice' – that wells specifically out of 'the postmodernist deconstruction of "master" narratives' (*Yearning*, p. 27) leads her to pass perhaps too quickly over the underlying observation that the attack on essentialism has resulted not only in positive re-evaluations of the 'identity trap' of Blackness but also in disempowering the voice of a very real oppositional status. Her citation of a common and negative response to discussions of postmodernism is made in order to open out and further explore the possibility of re-directing postmodernist thought into Black politics. This common response is, however, salutary:

> 'Yeah, it's easy to give up identity, when you got one'. Should we not be suspicious of postmodern critiques of the 'subject' when they surface at a historical moment when many subjugated people feel themselves coming to voice for the first time.
>
> (*Yearning*, p. 28)

The novels by Morrison, Ellison and Naylor discussed in Chapter 3, when read alongside these debates within postmodernist aesthetics and politics, make it clear that the mythical structures of Black communities, the enforced creative oralities of what have become 'Black' histories, and the contradictory re-definitions of human autonomy and freedom, already contain the 'new' radical perspectives and insights that postmodernism fixes as fin-de-siècle or late capitalist phenomena. Re-applying these issues concerning the histories of migration, the politics of postmodernism and the theorisation of racial identity, this chapter begins by suggesting how the textual preoccupations of African-American novels can be interrogated within British debates, picking up the historical threads of Chapters 1 and 2, which signalled to Britain's position within Black African and Caribbean writings.

Discussing the idea that the 'postmodern age' has come to focus or centre itself on the figure of Black migration or Diaspora, Stuart Hall writes of the place of Caribbean migrants in Britain:

> Thinking about my own sense of identity, I realise that it has always depended on the fact of being *a migrant*, on the *difference* from the rest of you. So one of the fascinating things about this discussion is to find myself centred at last. Now that, in the postmodern age, you all feel so dispersed, I become centred. What I've thought of as dispersed and fragmented comes, paradoxically, to be *the* representative, modern experience! This is 'coming home' with a vengeance.[5]

Side-stepping this train of optimism for a moment, I locate something in the new narratives of displacement and fragmentation which work, not to challenge the old hierarchies of metropolitan centre and colonial peripheries, but to enforce them in new ways. Hall finds himself, in the midst of his joke, caught disturbingly between the universal and the particular. The Grand Narrative of Migration, of leaving the imagined plenitude of home for what is predicted to be a circular journey, is both everyone's story and no one's. Within the grandeur of the racial or political collective is the isolated yet (as Hall calls it) 'universal story of life. One is where one is to try and get away from somewhere else' (p. 44).

If the 'Big Story' (p. 44) is the plurality of cultural relativism and the escape from one's family, Blacks in Britain are at once centred and lost. When all of us are equally fragmented and dispersed, when identity officially adds up to a series of temporary, non-finite hallucinations, some of us are more equal than others. bell hooks provides a useful warning here:

> Postmodern theory that is not seeking to simply appropriate the experience of 'Otherness' to enhance the discourse or to be radically chic should not separate 'the politics of difference' from the politics of racism.
>
> (*Yearning*, p. 26)

This is a major corrective to the liberal notions of a multi-racial, multi-ethnic, multi-different British society – it is also different in quite particular imbalanced ways. Salman Rushdie's point, in his essay, 'The New Empire Within Britain', is worth repeating here:

> Racism is not a side-issue in contemporary Britain; it is not a peripheral, minority affair. . . . It is a crisis of the whole culture, of the society's entire sense of itself.[6]

How does racism, then, introduce a new term into the postmodernist idea of a shared crisis of advanced industrialism and cultural difference? Stuart Hall suggests the radical potential of the term 'ethnicity' as a way towards undoing such grand, universal oppressions as nationalism and national identity. This is a significant point, feeding into the push to make Whiteness strange, to insist that, as Hall says:

> Every identity is placed, positioned, in a culture, a language, a history. Every statement comes from somewhere, from somebody in particular.
>
> ('Minimal Selves', p. 46)

It undoes the 'natural' link between race, immigrant and Blackness, the askew balance between neutral centre and racial periphery. But once racism and discrimination are added to cultures or ethnicities, an important political reading is demanded, which takes the new-found safety out of relativism, plurality and the one-world time of decentred subjectivity.

The problem seems to be about whose voice defines whose 'collective' experience, and what exactly is being opposed or (re-)claimed. If identities are given a political reality in racist Britain, where difference is emphatically not equal, can we talk of (a) narrative(s) of Black identity? Even if we disengage narrative from notions of stable origins, historical beginnings and endings, terrible – because insistent – choices come all at once onto the agenda.

Paul Gilroy, in an essay on diasporic identification,[7] discusses how Black identity or resistance doesn't always add up to the same thing. Like Womanness, Black-ness is a diverse, complex, sometimes contradictory category which forms itself in opposition to a multiplicity of oppressions, and in response to different creativities. Gilroy asks:

> What is being resisted and by what means? slavery? capitalism? coerced industrialisation? racial terror? Or ethnocentrism and European solipsism? How are the discontinuous histories of diaspora to be thought, to be theorised by those who have experienced the consequences of racial domination?
>
> (p. 4)

Pratibha Parmar's statement that 'Black British women are part of many diasporas',[8] makes the general point that the term 'Black' in Britain covers a range of cultures, races, even nations, and the more radical point that each of these ethnicities contains a stunning and difficult range of narratives, of meanings.

Turning away from opposition to a politics of articulation 'in and for ourselves', Parmar discusses the need to re-centre, to refuse otherness, to begin at a range of contradictory starting points, a need which also includes a heady range of anxieties. Parmar makes a statement which seems to militate against racism being the only or the ultimate identifying term for Black people in Britain:

> In these postmodernist times, the question of identity has taken on colossal weight particularly for those of us who are post-colonial migrants inhabiting histories of diaspora. Being cast into the role of the Other, marginalized, discriminated against and too often invisible . . . black women in particular have fought to assert privately and publicly our sense of self.
>
> (p. 106)

The tension here is between the individual and the collective, between a racially defined subjectivity and humanity, between invisibility and over-determined presence. The phrase, 'our sense of self', with its emphasis both on group identity and on singularity, encapsulates what appears to be an ongoing and problematic dance in Black or race politics in Britain and the West.

How has this sense of self been asserted within Black politics and feminism? How has essentialism become, on one hand, a danger, negating heterogeneity and plurality, and, on the other hand, become an important political tool, a way of claiming a voice from a strong and valid position? The prescriptiveness or not of claiming the essential nature of any racial or political group does, of course, rely on how you read 'essentialism', or how metaphysically absolute the category becomes. What colonial histories show is that, however much we can deconstruct concepts such as race, nation and culture, reveal their instabilities and illogical natures, they still operate actively to oppress groups of people and materially, psychologically and violently affect their lives. Has a recognisable, separate and valid history and identity been created, and does this positively define Black people? From which predicates can we begin? Going back to Hall's evocation of migrancy as a key focus of Black identity in Britain, the narrative of Diaspora can be, and has been, inter-preted in different ways.

Comparing V.S. Naipaul's *The Mimic Men*[9] and Sam Selvon's *The Lonely Londoners*,[10] for example, two different political conclusions and interpreta-tions emerge. Both provide different narrative responses to the postcolonial migrations of the 1950s and 1960s from the Caribbean and other ex-colonies to Britain.

Naipaul's Ralph Singh describes migration as the loss of history, the loss of a narrative of identity:

> Those of us who came to [the city] lost some of our solidity; we were trapped into fixed, flat postures. . . . Not the panic of being lost or lonely; the panic of ceasing to feel myself as a whole person.
>
> (p. 27)

He describes being 'flung off the world' (p. 69), being shipwrecked and always awaiting rescue (p. 111), the feeling that 'home' is eternally elsewhere. Feel-ing a migrant in London, Singh also feels that the Caribbean is a place of transit for the East Indian, whose racial origins are in the Indian sub-continent, so London is simply 'a greater shipwreck' (p. 180) than the fictional Caribbean island, Isabella. Singh's philosophy emerges in his nihilis-tic vision that:

> To be born on an island like Isabella, an obscure New World trans-plantation, second-hand and barbarous, was to be born to disorder.

From an early age, almost from my first lesson at school about the weight of the king's crown, I had sensed this.

(p. 118)

Failing to find, for himself, the centre of the Empire in London, Singh also fails to create a position of resistance or an oppositional political identity. His sense of a collective identity is based on chaos and despair, on being forever on the margins, off centre and adrift. Always imagining a lost 'ideal landscape' which represents an unreturnable homeland, Singh's sense of self refuses to be translated into a Black politics or a sense of belonging in the Caribbean or in London. He says that:

I am like that child outside a hut at dusk, to whom the world is so big and unknown and time so limitless; and I have visions of Central Asian horsemen, among whom I am one, riding below a sky threatening snow to the very end of an empty world.

(pp. 81–2)

Sam Selvon's *The Lonely Londoners*, published in 1956, provides a different interpretation of this situation of migrant-ness. Here is a profound recognition of the effect of displacement on a sense of self – that a hostile environment can affect the certainty of one's own body. In a passage reminiscent of Fanon's description of being Black in Paris,[11] Selvon's narrator, Moses, describes Galahad's feeling of being Black in London:

In the panic he start to pat pocket to make sure he have money on him, and he begin to search for passport and some other papers he had. A feeling come over him as if he lost everything he have – clothes, shoes, hat – and he start to touch himself here and there as if he in a daze.

(p. 42)

The magic of the mythology of London is described as a fantasy and a way of dreaming the city from the margins, and part of this dreaming involves the pain of alienation, the violence of despair, the longing for a home which is always elsewhere. As Moses says:

You know what I would do if I had money? I go and live Paradise – you know where Paradise is? Is somewhere between St. Joseph and Tacarigua, is a small village . . . that is life for me, boy. I don't want no ballet and opera and symphony.

(p. 130)

But out of this pain, this 'aimlessness . . . restless, swaying movement' (p. 141)

143

of exile, the sense of a *new* collective identity is formed. Migrants from Africa and different Caribbean islands, with distinct languages and dialects, form a new Black British identity in response to migration and racism, and radically change the identity of London itself, *claiming* London for their own. In a passage reminiscent of Stuart Hall's words about being centred, Galahad's experience of London reclaims it:

> Every time he go there, he have the same feeling like when he see it the first night . . . people sitting and standing and walking and talking and laughing and buses and cars and Galahad Esquire, in all this, standing there in the big city, in London. Oh Lord.
>
> (p. 90)

The idea of going home, or the predication of home elsewhere, becomes a vital part of Black imagining in the West, and incorporates itself as an oppositional reading of history, positive identities and continuity. The validity of this for a sense of collective identity emerges in, for example, Rastafarian notions of an African home, or simultaneous, often contradictory notions of home, such as the notion of being between 'home' and 'back home'.

The arrival of the Empire Windrush from the Caribbean in 1948 is popularly seen as the first modern wave of Afro-Caribbean immigrants to Britain. The Declaration of Human Rights, adopted by the General Assembly of United Nations, 10 December 1948, claims that:

> All human beings are born free and equal in dignity and rights. Everyone has the right to leave any country, including his own, and to return to his country. Everyone has the right to work . . . and to protection against unemployment.[12]

This shows both how law becomes incommensurable with politics, and why citizenship is so important.

The panic about immigration into Britain did not begin in 1948. Major William Evans Gordon, the Tory MP for Stepney, made an amendment to the Queen's Speech in 1902 in which is manifest the horror of immigration into Britain:

> Not a day passes but English families are ruthlessly turned out to make room for foreign invaders. . . . It is only a matter of time before the population becomes entirely foreign. . . . The working classes know that new buildings are erected not for them but for strangers from abroad . . . they see the schools crowded with foreign children and the very posters and advertisements on the walls in a foreign tongue. . . . A storm is brewing which, if it be allowed to burst, will have deplorable results.[13]

In this same speech, Major Evans panics about numbers, the growth of crime, the immigrant as an individual outside the law. Foreign-ness is here used as an essential, an unchanging, unchangeable feature of the migrant. Time moves like a whirlwind while 'strangers from abroad', 'foreigners', 'invaders' oppose English-ness on its own territory and get ready to fight. One thinks, of course, of Enoch Powell whose own speeches of 1968 and 1969 reflect 'the nation' in terms of a static 'English' people fixed to stable places. For Powell, nation-ness is about geography and 'race' bonded tightly and immovably together, so that the effect of the immigrant on an area – clinched in terms of numbers – is one of national alarm. Hence this passage in his Eastbourne speech of November 1968:

> The very growth in numbers would increase the already striking fact of dense geographical concentration, so that the urban part of whole towns and cities in Yorkshire, the Midlands and the Home Counties would be preponderantly or exclusively Afro-Asian in population. There would be several Washingtons in England. From these whole areas the indigenous population, the people of England, who fondly imagine that this is their country and these are their home-towns, would have been dislodged – I have deliberately chosen the most neutral word I could find.[14]

From this position, Powell can speak of 'The English as a nation' who should turn their hearts towards repatriation 'as a national duty'. Naturally, so 'neutral' is Powell's choice of words that the 'native' English have children while immigrants have 'offspring' and even 'piccaninnies'. Foreign-ness – the stigma of migration – sticks. Whether 'first generation' or 'second generation', or 'third', one is still *in passing,* one inherits ones migrant-ness through the genes. So Powell can claim in the same speech that:

> The West Indian or Asian does not, by being born in England, become an Englishman. In law he becomes a United Kingdom citizen by birth; in fact, he is a West Indian or an Asian still. Unless he be one of a small minority – for number, I repeat again and again, is of the essence – he will by the very nature of things have lost one country without gaining another, lost one nationality without acquiring a new one.

(p. 77)

So citizenship is a matter of law, and nationality a matter of race, of being. If a law flouts nation-hood it can, of course, be changed. It is nationality which guarantees freedom under the law. This state of limbo, this state of immigrant-ness, changes the holder of a British passport from Antigua, from Barbados, from Jamaica, from citizen to incurable alien.

145

Powell's justifications for this contradict each other. The problem, he claims, is that immigrants do not settle into an exclusive identification with Britain but, to quote again from the Eastbourne speech, 'even those born here in Britain, remain integrated in the immigrant community which links them with their homelands overseas' (p. 77) and 'there are many cases where individuals have uprooted themselves to come here, but . . . they are still to a large extent a part, economically and socially, of the communities from which they have been detached and to which they regard themselves as belonging' (p. 75). The problem is also, however, that the 'Briton . . . feels himself' to be 'the "toad beneath the harrow" in the areas where the immigrant population is spreading and *taking root*' (p. 66; my emphasis). Settling, harking back – either state is dangerous, irresponsible, destabilising.

Such oblique logical moves help to confuse the issues further, as does Powell's confusion of the words 'integration' and 'assimilation' in his Birmingham Speech of April 1968. If 'to be integrated into a population means to become for all practical purposes indistinguishable from its other members',[15] then the preoccupation is with a mythically static identity rather than – oddly – with numbers. Where there are too many foreigners, there will be an obliteration of Englishness. These premises would explain the rather strange obsession with such stories as that of the lone White child in a class surrounded by Blacks or the lone White occupant in a street taken over by 'the coloureds'. Or would they? For he has taken an unquestioned leap here from foreignness to colour, from immigrant to Black, and having made this leap, he finds Black-ness ringing with all the terrors of unbelonging, of infection, of invasion. The horror of an England ousted from its national space takes on the widespread taboo of miscegenation. Or, as Sir Cyril Osborne wrote in 1964:

> Those who so vehemently denounce the slogan 'Keep Britain White' should answer the question, do they want to turn it black? If unlimited immigration were allowed, we should ultimately become a chocolate-coloured, Afro-Asian mixed society. That I do not want.[16]

He still speaks of 'we' and 'Britain', yet such a generational melting-pot would at least create an inability to distinguish between the nation's members.

Culture and race as essentials, nationality as static and rooted, applies differently to the concurrent invisible emigrations of White British citizens to the dominions in their thousands, to colonies closed to Blacks of the same Commonwealth. If Whites are free to travel the borders of Australia, Canada, South Africa, then nationality is not an issue of place and space, but one of narrative, myth and emotion.

This question of colour, of being on the edges of the nation, has been an issue of Black migration through a long and wandering history. The conflation of immigrant with 'Black' in modern Britain has been the cause of a separation between citizen and ethnicity, between British and foreign, so that home and unbelonging take on confusing and harrowing dimensions. Sam Selvon's Galahad, in *The Lonely Londoners*, draws attention to this peculiarly devastating plight of Black identity in 1950s England. Tormented by the loneliness of racism, this immigrant Trinidadian discovers a sudden split between his identity as a British citizen and the Blackness which keeps him continually in transit:

> And Galahad watch the colour of his hand, and talk to it, saying, 'Colour, is you that causing all this, you know. . . .' So Galahad talking to the colour Black, as if is a person, telling it that is not he who causing botheration in the place, but Black, who is a worthless thing for making trouble all about.
>
> (pp. 72–3)

Dilip Hiro, discussing the problem of labels and terminology for Black peoples in Britain, describes how the language has changed throughout the years. He asks whether racial minorities are 'to be defined in terms of colour or their regional or continental origins?'. The word 'coloured' in Britain has moved to 'Black' and to nationalist or regional representation, like 'Afro-Caribbean' or 'Asian'. This change has occurred due to a need to claim an equal political identity in opposition to White, and to assert an autonomous, positive national identity while excluded by British nationalism.

Hiro, while pointing out the multi-racial or multi-cultural nature of Caribbean and Asian societies, decides to divide Black people in Britain into two kinds of racisms and identities. He writes:

> Since White prejudice against Afro-Caribbeans and Africans stems primarily from racial/colour differences, the term 'black' seems most appropriate particularly when it has the advantage of covering people from different regions of the world: the West Indies and Africa. Prejudice against Asians, however, stems as much from colour considerations as cultural. . . . So the group needs to be identified by its regional background: Asian or South Asian.[17]

This logical separation actually denies the irrational nature of British racism, which confuses culture, race and inter-ethnic difference in the same way that it makes up and confuses something called English or British culture with an Anglo-Saxon race. As we can see, racism may rely on history, but history depends on how you interpret it.

To attempt an answer to my earlier question – can there be a narrative of Black identity? – I would be forced to insist both on the narratives and on their significant difficulty.

'Were we in winter or summer?': inter-racial fantasy and African migration

The inquiries into the social construction of racial identities and the politics of postmodernism in the first section focused on how 'race' operates as a discursive frame in relation to the figure of migration. This section of the chapter continues these analyses through readings of two narratives of migration that take up the preceding inquiries into colonial racisms and cultural interchange and re-examine the possibilities and conditions of inter-racial dialogue and cross-cultural feminisms.

Tayeb Salih's *Season of Migration to the North*,[18] translated from Arabic and first published in English in 1969, is a narrative of border crossings between 'North' and 'South', creating sexualised interlocution between the racialised geographical metaphors of England and Africa. As a reverse journey from an African landscape to London, self-conscious allusions to Conrad's *Heart of Darkness* are manifest. Naipaul's *A Bend in the River*[19] was published ten years after *Season of Migration to the North*, and the texts can be read together as intertextual revisitations of the colonialist metaphors of Africa which structure Conrad's tale.

Like *Heart of Darkness*, Salih's tale is framed as a narrative within a narrative, where the opening oral voice – addressing a male audience – is primed to give way to the core first-person narration of Mustafa Sa'eed, another Sudanese traveller to the West. Erupting from the heart of the novel, framed by the discourse of the nameless first narrator, Sa'eed's autobiographical memories emerge as mysteries to be decoded, the ultimate meanings of which are made enigmatically elusive. Figured between the contrasting images of stability, rootedness and origins that open the novel, Sa'eed's story is one of migration and restlessness. The novel repeatedly echoes images of conquest and domination, entering the spaces of stereotype and sexuality, questioning notions of resistance and cultural manipulation through sexual and psychic trauma.

The possibilities of communication between a colonial subject on the brink of independence and the imperial metropolis are interrogated to provide a startling vision of the role of racial myths in a postcolonial world. The layering of narrative voices produces a protagonist who occupies the teasing, elusive spaces of the ghost-figure, the legend, the text within the text. Sa'eed's conscious manipulation of sadistic sexual roles, while being trapped within the racial codes that in turn seduce and manipulate him, creates a hilarious account of the ways in which racism is figured through sexuality, where carnal relations between Black and White (again complicated by gender roles) act out a plethora of racial signifiers. Having completed an English education in Cairo, Sa'eed enters university in England, where he is at once prey to the complexities of a desire signposted by colonial racisms. In the voice of his White lover can be heard the colonial lust for subjugation of a climate that appears to be far more intense, richer, more brutally sensual than one's own, and Sa'eed's body becomes the geography of more than one 'Black' continent:

> I want to have the smell of you in full – the smell of rotting leaves in the jungles of Africa, the smell of mango and the pawpaw and tropical spices, the smell of the rains in the deserts of Arabia.
>
> (p. 37)

Sexual passion for a Black African subject becomes a lust for 'Africa'. Black is the 'colour of magic and mystery and obscenities'. The novel is a cycle of masquerades in costume with White lovers donning 'Arabian' garb and Sa'eed recreating his past and living his present in a conglomeration of Western stereotypes. For example, he meets a White English girl whom he has never before seen and, in an extraordinarily theatrical scene, they act out a procession of projected Western fantasies that rely on a particular dreaming of distance, climate and environment:

> She would tell me that in my eyes she saw the shimmer of mirages in the hot deserts, that in my voice she heard the screams of ferocious beasts in the jungle. And I would tell her that in the blueness of her eyes I saw the far-away shores of the North.
>
> (p. 145)

The respective places of victim and aggressor in these sexual scenarios become difficult to determine. Sa'eed's manipulation of White English women, which frequently induces in them a fatal despair, is framed in a mise-en-scène where he becomes the victim of his own stereotype, painfully longing for the cancellation of the chasm between North and South. The analysis of desire as the mutual thirst for other landscapes, embodied in the racialised flesh of natives, is offset by the constant objectification of Sa'eed's own body as the principal focus of racialised desire. The first narrator's investigation of Sa'eed's secret room at the end of the novel, heralded as the ultimate moment where Sa'eed's Unconscious will be revealed, becomes instead a series of mirror images, reflecting only the source of the gaze which objectified him. Entering the secret room, the narrator encounters someone he believes to be Sa'eed, revisiting a scene from *Heart of Darkness* where Marlow meets Kurtz's picture of

> a woman, draped and blindfolded, carrying a lighted torch. The background was somber – almost black. The movement of the woman was stately, and the effect of the torchlight on the face was sinister.
>
> (*Heart of Darkness*, p. 523)

The narrator in *Season of Migration to the North* opens the door on a similar scene of light, blindness and approach:

> The light exploded in my eyes and out of the darkness there emerged a frowning face with pursed lips that I knew I could not place. I moved towards it with hate in my heart. It was my adversary Mustafa Sa'eed.
>
> (p. 135)

This scene of encountering the Other is exposed as a meeting with the reflected self: 'The face grew a neck, the neck two shoulders and a chest, then a trunk and two legs, and I found myself standing face to face with myself' (p. 135).

The uncanny encounter contrasts with the innocence of self-recognition at the beginning of the novel, where the narrator's sense of home and stability is expressed in the lack of division between self and image: 'I was happy during those days, like a child that sees its face in the mirror for the first time' (p. 4).

Salih's text can be situated within an analysis of colonial imagery through Homi Bhabha's theoretical readings of Fanon. Bhabha reads otherness as an ambivalent space, and negotiates a position of resistance from the dismantling of colonial power as a unified, homogeneous, univocal source. His dissolution of the colonial subject as power and intent, versus the dominated as victim, rests on an interrogation of representation as psychic fantasy, as the operations of desire and anxiety – as a psychic enactment of visual and spatial difference.

By attempting to approach a concept of identity from different theoretical standpoints – psychoanalytic, cultural, post-structuralist – Bhabha succeeds in revealing identity as process, a problem, a panic. Here – at the moment of dissolution, at what Bhabha calls 'the end of the "idea" of the individual' – an enabling point of resistance can be staged. Undoing the notion of a 'personal identity' in favour of a problem of psychoanalytic and cultural identification, Bhabha argues against Fanon's restless drive to restore – despite his radical insights into psychoanalytic ambivalence – the phenomenological place of the 'I', the 'presence of the marginalized'.[20]

What is significant for a politics of resistance, providing a way out of the trap of already constituted colonial divisions, is Bhabha's insistence on the transformative, on the need for patterns of response that recognise the association of time and identity with the ambivalent institutions of power. The process of decolonisation is seen as a challenge to the epistemological bases of History, rather than as an acceptance of the status quo that merely embarks on a reversal of the dialectic.[21]

Examining the visual/spatial language of stereotype, Bhabha recognises the racist gaze as that 'epistemic violence' which Fanon describes in *Black Skin, White Masks* as a splitting of the Black body into a neurotic concentration of three narrative and historical spaces. The intensive fusion of the immediately visual – the individual, present body – with the mythical unity of 'race' as trans-geographical and originary, creates, for Fanon, the specific, dizzying neurosis of Black identifications:

> It was no longer a question of being aware of my body in the third person but in a triple person. In the brain I was given not one but two, three places . . . I was responsible at the same time for my body, for my race, for my ancestors . . . and I was battered down by tom-toms, cannibalism, intellectual deficiency, racial defects, slave-ships.[22]

Remembering Bhabha's distinction between mask and masquerade in his reading of Fanon's 'Algeria unveiled', resistance can be written at the level of manipulation of stereotype. If truth and identity are always moments of slippage and unease, resistance within 'Postmodernist' cultures may fruitfully reside in a certain playing with metaphor and cultural code, which does not rule out a certain operation of violence, albeit at a psychic/visual level.

In *Season of Migration to the North*, the journey to the heart of Sa'eed's self, represented by entry into his room, operates as a double echo of Kurtz. Meeting his own reflection, the narrator follows Kurtz's movement into the heart of Africa, where Kurtz discovers only the darkness of his own heart. Entering the room, the narrator sees surface, not depth, as Kurtz, in *Heart of Darkness*, is discovered to be 'hollow at the core'.[23] The narrator's excitement on discovering Sa'eed's diary echoes Marlow's joy at seeing the book in the riverside hut:

> Such a book being there was wonderful enough; but still more astounding were the notes penciled in the margin, and plainly referring to the text. I couldn't believe my eyes! They were in cipher!
>
> (p. 543)

This mistaken interpretation of the marginal notes as cipher is referred back onto the scene in *Season of Migration to the North* where, instead of text, the narrator discovers a cryptic address and a blank page: 'To those who see with one eye, speak with one tongue and see things as either black or white, either Eastern or Western' (*Season of Migration to the North*, pp. 150–1). This indication of the depthlessness of racist projection, that the image presented by Sa'eed to Western (Northern) eyes is a mirage conceived by the gaze itself, concurs with Fanon's account of Blackness. Sa'eed's vision, early in his life, that the sea which leads from Africa to Europe is a desert of mirages – 'ever changing and shifting, like the mask on my mother's face . . . a desert laid out in blue-green, calling me, calling me' (*Season of Migration to the North*, p. 27) – is echoed by the narrator's predicament at the end of the novel, where he is

151

caught in the middle of the Nile, drowning (recalling Kurtz's death on the Congo), unable to reach either shore:

> I continued swimming and swimming, resolved to make the northern shore. That was the goal. . . . In front of me I saw things in a semi-circle. Then I veered between seeing and blindness. . . . Turning to the left and right, I found I was half-way between north and south. I was unable to continue, unable to return.
>
> (p. 167)

The idea here of an inability to reach the other, reminiscent of Fanon's 'evanescent' other (*Black Skin, White Masks*, p. 112), acts as a commentary on the reality of racial and cultural stereotyping, and the difficulties in fixing the meaning of other cultures and races. To understand the imagining of Africa (as discussed in the preceding chapters) becomes, not a matter of discovering the 'truth' behind the image, but of recognising the metaphorical, intertextual frame in which 'Africa' is conceived, *creating* it as an object. The narrator's closing description of himself in *Season of Migration to the North* emphasises the performativity of African identity, and its entrapment in parody, imitation and metaphor: 'like a comic actor shouting on a stage, I screamed with all my remaining strength, "Help! Help!"' (p. 169).

Ama Ata Aidoo's *Our Sister Killjoy*[24] is also structured as a reverse journey from Africa to the continent of Europe, exploring the parameters of race and sexuality through the exigencies and possibilities of love. Readable within a feminist framework of sisterhood and female autonomy, the novel takes the figurative structure of Conrad's *Heart of Darkness* and, by reapplying its paradigmatic schema of Africa, 'probes' the heart of Europe.

Sissie, a name that places her in relation to and as representative of other African women, having flown over the strange landscapes of Europe, finds herself on territory that bears the imprint of historical events. The text, moving between prose and poetry, allows subjective and general commentaries to intersect and complement each other. Sissie's personal experiences of alienation in Germany, located as historically central to Europe, are placed between poetic allusions to the indelibility of time and the centrality of Europe's racist histories:

> A Little
> Black
> Woman
> . . . would
> Not
> Have been
> There
> Walking

> Where the
> Führer's feet had trod
> A-C-H-T-U-N-G!
>
> (p. 48)

The inseparability of European landscape from the painful histories of racist massacre is used to echo Conrad's reading of African landscape and natives (interchangeably) in terms of time and historical or (pre-historical) meaning. Marlow's penetration 'deeper and deeper into the heart of darkness' (p. 539) is mirrored by Sissie's descent into the heart of a nightmarish European scene where her 'anti-Western neurosis' (p. 119) teaches her to concentrate on and objectify Whiteness as a racial difference:

> And it hit her. That all that crowd of people going and coming in all sorts of directions had the colour of the pickled pig parts that used to come from foreign places to the markets at home.
>
> (*Our Sister Killjoy*, p. 12)

Remembering Marlow's rumination on the possibilities of human relationship, of 'remote kinship' (*Heart of Darkness*, p. 540) across the barriers of race, Sissie's relationship with Marija, a German Hausfrau, is fraught with her inability to ignore objective racial differences as biologically and psychologically significant. In Sissie's mind, 'being white' has become a condition of exposure, of scrutiny, of uncovering:

> But oh, her skin. . . . It made you awfully exposed, rendered you terribly vulnerable. Like being born without your skin or something. As though the Maker had fashioned the body of a human, stuffed it into a polythene bag instead of the regular protective covering and turned it loose into the world.
>
> (*Our Sister Killjoy*, p. 76)

The possibility of love across the barriers imposed by race and history is charged with sexual fantasies that are a condition of migrancy, and which have stereotypically gendered patterns: 'what a delicious love affair she and Marija would have had if one of them had been a man' (p. 61). The sexual myths which generate the possibilities of inter-racial love are themselves generated out of divisions that, Sissie claims, have originated from the determinations of history:

> We are the victims of our History and our Present. They place too many obstacles in the Way of Love. And we cannot enjoy even our Differences in peace.
>
> (p. 29)

Histories of imperialism and the realities of racism and exploitation under-
lie Sissie's analysis of inter-continental migration and inter-racial friendship
between women. The peculiarities of this text, besides its blending of poetry
and prose, of letter-form, autobiographical address and third person narrative, are the simultaneous recognition of the oppression of Africa and the violence of racism, and the representation of a relationship between two women
that curiously *reverses* the expected power structure. The merging of genres
and the shift in authorial address places attention on narrative voice and
expression – on the importance of narrative control. In this way, the relationship between Sissie and Marija is related from a position of *knowledge*, with
Sissie taking up a 'masculine' position against Marija's emotional *dependence*.

The effect of this is a narrative that promotes African subjectivity to the
place of observer, definer and historical judge. Reversing dominant perspectives, African female subjectivity presents European history, landscape,
people and language as ethnographically strange, with Marija's German
English placed at a similar expressive disavantage as pidgin in European
ethnographies/novels. The feminism of the text is, then, deliberately and
inescapably placed within specific cultural locations, at the point of conflict
between dominant and subordinate national identities. 'Black feminism', in
relation to this text, is both a re-evaluation of African femininity in respect of
African communities and men, and a re-examination of racial and cultural
differences between women.

The letter that moves towards the conclusion of the novel emphasises
Sissie's 'anti-western neurosis', and her fear of the loss of African identity –
particularly African femininity. As a letter addressed to an African man, the
text refuses a direct engagement with the politics or feminisms of 'the West'
and yearns instead for the autonomy of definition:

> That is why, above all, we have to have our secret language. We must
> create this language. . . . So that we shall make love with words and
> not fear of being overheard.
>
> (*Our Sister Killjoy*, p. 116)

Wigs and veils: cultural constructions of the body

The interrogations of sexuality and race that emerge from Salih's and Aidoo's
texts ask questions around the difficulty, or impossibility, of finding a basis
for racial identity. Investigating how race is mobilised in terms of Black or
feminist resistance, and how gender and race intersect or become significant
in identity politics, it becomes necessary to explore the relationship between
cultural signifiers and the body, or rather the *acculturation* of the body, its
invention as an object of analysis and knowledge. The argument in this section will be framed by a reading of Frantz Fanon's essay, 'Algeria Unveiled',

which introduces key issues around gender, racial difference and the meaning of the body in contesting political contexts.

Fanon's essay develops the conceptualisation of race through displaced signs and images of the body. The grounding quote from this essay is in Fanon's words:

> It is the white man who creates the Negro. But it is the Negro who creates negritude. To the colonialist offensive against the veil, the colonized opposes the cult of the veil.[25]

The male subject and object of this scenario, the colonialist White man and the colonised Negro, makes clear who are the main protagonists in his argument. The female subject – the veiled Algerian woman – slips into the space between the two, obliquely gestured towards as a site of interpretation. The operation of racial meaning through images of the female body – as sexual, gendered, revolutionary or object (abject) – has a significant impact on Black feminisms and on theories of essentialism and race. The place of the female body within the politics of racial representation – under the scrutiny of the gaze – is both fixed and radically indeterminate. Fanon's claim in 'The Fact of Blackness', to being 'fixed by a dye' as well as 'burst apart' and 'in a triple person',[26] signals to the negative activity, the *intensity* of third person consciousness and the instability of racial metaphors as incomplete, *illusory* and yet *insistent* ideologies. (The intensity of third person consciousness is precisely the economy of African identities and the 'meaning' of Africa.)

This insistence is not, of course, the prerogative of the White racist gaze. Its location as Black self-consciousness has important reverberations for the possibilities of Black and feminist politics, where the role of self-objectification, self-obsession and self-classification is at the borders of gender and racial consciousness. If race is itself conceptualised through (or with) constructions of sexuality, its meaning, resting precariously on the shifting sands of context and perspective – and yet with an emphatic external *fix* – particularly circumscribes the possibilities for an anti-essentialist Black or feminist politics.

Fanon's 'Algeria Unveiled' focuses on the interplay of body, dress and cultural identity, not only as sites of metaphor and play, but as areas of crucial contestation in the Algerian war of independence. Clothing becomes emblematic of a cultural or racial group, representing a colonial relationship that is at once gendered and sexualised. The feminising of colonised territory is, of course, a trope in colonial thought. In Fanon's analysis, Algerian women are placed in a metonymic process where both veil and woman become interchangeable, scopic signifiers of colonised Algeria itself – as oppressed, inscrutable and dispossessed.

It is under the aegis of a displaced feminist politics that a specifically colonial battle, on one level, becomes waged. Fanon characterises the French colonial resolve in the phrase: 'we must first of all conquer the women; we must go and find them behind the veil where they hide themselves and in the houses where the men keep them out of sight' (pp. 37–8). This 'kind of violence', where 'unveiling' equals 'revealing . . . baring . . . breaking her resistance . . . making her available' (p. 43), is confused with a mission of female liberation and a paternalistic notion of empowerment which, in practice and at base, is a politics of ownership and control: 'the European faced with an Algerian woman wants to see' (p. 44). The familiar discourse of rape between the coloniser and the colonised country[27] becomes elaborated through images of rending veils, of exposing bodies and forbidden horizons 'piece by piece' (p. 42).

The 'morbid infatuation' (*A Dying Colonialism*, Preface, p. 27) of which Fanon accuses the French in their colonisation of Algeria remains to inform the tenets of his own argument. Fanon's detailed dressing and undressing of the Algerian woman, seeing her body as an instrument, an object of war, operating to disrupt the 'obvious' divisions between White and colonised, never allows for a determining subjectivity beyond that of male perception, organisation, recognition. Wanting, ultimately, to 'discover the man behind the colonizer' (Preface, p. 32), Fanon does not attempt a similar humanist move towards the woman behind the veil.

This hidden body, always removed, always at a distance, comes to define – through the metonymy of the veil – that which is ultimately indefinable: 'The Algerian woman, in the eyes of the observer, is unmistakably "she who hides behind a veil"' ('Algeria Unveiled', p. 36). The centrality of the veil as sign for the Algerian woman becomes evident at precisely the moment when the body emerges *outside*. Once revealed, 'offered . . . to the bold and impatient glance' (p. 43), Algerian womanhood – already undefined – merely *disappears*. Once freed, once ushered into light, the 'Algerian woman' is no longer *there*. The veil as colonial border also marks a racial boundary that, once crossed, reveals not a truth but a further absence, which is in itself ambiguous. Beyond the 'confinement' (p. 49), the 'discipline' (p. 58) of the veil, Fanon discusses the experiences of Algerian woman as alternately (or simultaneously) encountering and losing the self. Her legs are at once 'given back to themselves', with 'hips . . . free' (p. 58), and her body *taken from* her. Walking, unbounded, with 'easy freedom' (p. 58), beyond the veil, the Algerian woman is also 'exposed' (p. 51), 'stark naked', 'put adrift' (p. 59). Out of the concurrent isolation *and* reassurance of the veil lurks liberty, self-invention *and* disintegration: 'the unveiled body seems to escape, to dissolve' (p. 59).

Evoking the multiplicity and ambiguity of 'the' Algerian woman, Fanon is compelled to draw attention to the unceasing modification of the veil and to its shifting meanings – as revolutionary camouflage, as a signifier of tradition, as an entrenched symbol of Algerian culture and resistance. Moving implicitly from and between *the* Algerian woman to Algerian women, from *the* veil to veils, Fanon's essay may act as a starting point for interrogating the signification of race, cultural identity and sexuality in wider contexts. This needs to be achieved with the necessary proviso that Fanon's own central-isation of Algeria and Algerian examples as *primarily* representational of Africa or *the* colonial situation *as a whole* be resisted. The emphasis on the colo-nist as *observer* and the Algerian woman as the body under scrutiny, presents a text that is unavoidably implicated in the voyeurism it examines. The 'Algerian-ness', and, *at the same time*, the *sexuality* of the veiled and un-veiled woman exist in a strip-tease of racialised metaphors where 'what you see' and 'how you see it' remain paramount.

The sexuality that is implicit in Fanon's description is clearly indicated in his discussions of the Algerian woman's sexual maturity. The veil itself signals the onset of puberty with its unequivocal message for the (male) observer: 'It is of course possible to remain hesitant before a little girl, but all certainty vanishes at the time of puberty' (p. 36).

For the Algerian woman herself, she learns to recognise her body through both its sexualisation *and* its veiling:

> The body of the young Algerian woman, in traditional society, is revealed to her by its coming to maturity and by the veil.
>
> (p. 58)

Fanon's interest in the Algerian woman is centred on her role as crosser of borders. The 'now you see it, now you don't' ambiguity of her racial identity shifts racial signifiers into play with sexuality and gender. Her Algerian-ness, signalled by the gendered veil, is always under the uncertain promise of being lifted.

The significance of the veil as a racial metaphor can be read through W.E.B. DuBois' *The Souls Of Black Folk*, where the veil represents the barrier between Black consciousness and a White world. As a *racial* signifier, the 'veil' acts as the 'shadow' between Blackness and humanity – or the *un-racialised* consciousness. Recognition of oneself as a racialised being and the intensity with which this 'knowledge' disciplines both the body and the mind is articu-lated by DuBois' use of physical images, his 'desire to tear down that veil, to creep through'.[28] For DuBois, the Veil marks an absolute boundary between two consciousnesses, two worlds, and yet it is a boundary that can be trans-gressed, objectified, struggled with. As the Algerian woman, in Fanon's account, manipulates – within the constraints and ambiguities of racialised and gendered meanings – the signification of the veil, so DuBois offers a glimpse of Blackness as a consciousness lived out on the borders:

> Leaving, then, the white world, I have stepped within the Veil, raising it that you may view faintly its deeper recesses.
>
> (p. 209)

This notion of borders, worlds, physical limits – linked to the production of

Africa as a world beyond – is echoed in the novel contemporary with DuBois, James Weldon Johnson's *Autobiography of an Ex-Coloured Man* (1912).[29] Here, realisation of a Black heritage is accompanied by the protagonist's: 'transition from one world into another; for I did indeed pass into another world' (p. 403).

The link beween race and sexuality, taken up by Fanon in 'Algeria Unveiled', is one that allows for, in specific ways, the *sexualising* of race. The use of the 'veil' as a border metaphor for the objectifying gaze, and for the shadow of (self-)consciousness (as a 'mask' against the face), emphasises both the superficiality *and* the tangibility of Blackness and femininity.

In many West African countries, 'the colonialist offensive against the veil' is replaced by the missionary offensive against the breasts. Here, it is the very *exposure* of the female body, its unabashed exhibition, which likewise stands for an unacceptable misuse of women and characterises, for the Western mind, the African man's primitive promiscuity and possessiveness. Civilisation and Christianity in this context typically lies on the road to covering up, concealing, neutralising and taming the body. These static, and yet contradictory, representations of the colonised woman, or the Black subject, emerge from a network of European knowledge systems which Fanon identifies as 'written accounts . . . photographic records . . . motion pictures', and the gaze of 'the tourist and the foreigner' ('Algeria Unveiled', p. 35).

In this way, 'ethnic' dress becomes interchangeable with tradition and essentialism, and the female body enters an unstable arena of scrutiny and meaning. In a similar way, cultural images of the body – of hair and fashion – are manipulated through forms of stereotype, appropriation and resistance. Pratibha Parmar has written that a major problem 'that has been more specific to black women and the black communities is that of shifting definitions of black identity'.[30]

In Fanon's analysis, the veil, as an unstable signifier of colonised identity, becomes both a solid wall of defiance, and a fluid and misleading cultural signpost. Singled out for colonial manipulation, the body can act to transgress colonial boundaries of space, time and identity. The veil marks the territory of the body, protects its borders, disciplines its bounds. The crossing of these lines, symbolised in a strategic lifting of the veil, re-creates the terms of the Algerian struggle. In this way, the Algerian woman is written into – and becomes representative of – the nationalist cause in a way similar to the Irish and the Palestinian terrorist in Clair Wills' analysis of counter-terrorism in the Western media: as she says, 'When all Palestinians are terrorists it can hardly be denied that theirs is a national struggle'.[31]

The veil, as an essentialised article of clothing in the Algerian struggle, marking significant political and religious difference, is often replaced by a cultural politics of hair in Black identifications. In contemporary Britain, the United States and South Africa, the style, the texture, the colour of hair often stands as a crucial marker of racial identity and – more than that – of political and cultural affiliation.

Kobena Mercer's exploration of the phenomenon of Michael Jackson, who is popularly advertised as a prime Western example of an unhealthy Black subjectivity longing to be White, is a useful locus for seeing how hair becomes politically meaningful. Jackson's recent assertion that 'It doesn't matter if you're Black or White'[32] won't wash in a society where the panic about race repeatedly rests on how it's made visible or, in Jackson's case, invisible.

If hair holds the latent traces of Blackness as, or more, tenaciously than skin colour, it is also subject to acculturation, the meanings of which shift as regularly as fashion. Hair functions, then, as a sensitive arbitrator between body and dress, nature and culture, and the burden of its African-ness or European-ness depends both on history and context. According to Kobena Mercer:

> We require a historical perspective on how many different strands – economic, political, psychological – have been woven into the rich and complex texture of our nappy hair, such that issues of style are so highly charged as sensitive questions about our very 'identity'.[33]

In West African countries, the battle over the cultural or racial affiliations of hair styling has often been waged most visibly in terms of women's hair. Ama Ata Aidoo's short story, 'Everything Counts', describes a kind of male policing of African values around the politics of women's wigs. On one level, the argument is one about beauty, fashion and masquerade; on another, it is a debate about racial masks:

> The wig. Ah, the wig. They say it is made of artificial fibre. Others swear that if it is not gipsy hair, then it is Chinese. Extremists are sure they are made from the hair . . . of dead white folk. . . . Second-hand machinery from someone else's junkyard.[34]

Sissie's assertion that 'the wig was, after all, only a hat' (p. 3) is faced by a barrage of emotional warfare from the 'brothers' that the wig does, in fact, need attention in Ghana's cultural revolution: 'Because it means that we have no confidence in ourselves' (p. 2).

What seems ludicrous about this psychologising of hair becomes of contextual importance if we think about the terrible pressure of colonial racism on Black bodies and minds. The wig in Aidoo's story is, in some cases, accompanied by what is called 'a terrible plague' of skin bleaching and a subterranean yearning for what Sissie calls 'mulatto' beauty. As one of the 'boys' says: 'you've still got to admit that there is an element in this wig-wearing that is totally foreign. Unhealthy' (p. 6).

The nature/nurture argument in feminist analyses has been supplemented by a row about cultural authenticity which has strangely changed places. Kobena Mercer points to an underlying process of appropriation and envy in the subcultures of style and fashion, which, in the West, works to determinedly neutralise the oppositional power of Black styles and attempts to absorb them into mainstream fashion. In this way, 'authentically' Black hairstyles such as the Afro, dreadlocks, braids and even that supposedly 'White' look, the curly perm, have become as decontextualised, fluid markers of Western fashion markets as so-called 'ethnic' jewellery and clothes.

Having emphasised the non-essentialist nature of Blackness, it remains crucial to underline the importance of these Black signifiers for continuing re-interpretations and staking out of Black spaces in the contemporary West as well as in post-independence countries. The veil changed its meaning from a negative marker of oppressive tradition and immobility to a symbol of nationalist pride and, when strategically manipulated as a revolutionary device, its removal acted, not as revelation, but as camouflage.[35]

Similarly, the changing meanings of Black styles and fashion in music, dress and hair point to a healthy and active resistance in a society which mobilises a dizzying range of weaponry against the representation of positive Black images. As Stuart Hall writes:

> Young black people in London today are marginalised, fragmented, unenfranchised, disadvantaged and dispersed. And yet, they look as if they own the territory.[36]

Racialised bodies and sexuality

This section of the chapter moves from the discussions of the body as it is signified through the cultural codes of dress and hairstyling to concentrate on the way the body becomes essentialised and racialised. The reading of racial and sexual signifiers on the site of the physical body and the political circulation of these racialised and gendered meanings is an important part of the colonialist ethnographies examined above. The reappearance of these issues in feminist analysis and in literary representations of psychic trauma reveals the historical *insistence* of racial and sexual codes.

The emphasis on performativity and theatre in Tayeb Salih's *Season of Migration to the North* can be read through Fanon's analysis of racial *self*-consciousness through objectification. Fanon's re-reading, particularly of Hegel and of psychoanalysis, to insist on a *third* or extra term in the establishment of self-consciousness – that of race, or of Blackness – is crucial for an inquiry into racialised subjectivity.

The insistence, in both Fanon and Salih, on Black subjectivity puts the emphasis on Black consciousness itself as being profoundly implicated in the racial scene. In Fanon's 'Fact of Blackness', following the external stimuli, the assault of a racist epithet, 'Look, a Negro!',[37] the racialised subject – the

Black man – is immediately at one remove from this identified, body. What Fanon calls the 'dialectic between my body and the world' (p. 111), suffers a further split where 'completely dislocated . . . I took myself far off from my own presence, far indeed, and made myself an object' (p. 112).

This fixing of Blackness as an object, as a race, where Whiteness remains un-racialised and un-coded, gives the dread authority of the gaze its neutral objectivity. Who is looking in Fanon's text as he describes his own, mediated reaction to his body?

That this 'fact of Blackness' is unswervingly masculine is there in the racist word, 'A Negro!' Its fixity as an object of fear and aggression is a masculinised image that, paradoxically, robs the Black male of his manhood. Grieving the fact that he is 'a master' forced into humility (p. 140), what is being examined throughout *Black Skin, White Masks* is Black *masculinity*. Even in his chapter entitled 'The Woman of Color and the White Man', Fanon's real focus is revealed in his framing statement: 'we must see whether it is possible for the black *man* to overcome his feeling of insignificance' (p. 50; my emphasis).

When approaching the subject of the Black woman, Fanon's text falls into ellipsis. The third person consciousness that splits Black male subjectivity into neurosis becomes, for the Black woman, a consciousness of Black masculinity. What she apparently sees as displaced from herself is not Black woman-hood, but 'the Negro', the Black *man*, *the* object from whom she must escape at all costs.

The male-centredness of Fanon's analysis, insisting that the pain of Blackness, its immoveability, its weight, is intrinsically masculine, begs the question of what it would mean to apply this to female consciousness. What has been left out of Fanon's account seems to be the image of the female body itself. Going back to the earlier question '*Who* is *looking* in Fanon's text?', it is clear that, for Fanon, it is the White *man* – or the White *boy*.

For Mayotte Capécia, in 'The Woman of Colour and the White Man' (in *Black Skin, White Masks*), her debut into the White society of her lover, Andre, is made under the speculation of White *women*. In her autobiography, she claims:

> I felt that I was wearing too much makeup, that I was not properly dressed, that I was not doing Andre credit, perhaps simply because of the color of my skin.
>
> (p. 43)

Skin colour – Blackness – appears at the end of her list of responses. The racialised glare of the women, that makes of her a spectacle, estranges her from her make-up, her clothing. For Fanon, the 'uniform' of which he becomes aware is his own body. For Mayotte Capécia, race is signified through gendered and sexualised figures that *over*-represent her body.

This reading of the racialised female body through, so to speak, *secondary* codes of gender, sexuality and dress, can perhaps be mapped back onto Fanon's discussions of Black masculinity in 'The Fact of Blackness'. Racial difference, in his description, is fixed as a surface phenomenon from *behind* which self-consciousness peeks and dissembles. *Blackness* as a mask separates it from an essential body beneath, which is, of course, always escaping definition. The identity of the one who is looking may always be the same. Fanon's dialectical argument through negrophobia and negrophilia, seeking to essentialise the body, finally confronts the Nothingness and Infinity of its impossibility.

Returning to the debate within Alice Walker's *Possessing the Secret of Joy*,[38] a major issue in Western feminisms involves the representation, discussion and manipulation of Third World women. Here the debate moves to a different kind of acculturation of the body, where what is literally inscribed in the flesh, and, by implication, in the sexual freedom and expression of African women, is placed as a difficult agenda for Black and White women.

The taboo of female circumcision in certain feminist writing is so obscured by myth and conflation that it is the representation and meaning of this issue in feminism which I wish to explore. That is, how does this range of practices and their differing degrees of severity, meaning and importance in the male and female worlds of African societies become *one* polarised argument about the very basis of female or feminist identity? 'Female circumcision' has become almost a dangerous trope in Western feminisms for the muting and mutilation of women physically, sexually and psychologically – and for these women's *need for* Western feminism. Circumcision, clitoridectomy, infibulation become one visible marker of outrageous primitivism, sexism and *the* Third World woman. I don't wish to invalidate the varying degrees of pain or the struggles of certain African women to change some or all of these practices, but I do wish to militate against how the subject of feminism in Africa is often seen to be the circumcised – hence, damaged and oppressed – Black Third World woman.[39] The representation of the body characteristically oscillates between, and confuses, natural and cultural attributes in discussions of race, and constructions of femininity are crucially related to these confusions.

Bessie Head's *A Question of Power*,[40] situated in late twentieth-century South Africa, explores the trauma of racist conceptualisations of the female body through the neurosis of mixed race subjectivity. Here, rigid notions of racial difference, legalised and socialised by the South African state, reveal their dangerous irrationality in the torment of Elizabeth's mind. Where does racial identity lie? Elizabeth's panic at the madness of her own uncertain identity is expressed through a shattering of her own physical attributes in synecdochic images of Black or sexual body parts and body types. Told, amongst other things, that her 'hair is not properly African', Elizabeth is attacked by a sense of impurity and inauthenticity, subjected to an imagined parade of women who are reduced to racist or misogynist stereotypes:

Who were they? Miss Pelican-Beak, Miss Chopper, Miss Pink Sugar-Icing, Madame Make-Love-On-The-Floor where anything goes, The Sugar-Plum Fairy, more of the Body Beautiful, more of The Womb, a demonstration of sexual stamina with five local women, this time with the lights on, Madame Squelch Squelch, Madame Loose Bottom – the list of them was endless.

(p. 148)

This segmenting of sexuality into overblown body parts emerges from a confusion of racial impurity with sexual degeneration: 'she was mixed breed. What a plague that was!' The pathological depiction of Coloured men as grinning homosexuals in drag is part of a panicked internalisation of the social parameters of race and gender:

The records went round and round in her head the whole day . . . the poor man had been sent into the job with a leprosy-like fear of Coloureds or half-breeds. That was one of his favourite records. He was afraid he might have to touch the half-breed at some time and contaminate his pure black skin . . .

(p. 127)

The preoccupation in the novel with binary oppositions – good/evil, man/woman, normal/abnormal, sane/insane, inside/outside – is presented as the direct result of living in a South Africa that legalises, enforces and normalises a rigid divide between Whites and Blacks. Elizabeth's position on the borders of race, as a mixed race woman, and also her exile in a foreign African state, Botswana, leads to an intense concentration on African-ness. Her identity as a racial and national outsider is analysed as the exclusion from a 'real' Africa, a 'tribal' Africa, whose social, institutional and psychological patterns remain beyond her reach: 'I am not a tribal African. If I had been, I would have known the truth. . . . There aren't any secrets among tribal Africans. I was shut out from the everyday affairs of this world' (p. 145).

The understanding of 'African-ness' as a race, a sexuality and a psychology constructs the metaphors of Elizabeth's nervous breakdown. The figures that stalk her mind, Dan, Sello and the Medusa, are figures representing the polar extremes that racist society legitimises. Dan's embodiment of Africanness is, basically, that of a penis: 'he thrust black hands in front of her, black legs and a huge, towering black penis. The penis was always erected' (p. 128). Her fear of 'all things African', informed by racist imagination, such as 'the African man's loose, carefree sexuality' (p. 137), impacts on her own sense of racial ambiguity, labelling her with sexual impotence and non-identity.

The longing for an Africa that is un-structured by racial barriers is immediately expressed at the novel's opening, where, confronted by Sello, Elizabeth clings to his 'universalism': 'It seemed almost incidental that he was African' (p. 11). In the paranoid construction of Elizabeth's mind, racism is seen to operate by forcing an identification with its doctrines, and Elizabeth's insanity passionately produces racist terms. 'Africa' circulates as a term of savagery, secrecy, lust, aggression and evil, by which Elizabeth is possessed and banished. Elizabeth's concentration on perversion, as a figuring of her own 'perverse' status as Coloured, demonstrates the fear that her own existence produces in racist thinking. Reproduction between a Black man and a White woman, presented as abnormal, insane and illegal, where the introduction of Blackness into the White body is abhorrent, is at the root of Elizabeth's identity.

Unable to escape the 'perversion' of her own biology, Elizabeth's glimpses of hope and self re-interpretation lie in natural metaphors. Dominated by the Botswanan landscape, which is presented in the stark reality of weather, darkness, space, a landscape that she cannot confront in the terms of local practices, she still succeeds in recognising herself in its natural manifestations. Cultivating the soil, she recreates her own conditions of being:

> a complete stranger like the Cape Gooseberry settled down and became a part of the village life of Motabeng. It loved the hot, dry Botswana summers as they were a replica of the Mediterranean summers of its home in the Cape.
>
> (p. 153)

Forced on the edges and the in-betweens of racial boundaries, Elizabeth's dreams of a utopian future centre on the peaceful resolution of a non-racial 'brotherhood of man' (p. 206), where 'women were both goddesses and housekeepers and there was a time for loving' (p. 201).

The analysis of race with female sexuality in Head's novel reveals how the racialised body becomes a politicised object, used to play out social divisions and figured in psychological anxiety. Sembene Ousmane's *Xala*[41] restages these issues through the representation of a Black male body as a locus for political meanings. Ousmane's novel studies the issues of postcolonial identity through a powerfully metaphoric staging of the Black body as a hysterical symptom of colonial legacy. El Hadji Abdou Kader Baye, a product of colonial Christian education and the post-independence backlash to an earlier, Muslim self-identification, seeks economic profit from his embodiment of uneasy cultural balance. Taking a third wife as signifier of wealth and property, the dangers of self-doubling at this splitting point of two 'cultures' become etched upon the body. The terror of castration through the metaphor of impotence heralds the return of repressed colonial violence. Circling the intimacies of his family home in distressing images of sexual humiliation and cruelty, the novel reaches its catharsis with a parable of punishment for inter-African oppression. The final scene of external mutilation and disease emerging from the burial of spiritual decay scourges the Black body as a focal-point and emblem in an outcry against internal Black suppression and hypocrisies:

> I am a leper! I am a leper to myself alone. To no one else. But you, you are a disease that is infectious to everyone. The virus of a collective leprosy!
>
> (p. 110)

The examination, in these two novels, of the meaning of African-ness as a race, as a physicality and as sexually defined, where African-ness is, literally and figuratively, etched upon the body, also reveals the possibilities and the dangers of transgression. African identity, as a product of surveillance, of cultural and moral policing, and of psychological suffering, is presented as a constantly negotiated space. To be 'between' cultures or 'between' races is to be at the fraught and dangerous interstices of sanity, community, self. It is to be in 'the middle passage' between worlds.

Toni Morrison's *The Bluest Eye*[42] traces the extent to which racism affects the identity, the fantasies and the sexuality of Black women (and men) in the United States. Here, third person consciousness of self results, through racism, in a profound psychic splitting and neurosis. The development of desire and understanding, of self-articulation and its source, is expressed in Pecola Breedlove's childhood and adolescent encounters. Living in a world which is run by White domination, which informs the discourses of 'normality', of beauty and of worth, Pecola is continually slammed up against an image of herself that is sharply at odds with the White 'norm'. The novel opens with the script of a child's storybook:

> here is the house. It is green and white. It has a red door. It is very pretty. Here is the family. Mother, Father, Dick, and Jane live in the green and white house. They are very happy.
>
> (p. 7)

This is the doorway through which Black and White children will enter into the social discourse, a discourse which will form the shape of a child's contact with the world around her. The script is repeated three times, each time letting the words seep closer together until a tightly woven fabric is created:

> othermotherisverynicemotherwillyouplaywithjanemother laughslaughmotherlaughseefatherheisbigandstrongfather.
>
> (p. 8)

If this is the 'normality' with which a Black child must identify, the result can only be a deep sense of alienation, of worthlessness, a barrier between the self and the world, created by the standard, literary discourse. Ngũgĩ Wa Thiong'o writes that:

> The second aspect of language as culture is as an image-forming agent in the mind of the child. . . . But our capacity to confront the world creatively is dependent on how those images correspond or not to that reality, how they distort or clarify the reality of our struggles. . . . Language is mediating in my very being.[43]

Looking around her, Pecola sees only images that are disjointed from the language of her reading. She sees a Black father enraged with the impotence which burned in his body when White men enacted a vicious visual rape, a Black mother whose fancied identity with the White film stars of the dark cinemas is smashed along with her front tooth, and a grey and ugly home.

Blackness becomes a concept of excruciating visibility with the suffocation of all other differentiation beneath itself. If there is no place to position the self within this discourse, the result is a form of self-annihilation that, beginning in the mirror of White society, becomes a conscious and then an internalised unconscious activity. Pecola's visit to the sweet shop, owned by a White shopkeeper, is an episode that reveals the role of Blackness in the formation of identity:

> But she has seen interest, disgust, even anger in grown male eyes. Yet this vacuum is not new to her. It has an edge; somewhere in the bottom lid is the distaste. She has seen it lurking in the eyes of all white people. So the distaste must be for her, her Blackness. All things in her are flux and anticipation. But her blackness is static and dread. And it is the blackness that accounts for, that creates, the vacuum edged with distaste in White eyes.
>
> (*The Bluest Eye*, p. 47)

At this point, Pecola is aware of the White gaze as an outside force, translating who she is by virtue of her skin and features. Within her, another awareness ebbs and flows, the same awareness which appraised the dandelions on the edge of cultivation as 'pretty' and which gave her an immeasurable joy in her own reality. She knows the language her mind speaks, the 'codes and touchstones' which are available to her, the beauty upon which she relies and understands as her own: 'And owning them made her part of the world and the world part of her' (p. 47). The part of the world she is able to articulate, however, has no corresponding moment in White consciousness and before the White shopkeeper she finds herself robbed of language and dumb in the loneliness of her perceptions: 'he cannot see her view – the angle of his vision, the slant of her finger, makes it incomprehensible to him' (p. 48).

Such is the power of White discourse that it forces its values deeper than the surface, making Pecola internalise the scales of worth which are held before her. As her shame heats up the surface of her skin, the 'dread' Blackness melts down through her pores, filling up the cracks of her imagination with the 'vacuum edged with distaste' (p. 48) that 'white eyes' attached to it: 'the shame wells up again, its muddy rivulets seeping into her eyes.' Believing that the dandelions after all *are* ugly. They *are* weeds' (p. 49), Pecola's first move is self-extermination. Praying to the same God which Cholly conceptualises as 'a nice old white man, with long white hair, flowing white beard, and little blue eyes' (p. 124), there is only one plea at the centre of her mind, to blank out the ugliness in the only way possible. ' "Please, God", she whispered into the palm of her hand, "Please make me disappear" . . . little parts of her body faded away' (p. 44). In the gap, slotting into the place at the centre of her dreams and at the tender core of her erotic fantasies is the persona of a White girl, the epitome of that which a White-dominated society sanctifies as beauty:

> A picture of little Mary Jane, for whom a candy is named. Smiling white face. Blonde hair in gentle disarray, blue eyes. . . . To eat the candy was somehow to eat the eyes, eat Mary Jane. Love Mary Jane. Three pennies had bought her nine lovely orgasms with Mary Jane.
>
> (p. 48)

This is the language of a little Black girl's unconscious. Her utopian fantasy splits her in two and she creates another mirror in which to view her new, blue eyes, another dialogue within which to articulate herself in relation to the world:

> Oh yes. My eyes. My blue eyes. Let me look again. SEE HOW PRETTY THEY ARE. Prettier than Alice-and-Jerry storybook eyes? OH YES. MUCH PRETTIER THAN ALICE-AND-JERRY STORYBOOK EYES.
>
> (p. 49)

This concentration on the body as a site of scrutiny and excess emerges at once from a history of exhibition and vilification of Black and women's bodies, and a narcissistic, oppositional redressing and re-presenting of their meaning.

Black and female identities are not simply figurative or superficial sites of play and metaphor, but occupy very real political spaces of Diaspora, dispossession and resistance. What is complicated is the simultaneity of suffering and power, marginalisation and threat, submission and narcissism, which accrue to Black and women's bodies and their representation in racist culture.

To go further than Mercer's query – 'So who, in this postmodern melee of semiotic appropriation and counter-creolisation, is imitating whom?' (Black Hair/Style Politics, p. 52) – I would like to end with the question: 'On whose terms is this celebration of postmodern plurality and difference being conducted?'

Across the line: transgressing Whiteness and desire

This section explores fantasies of race and the articulation of Blackness in White texts. John Howard Griffin's *Black Like Me*[44] and Christopher Hope's *My Chocolate Redeemer*[45] are analysed as texts which perpetuate a range of stereotypes and myths through the image of crossing racial borders – either through inter-racial desire or through 'race-crossing' and masquerade. Finally, the section will conclude with a reading of Nella Larsen's novels, *Quicksand* and *Passing*.

I want to take up Fanon's particularly masculine analyses here in two ways: first, by examining his staging of a combat between the gaze of the White man and the 'humanity' of the Black man; and second, by exploring how much this is readable within female consciousness. By looking at narratives that occupy the borders of racial identity – narratives of passsing, of mixed race and of racialised desire – the identity of looker and object, and the location of racial readings of the body, become peculiarly complex.

Reversing Fanon's title to *White Skin, Black Masks*, I want to look first at John Howard Griffin's *Black Like Me*. This is one of the most startling examples of a White subject, not only wanting to see, but to *experience* Black subjectivity under the guise of sympathetic journalism. His bizarre, voyeuristic travelogue of the American Deep South of 1960 reads like a case of White pathology. Griffin's obsession is not only with how Blackness writes itself into the body but how White identity can be expunged to allow him privileged entry into the Black psyche, in order to report on and speak for Black people.

Griffin's text, first published in 1964, was hailed as a triumph of liberalism and understanding that 'courageously' marked a plea for justice and equality in the USA's Deep South. Claiming, as a White Southerner, his intentions to report on and to speak for Black people, Griffin's preface presents his account as revealing 'what it is like to be a Negro'. What defines a 'Negro' is 'skin colour' and experience, an experience that is impenetrable to Whites. Black men guard the secret within themselves and 'will not tell the white man the truth'. This leads to Griffin's conviction that 'How else except by becoming a Negro could a white man hope to learn the truth?' (p. 9).

However, this particular 'truth', so completely locked away, is also banally 'universal'. As Griffin claims: 'I could have been a Jew in Germany, a Mexican in a number of states, or a member of any "inferior" group. . . . The story would be the same' (Preface).

Armed with this vision of the universality of Whiteness to both interpret and to simply take on 'inferior' identities, Griffin envisages his task as one of entry and penetration. Collapsing and crossing racial barriers involves, particularly in 1959, a difference in physical movement within the city. The freedom to transgress as strict a code as racial identity and its allotted geographical space (part of the current narrative of North American nationality) involves the liberty of taking on alternative subjectivities. Griffin's decision, as a White American, to take on a Black identity is part of a desire for unfettered travel:

> I searched for an opening, a way to enter the world of the Negro. . . .
> My greatest preoccupation was that moment of transition when I
> would 'pass over'. . . . To get from the white world into the Negro
> world is a complex matter. I looked for the chink in the wall through
> which I might pass unobserved.
>
> (p. 15)

This mission to see and not be seen, to find the peep-hole into an other dimension of the same space, finds an uncanny echo with his previous visit to New Orleans, which he made while blind. Having learned to negotiate the city without sight, 'cane-walking' (p. 13), Griffin now has to learn Black codes of travel and ways of seeing.

The adding of Black signifiers to his body through medication and skin dyes in order to manipulate the visibility of racial borders allows Griffin to begin his gate-crashing of the hidden nooks and crannies of Black experience. Suddenly faced with his own transformation, Griffin gives an immediate account of the major elements of Black subjectivity. The objective move is also deeply spiritual. It is a massive historical leap. Not only has he got behind the veil, he wears it:

> Even the senses underwent a change so profound it filled me with distress. I looked into the mirror and saw reflected nothing of the white John Griffin's past. No, the reflections led back to Africa, back to the shanty and the ghetto, back to the fruitless struggles against the mark of blackness.
>
> (p. 19)

Black identity opens up a whole new trajectory of past and present which the daubing of a skin dye allows the White John Griffin to represent. This scene of the alienated mirror image, fixed in its difference at one remove from the self, is reminiscent of Fanon's descriptions in 'The Fact of Blackness'. However, here there is no doubt as to the identity of the gaze, as Griffin stares, afraid, at the other, 'the utter stranger'. This split between *two* men, who Griffin describes as 'the observing one and the one who . . . felt Negroid even into the depths of his entrails' (p. 19), is the split between a neutral voyeur and another species.

Griffin, forcing himself to confront the mirror and banish darkness with a 'flood of light against white tile' is immediately steeped in terror at his own – the Other's – image. He describes the reflection that 'in no way resembled me' as 'a fierce, bald, very dark Negro' (p. 19). This recognition of an image that is 'naturally' hostile and whose degree of darkness actually intensifies hostility reveals Griffin's complete investment in racialised ways of seeing. It also contradicts his earlier opposition to the idea that the darker the Negro the less trustworthy he is (pp. 16–17). The significance of baldness is revealed later in the narrative where Griffin allows it to represent excessive sexuality (p. 22). For Griffin, the 'Negro' is not a surface image, but Negro-ness 'permeated my whole being'. What he calls 'The completeness of this transformation' leads him to claim that

> I knew now that there was no such thing as a disguised white man, when the black won't rub off. The black man is wholly a Negro, regardless of what he once may have been.
>
> (p. 19)

This meditation on consciousness, history and biology is curious from a text that is obsessed with sight. The discussion of the privilege of White male scrutiny, where White John Griffin is constantly invited to stare at semi-nude White women in bars (p. 13) and, as a Black man, is firmly forbidden entry (see p. 72), allows the narrator to focus on his family. Haunted by the vision of return home, as a Black man, to his White family, Griffin rehearses his children's blank stare barring the door (p. 19). The role of husband, father and patriarch is central to Griffin's White identity (p. 12), while the wandering isolation of the bald Negro, shorn of youth, manhood and power – and yet a threat to the security of family – comes to represent Black experience.

Griffin's claim to be presenting the 'truth' of Black consciousness in the Southern States is constantly jarred by a text that remains shadowed by this figure of the other, the negative double that threatens to break in from the outside. He claims that: 'I could feel no companionship with this new person. *I did not like the way he looked*' (p. 20; my emphasis). This last sentence holds the ambiguity that saturates the text. Griffin's obsession with the *appearance* of this Negro is also an obsession with the Negro's gaze. The fierce Negro 'glared at me from the glass' (p. 19).

The narrative slides fitfully between the identity of stalker and stalked. Followed and abused by a young White man in New Orleans, Griffin describes the 'deep terror' inspired in him by the chase (p. 45). This terror is, in other sections of the text, one that is inspired by his own extraneous image on which he looks in the sick separation of invisibility (p. 44). Repeatedly, his discourse on universality with which the Preface is concerned, breaks down in the temptation for racialised biology. Emerging, for the first time, into the darkness as a Black man, Griffin encounters 'the figure of a white man' who 'stared intently at me' (p. 20). Confused, Griffin breaks into a sweat and the narrator states:

> It was the first time this adult Negro had ever perspired. I thought it vaguely illuminating that the Negro Griffin's sweat felt exactly the same to his body as the white Griffin's.
>
> (pp. 20–1)

From his belief that White identity is negotiable and neutral, Griffin is able to launch himself into a reportage that rambles into homes, beds, conversations and intimacies, representing and re-interpreting Black experience and subjectivity as his own. The fluidity and temporality of his Negro identity – his choice of removing the stain, escaping the threat – provides Griffin with the licence to explore and to trespass with an extraordinary, dizzying liberty:

> I developed a technique of zigzagging back and forth. . . . It was hazardous, but it was the only way to traverse an area both as Negro and white. . . . I would go through the area as a Negro and then, usually at night, remove the dyes with cleansing cream and tissues and pass through the same area as a White man.
>
> (p. 12)

At one point, having endured the final racial slur, Griffin has 'had enough' – 'suddenly I could stomach no more of this degradation – not of myself but of all men who were black like me. Abruptly I turned and walked away. . . . I took out my cleansing cream and rubbed it on my hands and face to remove the stain' (pp. 153–4). This identification with 'all men who were black like me' comes at precisely the moment of its denial.

This White liberal tourism of justified cross-dressing allows Griffin the honour both of neutrality and of voice. His trickery before Black companionship is explained as the prevention of misunderstandings – that is, to avoid the swift conclusion that he is, not a Black representative, but (and I see this as a negligible semantic move) 'a spy for the whites' (p. 66).

Not only do these speedy trips across historical and political placements allow John Griffin the huge privilege of an unchained gaze over blocked horizons, they also keep the door of 'universality' and appropriation wide open. Or, as he claims, 'because I was a Negro for six weeks, I remained partly Negro or perhaps essentially Negro' (p. 156).

This final identification with Blackness is immediately followed by the text's conclusion – a disapproving assessment of what he calls 'racism among Negroes' (p. 187). Black radicalism, or what he designates as the preaching of 'Negro superiority', will result in a 'holocaust that will drag down the innocent and right-thinking masses of human beings' (p. 188). This is, of course, an immediate recollection of Griffin's earlier, haunted vision of the fierce Negro at the door.

The earlier American novel, James Weldon Johnson's *Autobiography of an Ex-Colored Man*, explores similar ideas of crossing between the Black and White 'worlds'. For the main character, moving from Black to White territory also involves acting a role, assuming a part. 'Playing' a White man is a precarious role, relying on the *manipulation* of the gaze – in this case, on *concealing* what *cannot* be seen. Anxious to hide a secret 'Negro-ness', both observer and observed are caught in the battle of gaze and counter-gaze: 'I watched her to see if she was scrutinizing me, to see if she was looking for anything in me which made me differ from the other men she knew' (p. 504). In fact, identity throughout the novel is reliant almost equally on what is *known*, what is *hidden* and what is *seen*. The revelation of his hidden identity to the woman he loves, for example, results in the traumatic transformation of what she *sees* – or, rather, of what the main character *perceives her to see*. Her gaze controls the stage and the conditions of the act:

> when I looked up, she was gazing at me with a wild, fixed stare as though I was some object she had never seen. Under the strange light in her eyes I felt that I was growing black and thick-featured and crimp-haired.
>
> (p. 507)

The importance of the specular in assuming racial identities emerges in the earlier mirror scene, where the protagonist re-acquaints himself with his own reflection after having, for the first time, discovered that he is Black. What is, somehow, a matter of blood and history re-surfaces in a way that threatens, not just racial, but also sexual identity. As in Head's *A Question of Power*, where the 'coloured men' are also transvestites (see p. 163), the ambiguous nature of the protagonist's race disturbs the fixity of gender and heightens the significance of the sensual:

> I noticed the ivory whiteness of my skin, the beauty of my mouth, the size and liquid darkness of my eyes, and how the long, black lashes that fringed and shaded them produced an effect that was strangely fascinating even to me. I noticed the softness and glossiness of my dark hair that fell in waves over my temples.
>
> (p. 401)

This idea of mixed race identity – of concealed 'Negro-ness' – as a disrupting, sexualising, *feminising* force contrasts interestingly with Griffin's assertion of brutal masculinity when 'becoming' a Negro. Blackness as aggressively or overtly sexual and mixed race identity as transgressively sensual and feminine links race and sexuality together in vital ways.

This playing with the signifiers of Black identity and migration over boundaries emerges in Christopher Hope's *My Chocolate Redeemer*, where the Black subject in exile on White French territory assumes a range of sexual metaphors and geographical threats. For the half-French, half-English, teenage Bella, already used to the easy slipping over borders of dual nationality, the exiled African leader becomes the representation of wide and distant spaces. The Black identity of the exile is something to be devoured, tasted, experimented with; it is a manifestation of desire, sweeter and richer than the narrow sterilities of familial life. On the fringes of her French and her English identity, mourning her dead father who was lost wandering in Africa, Bella's grief and lust for escape builds for her a huge myth of Black sexuality. The deposed Redeemer of Zanj becomes easily appropriated as Bella's own personal salvation. He is flight and freedom held temporarily to her earth, trailing images of Africa and a physicality which Bella experiences as a greedy consumer:

> The nose sits there waiting – with its wide wings like a jet plane on a runway, grounded. . . . Altogether he is as solid as a tree. A black oak darkening to violet. A very beautiful bruise – Plum dark, smooth as caramel! I lick my lips to let out the words.
>
> (p. 88)

Faced with this crosser of borders, this man in limbo on the outskirts of a viciously unwelcoming French nationalism, Bella gives him her own generic name and claims him as the representation of all her dearest free associations. Monsieur Brown is death and father manifest, a sexual addiction with a weight of history and exotic spaces, an aphrodisiac for a White unimpaired sensuality. His exile to France does not allow him national entry. He carries his political and cultural borders, drawn by 'race', very much with him:

> Several metres of wooden bench are now the stranger's territory and we all respect what politicians call its sovereignty. . . . The border could not be more clearly set if it were built of bricks and topped with barbed wire. . . . He has now become the dark continent, to be avoided at all costs, the subject of a hundred horror stories.
>
> (p. 138)

The Africa he brings to Bella is an easy-to-grasp comic reduction. It is history as child's play. The three tribes of the imaginary Zanj divide what can be called an African 'triple heritage': the traditional, the Muslim, the Western – three religions, three dress codes, three bounded preoccupations. Monsieur Brown is Bella's African present – in line with the little pieces of Africa her

173

father would bring. A gift for a child, a game, an adventure, a childish blessing for a sweet tooth:

> I can't help noticing how his neck rises from his perfect collar, like a column of pure – well, what can I say? – chocolate! No, cocoa-butter! In the shadows he is solid, silent and shorter than I remember him, pure Bournville, utter Nestle, simply Suchard from nose to toe . . . as if I am seeing the face just before it is wrapped in silver paper to be sent off to delight children, a walking, talking, chocolate troll . . . a most lickable fellow . . .
>
> (p. 122)

Bella's whim to slide familial barriers, to fly the constraints of family duty, lets her slip freely into an Africa whose national walls dissolve and re-build themselves in temporary, arbitrary ways. The borders of the licensed and the forbidden, split three ways, change their territorial spacing, allowing Bella's White fantasy to race easily into this travesty of an accommodating central African kingdom. Enthroned, by her own decision, as White queen and fifth wife, the colonising spirit of a Western, travelling sensuality allows Bella's reinterpretation of African cultural borders. She easily, glibly, mothers a nation on spec:

> All I need is time. . . . These are the early days of creation in the city of Waq, and, in that mysterious time behind the Planck Wall where telescopes may not spy, my universe is hot and young, and anything may happen.
>
> (p. 262)

I want to look now at two novels by Nella Larsen, *Quicksand* and *Passing*.[46] Both of these texts are, like Griffin's *Black Like Me*, concerned with race – with Blackness – and its meaning. Dealing with mixed race identities, the novels explore the liminalities of race, the possibilities of 'passing' and the signification of race as colour, behaviour, sexuality and procreation. As with *Black Like Me*, the novels are obsessed with *what can be seen*, and the relationship between self and image. As texts that explore female Black consciousness and racial ambiguity, the fluidity of racial significance and its manifestations is striking.

In *Quicksand*, the text's preoccupation with colour – both of complexion and dress – reveals the curious interchangeability of surface metaphors in describing race and sexuality. The novel opens with an immediate invitation to see colour and light, the *contrast* between shades of light and dark. Ushered in, as an 'observer' (p. 2) of the 'intensely personal' (p. 1), intimate isolation of Helga Crane, the reader is instructed to see her as a manifestation of *competing* colours, recognition of which moves from the evening light, to the furnishings and flowers of the room, to the vivid *competition* of colours in her clothes and, finally, to Helga herself. The relationship between clothing fabric and Helga's body is emphasised to the 'observer' by the description of her 'skin like yellow satin' (p. 2).

The *artistry* of observation and its relationship with projection and manipulation is carefully articulated by the creation of this opening scene and gestured towards in the sentence: 'An observer would have thought her well fitted to that framing of light and shade' (p. 2). The aestheticism of colour is closely related to sexual attraction. We are assured that 'the observer's attention would fasten' on 'sensuous lips', 'wayward, delightful' hair 'falling unrestrained' (p. 2).

Repeatedly, it is the various shades and textures of Black skin, the variety of combinations within a range of angles and frames, that structures the narrative. The pupils at Naxos school are a 'baffling' variety of 'ebony, bronze, and gold faces' (p. 4), Helga has 'biscuit-coloured feet' (p. 11) below 'the pale amber loveliness of her face' (p. 13), and a 'visiting girl' stands 'in relief, like old walnut against the buff-coloured wall' (p. 14). Later, marvellling at 'the gradations within this oppressed race of hers', Helga looks on at a Harlem dance:

> A dozen shades slid by. There was sooty black, shiny black, taupe, mahogany, bronze, copper, gold, orange, yellow, peach, ivory, pinky white, pastry white. There was yellow hair, brown hair, black hair; straight hair, staightened hair, curly hair, crinkly hair, woolly hair. She saw black eyes in white faces, brown eyes in yellow faces, gray eyes in brown faces, blue eyes in tan faces.
>
> (p. 59)

This sliding up and down the spectrum emphasises the fluidity of Black signifiers, the varying associations of colour and meaning, of 'ugliness and beauty, [the] semi-barbaric, sophisticated, exotic' (pp. 59–60). However, *beneath* this celebration of shade and change, the text draws attention to the dread, essential fixity of Blackness and its genealogy. *Beneath* scrutiny and the visibility or invisibility of race lies a truth. The dancers are 'shaking themselves ecstatically to a thumping of unseen tomtoms' (p. 59) and, afterwards, Helga feels with 'a shameful certainty that not only had she been in the jungle, but that she had enjoyed it' (p. 59).

Blackness as sexuality, passion and colour is at once accepted and reflected by the novel. Helga is said to love 'colour with a passion that perhaps only Negroes and Gypsies know', but *too much colour* makes her feel 'like a veritable savage' (p. 69). In Copenhagen, staying with her mother's rich relatives, Helga is 'excited, incited' (p. 74) by the colour of clothes, the profusion of which reads like the list of Black faces in the sexually explicit Harlem dancing:

> There were batik dresses in which mingled indigo, orange, green, vermilion, and black; dresses of velvet and chiffon in screaming colors, blood-red, sulphur-yellow, sea-green; and one black and white thing in striking combination.
>
> (p. 74)

The difference between this description and the earlier survey of Helga's room at Naxos is the clashing inappropriateness, the awkwardness of context and balance. The garments here are 'incongruously laid out in the quaint, stiff, pale old room', the colours scream with 'strange' danger and voluptuousness, and sensuality has crossed the border to sex (p. 74). What matters, besides context and blending, is *who is looking*. Axel Olsen's framing of Helga in his portrait of her, which Helga describes as 'some disgusting sensual creature with her features', and which she does not recognise as herself, acts as a refutation of the scene in *Black Like Me* where Griffin approaches the Negro in the mirror. Hega's refusal of the truth of the representation with 'It isn't, it isn't at all' (p. 89) shatters what is described as the sexual wickedness of the image.

This uneasy juxtaposition between lurid colour and sexuality on the one hand, and sensual tones on the other, between a racist gaze and racial awareness, remains curiously uncertain. Invited, as observer, to view Helga Crane, the reader also witnesses the dangers of voyeurism. Instructed to refute the sexual overtones of skin colour, the text nevertheless asserts the essential bonds of race, as 'Ties not only superficially entangled with mere outline of features or color of skin. Deeper. Much deeper than either of these' (p. 95). The shame of responding to the essential 'jungle' beat in Harlem returns within Helga as she goes back to join her race. Here, in New York, desire and the 'uncontrolled fancies' (p. 105) of Robert Anderson lead her to seek purification in marriage. Even here, however, there is no escape from the wild nature of racialised sexuality that is described as a savage depth within her:

> And night came at the end of every day. Emotional, palpitating, amorous, all that was living in her sprang like rank weeds at the tingling thought of night, with a vitality so strong that it devoured all shoots of reason.
>
> (p. 122)

The move from fabric to body, from surface colour to biology is shown as a disaster for Helga. The body as procreation and sex, as destroyed by the desire that lies embedded within her, closes the novel.

Fear of fertility as a threat to the body is also present in *Passing*. Here, procreation threatens the specular certainty of racial identity through its potential for bringing racial secrets to light. The discussion between Clare Kendry and Gertrude Martin, who both 'pass' for White, reveals the horror of reproduction as the danger of exposing the self's hidden image. Race as a genealogy, a history and a biology is evident in Gertrude's words:

> They don't know like we do, how it might go way back, and turn out dark no matter what colour the father and mother are.
>
> (p. 168)

The family 'joke' made by Clare's White husband because she is, as he sees it, 'gettin' darker and darker' (p. 171) is one that *relies* on the possible disjunction of surface image and 'actual fact'. As long as she is *not actually* Black, her darkness does not signify:

> I know you're no nigger, so it's all right. You can get as black as you please as far as I'm concerned, since I know you're no nigger. I draw the line at that.
>
> (p. 171)

Clare's secret Blackness, readable only to those 'in the know', is one that has a complex relationship with the visible and material. Irene's first encounter with Clare, while both are publicly 'passing', is one that focuses enigmatically on visual exchanges and codes of seeing. Irene's desire to 'outstare' Clare, the 'rude observer', is based on her own fear of exposure: 'Did that woman, could that woman, somehow know that here before her very eyes on the roof of the Drayton sat a Negro?' (p. 150). If 'appearances', as Irene knows, 'had a way sometimes of not fitting facts' (p. 156), both Irene and the reader/ observer become implicated in the hunt for 'clue[s]' (p. 151). The location of clues, codes and signs relies on what can be read as a complicated racial framework. It is not through, as White people imagine, 'finger-nails, palms of hands, shapes of ears, teeth' (p. 150), and particularly *not* through skin colour. For the purposes of the text, it lies within sensuality, beauty and the *eyes*: 'Ah! Surely! They were Negro eyes! Mysterious and concealing' (p. 161).

As with Mayotte Capécia, in Fanon's *Black Skin, White Masks* (see p. 161), and for Helga Crane, it is sexuality, dress and the context of colour and shade that finally determine the significance of race. In Clare Kendry's living-room, racial *fact* becomes part of a social exchange, subtly coded and understood within the veil:

> She gave them her attention now, pouring the rich *amber* fluid from the tall glass pitcher . . . and then offered them *lemon* or *cream* . . .
>
> (p. 168; my emphasis)

However, even within the circle, racial identity remains a *problem*, reminiscent more of Fanon's Jew than of his Negro. Irene's assertion to Hugh that you just cannot tell, 'Not by looking' (p. 206), applies also to White identity. The

177

late recognition of a supposed Black woman as White leads Irene to claim: 'It's easy for a Negro to "pass" for white. But I don't think it would be so simple for a white person to "pass" for coloured' (p. 206). The reason for this relies, curiously, on essential, absolute qualities, in this way flirting with the biological materialism that is found in *Quicksand,* and yet allowing it to slide into ambiguity: 'There are ways [of telling]. But they're not definite or tangible' (p. 206).

Fanon's analysis of Blackness as the split between image and self, with his perhaps doomed search for a 'new humanism' beyond race, his search for the man behind the Negro, is powerfully evocative of race as self-consciousness. The identity of voyeur and object becomes curiously overlapping as his text reveals its implication with a racialised gaze. Reading these literary texts through Fanon exposes the ways that each text implies the role of the specular and the reality of the object. Reading Fanon through these texts highlights the masculinised nature of his discussion, but also its incredible insight into Blackness as the trauma of image, context and frame.

Mixed metaphors: popular culture and hybridity

I remember when I was about seventeen, a girl asked me if it wasn't strange that my mother was a different colour. 'She must feel like she's not quite your mother.' She asked me if I wished I looked like my mother.[47]

Mammy why aren't you and me the same colour?[48]

This final section pulls together the preceding analyses in order to focus on modern British fantasies and psychological experiences of race. Examining a recent British sociological text, which discusses popular cultural representations of race, and a recent poetical exploration of mixed race identity – placing the *contesting* affiliations of family, race and national identity against each other – the section reveals how the discussions of earlier chapters become telescoped into the space of popular culture and politics in modern Britain.

Feminist theories, attempting to define the link between the personal and the political, have had to tackle or redefine the notion of feminine identity. What does it mean to be a woman? What have sexism, patriarchy and heterosexism taken away from us? How do we reconnect the 'true' histories, the forgotten 'origins'? How do we 're-mother' ourselves through rereading our mothers? Adrienne Rich's lines from nearly two decades ago sound a familiar feminist chord for the act of rewriting the feminist self: 'Birth stripped our birthright from us, tore us from a woman, from women, from ourselves so early on.'[49]

The complications and difficulties of that identification – of political, national, class or racial difference – have been grappled with, denied, explained, transcended or dismissed. The absence of complicity between my story and hers, the break in the narrative thread, initiates a self-redefinition that insists on the possible overlaps, or dramatises the yearning rupture as the definitive moment of our feminist self-invention. I want to examine how Black politics and feminism have come together with a splintering set of contradictions around the imperatives of identification. Placing oneself within a historical narrative of identity, or retelling the narrative in new communal ways, has become a vital part of race, gender and class politics. Narratives of migration confusingly imagine the landscape of racial histories elsewhere, other father – or motherlands from which to ground the story's origins, or against which to place a new one, politically and culturally connected. Against some feminist urges for universal, horizontal female identification, Black feminism has asserted cultural solidarities, national particularities and antagonistic historical legacies. Being women is not all that we are.

The heterogeneity of Black cultures, their frequent political incommensurabilities, nevertheless admit of vital racial and historical narratives. For many Black feminist and women's texts, understanding one's mother, learning her story, becomes an act of racial and historical reassertion and self-understanding. It becomes a personal and cultural history. Denied a recorded literary heritage of the same recognition and visibility as that accorded to White literatures, artistic heritages have been traced through oral memories and unwritten (as well as written) creativities. Alice Walker's essay 'In Search of Our Mothers' Gardens' (1984) outlines this significant act of narrative pilgrimage, where Black self-expression begins at home:

> But this is not the end of the story, for all the young women – our mothers and grandmothers, ourselves – have not perished in the wilderness. . . .
>
> Yet so many of the stories that I write, that we all write, are my mother's stories.[50]

What are the contradictions when culture and familial heritage do not add up? When colour and culture do not coincide? When the racial story suffers a radical break between one's mother and oneself? When we explore metaphors of landscape, narrative and origins, the significance and difficulties of Black and feminist cultures of belonging reveal radical inconsistencies around the phenomenon of mixed racial identities.

Carolyn Steedman, struggling with the inconsistencies of her mother's life and its political contradictions, formed by desires and dispossessions which cut across traditional cultural narratives, makes a telling statement. Pointing to those repressed stories which do not fit in, the barbarous threads consigned to the wilderness outside traditional accounts of class heritage, Steedman writes:

> Personal interpretations of past time – the stories that people tell themselves in order to explain how they get to the place they currently inhabit – are often in deep and ambiguous conflict with the official interpretative devices of a culture.[51]

Identity politics has received a bad press in contemporary critical debates, where claiming a radical identity on the basis of belonging to a specific community has often been condemned as an unsophisticated belief in the authentic self. The borders between cultures, falsely reified, or races, flagrantly imagined, or sexes, socially constructed, blur or disappear under scientific or theoretical analysis. Those living on the margins, crossing the boundaries, ambiguously placed – as postcolonial or second-generation migrants, or refugees and mixed race people – are often seen as proof of the unhinging of static differences. The insistence on hybridity as a dislocating term points not only to a critical trend, but also to an awareness of recent (and less recent) histories of cultural change. Challenging the dictated limits of a communal identity and its official 'interpretative devices' is vital and necessary, precisely because those limits are not always dictated internally, and often *prescribe* as much as they *describe*. Avoiding the danger of coerced subscription to a rigidly coded set of behaviour, appearances or lineages, in order to have an 'authentic' voice within or of a community, must include a keen awareness of repressions, contradictions and uncomfortable realities at the edge of identity politics.

There are then two types of authenticity which have been – and should be – interrogated. The first is biological or 'natural' essentialism – the idea that Blackness, or woman-ness, or community, is simply and always born into, inherited and metaphysically inevitable ('this is what I am'). The second is political essentialism – the idea that Black consciousness, or feminism, or belonging, is dependent on certain cultural criteria ('this is what I am meant to be'). The temptation, in the face of these dangers, has been to insist on the dissolution of identities – whether racial, cultural or sexual. To claim a politics or a voice based on an identity to which one has an uncritical right has been placed under the essentialist label, then denounced.

The consequences of this are at once liberating (for some) and politically disempowering. It is evident that the limits of cultures, or 'races', are not always dictated internally, but often result from discourses and practices of power; from institutional, collective victimisation. However, in order to oppose these structures of exploitation, by which people are identified, anxiously, as discrete units, communities or cultures of resistance are and have been created, inherited and learned. Belonging may not be a simple biological fact, but may be signalled by inescapable codes of scrutiny. Having been robbed of the power of self-representation, owing to the experience of an external identification as Black and/or female, it is choking then to be robbed of the power to represent the validity of that experience and the reality of that identification. The borders between 'what I am' and 'what I am meant to be' are themselves blurred.

The difficulties arise around frozen conceptions of 'the Black woman' or, to be more specific, 'the Black British woman', that may, perhaps, insist on a relationship with African-Caribbean cultures, or with being working class, or 'loud', or other forms of stereotyping. However, there are certain kinds of experience, of politicisation, of racialisation, of mutual recognition and external hostility which enable a sense of positive belonging around the sign 'Black (British) woman' that is not endlessly movable or limitlessly able to be appropriated. What becomes a significant exploration *within* this sign 'Black woman' is the possibility and importance of articulating it in various political ways. The term 'mixed race' makes political sense *within* the category of Blackness, and as part of Black politics, in a different way from how it might be deployed within the category of Whiteness. Being a 'mix' of White English and White Scottish, for example, makes use of a different code of 'race' and its boundaries from being a 'mix' of 'White' and 'Black'.

The political consequences in terms of racial identity and racism are profoundly different. Black politics – in terms of organising against racism, gaining positive, collective empowerment, recognising certain aspects of experience or identification – do need to employ certain essentialist categories in order to have any kind of strategy or existence. Diana Fuss' contention that essentialism can be read or deployed in different ways, with different political effects, is a crucial one, and leads to the conclusion that the category Black is not always determined by negative racism, but can also be constructed through positive empowerment.[52] It is also a category that is variously determined by historical circumstance, geographical positioning, gender, class or sexuality. The boundaries around 'who's in' and 'who's out' and what being 'in' entails vary according to these contingencies. In order to make political interventions or to recognise operations of power, however, these contingent boundaries often need to be employed as (temporarily but actively) valid. As Fuss states:

> There is an important distinction to be made, I would submit, between 'deploying' or 'activating' essentialism and 'falling into' or 'lapsing into' essentialism. . . . 'Deploying' or 'activating' implies that essentialism may have some strategic or interventionary value.[53]

The creation of Black women's or Black feminist cultural traditions has largely relied on notions of community and heritage; on oral communications between mother and daughter; or on mourning and imaginatively reconnecting links broken through historical violence. When those links are absent owing to a transgression of cultural or racial or geographical limits, new possibilities and interrogations emerge, often through a process of revisiting the fragile links between culture, race and family. The constant interchangeability or confusion of these categories has led to unbearable tensions within the politics of identity.

The Colour of Love: Mixed Race Relationships (1992) provides a revealing insight into racial and racist codes and taboos, and the prevalent uncertainty about where the 'divisions' between races lie. The text is a series of interviews, marketed and organised around the prevailing principle of *visible* racial difference, with the chapters arranged and titled around scopic metaphors such as 'Love is Colour-Blind' and 'Ways of Looking', while the front cover shows a benevolent White man and a smiling Black woman (Stephen Komlosy and Patti Boulaye) in *juxtaposed* profiles of marital unity. The interviewees themselves move uncomfortably and with glib unawareness between problems of 'visible' racial difference, cultural issues, religious barriers, desire and imagination. They are largely from the middle classes, which allows an explicit celebration of supposed middle-class racial tolerance, while the text constantly reveals the opposite. Patti Boulaye, for example, is quoted making what becomes a familiar claim throughout the text: 'No one has said anything to our faces, although they may say it behind our backs. . . . We don't mix with people with a low mentality, you know, fools. Class makes all the difference.'[54]

The male and female narratives (the relationships are all heterosexual) are often placed side by side as gendered and racial alternatives. Patti Boulaye and Stephen Komlosy's narratives classically encode problematics of power and desire, while explicitly claiming otherwise. Patti Boulaye solves the problem of Black communities and family by positioning her White husband in the place of nurturance: 'He feels he has to protect me. I can't understand girls who want to be too independent and grown up. . . . And just like a father or mother, Stephen is always there for me to come crying to' (p. 37). Stephen's story is a curious minefield of surface disavowal and hidden problematics. Repeating phrases like 'But colour never occurs to me . . . just whether the person is attractive or not', he also claims: 'so my image of brown people were that they were very attractive' (p. 39). Having said about Patti 'as a Black woman maybe she evokes some folk memories in White men: of slavery, of Black women being available . . . you could do what you liked to them', he then typifies his role as anti-racist protector by telling an anecdote where his response to a White man saying about Patti 'I would really like to give her one' was 'well, I frequently do!' (p. 41).

Having marketed the text around the issue of 'colour' and the problems of visibility, the interviews teeter uneasily between colour, culture, class and nationality. Difference becomes encoded in sliding ways. Richard Gifford's reflection, as a White Englishman, on marrying a South Asian woman has to be read through a disguised set of assumptions: 'I suppose it might have been different if I'd married someone very different – from the Caribbean, for example' (p. 53). What it means to be 'very different' rather than just 'different' remains obscure. Colour and culture as terms of difference are analysed at times in ways which question their commensurability. Shyama Perera, while revealing the contradictions between the terms, manages to widen the racial issue by insisting on race as a more complex set of scopic signifiers. The dialogue between mother and daughter, although they are of the same 'race', is complicated not simply by cultural difference but by a different specular interpretation of culture, of being Sri Lankan:

> I knew I was Sri Lankan, but I didn't feel that it made me different. Whereas my mother dressed in a sari, and if she walked across a group of skinheads they'd shout out 'Paki', if I walked past they would whistle at me – the opposite reaction.
>
> (p. 114)

What is interpreted as the 'opposite reaction' emerges, through the interviews, as one which is in fact barely distinguishable. Asian-ness and sexual attraction are often assessed together in ways which compress the separated reactions to sari-ed mother and sexual daughter, and expose their continuum. Mark, a 'White English man' with an Asian girlfriend, discusses her sexuality in unmitigated racial terms, replete with cultural fantasies:

> Sexually too she doesn't try and make me feel inadequate, or compete with me. She appreciates me. I love her wearing her sari and all that – those feelings you get when you see a beautiful Indian woman in her sensual sari, it's unbelievable.
>
> (p. 291)

Mark's 'liberal' contention: – 'If I desire someone, why can I not have a Black or Asian or Chinese woman?' – is endlessly mirrored in the statements of other White men in 'mixed race' relationships. Under the chapter heading 'Blind Prejudice', Ian Gordon claims: 'I estranged one of my first girlfriends by confessing to her that my dream for the future was to experience sex with every race in the world' (pp. 85–6). This racial fantasy is sometimes explained in purely biological terms, where desire for what are perceived as other races becomes ultimately a matter of genes. Richard Gifford claims, for example:

> It seems to me that there's one basic thing that applies to mixed marriages – that it satisfies the instinct for what the anthropologists call exogamy, which is to cast your genetic net wider than the immediate circle. . . . It is as basic an instinct as the infant suckling on his mother's breast, it's inbuilt and has nothing to do with choice

or decision. . . . I am very conscious of broadening the gene pool in a
very wide and comprehensive way.

(pp. 48–9)

The notion of some people being 'more different' genetically than others,
through a kind of fantasy of Blackness, is again employed here. 'Colour' and
culture as popular fantasies cross over each other in implicit ways, until the
contradictions emerge in the statements of mixed race people who experience
race in radically fissured terms. Vicky Philipps, described as 'born of a half
Sierra Leonean, half English mother and an English father', confronts what
she calls 'that split between the self and the body', and questions the status of
'race' in between visibility, culture and experience:

> So it is very complex. When I look at myself I expect people to see me
> as white, though I am Black through my experiences, my cultural
> background and my value system, and the way I function. . . . I was
> brought up by my Black mother in an African country, so my appear-
> ance is something which is rather separate from myself.

(p. 276)

This gap between mother and daughter, explained as a break between
'myself' and 'my appearance', is a matter both of perception and of national
culture, or environment. The significance of perceived physical difference,
intruding in the dialogue between mother and daughter, is described as an
issue which, of itself, transgresses the 'normal' dimensions of motherhood.
Gill Danesh, a White woman with a Black daughter, discusses 'colour' as a
perceived division which can push the social constructs of racial difference
into a more valid place than family relationships, until they appear to be
'unnatural':

> I found it rather strange having an olive-skinned child at first. You
> automatically think when you have a child it's going to be a carbon
> copy of you – if it's not, you don't love the child any the less, but it's
> a strange experience . . . like a duck will kick a strange looking duck
> egg out of the nest.

(pp. 217–18)

Love itself, as a form of 'natural' communication between mother and child,
becomes perverted by the imagined impossibility of mutual identification.
The pull to identify with one's child across racial difference seems, in some of
the text's narratives, to have profound implications for the boundaries of
one's own racial identity. Ethal, a White woman with a Black son, discusses
her own sense of alienation from him:

I still couldn't get close to the boy, though. I didn't feel he had come from me. Mothers want their children to look at least a bit like them. . . . He thought I was his aunt or something. . . . I think I was ashamed of him.　•

(pp. 68, 70)

The internalised confusion leads her to a sense of racial self-mutation: 'At first I felt strange. . . . I think it was like changing colour' (p. 68) – a statement which is echoed by Sue Norris, another White mother of Black children, who claims: 'it hurts. It is like that film where you wake up one day and you are Black' (p. 223).

The text itself, by insisting on the primacy of vision, seems to disallow the fact that visible difference is itself a matter of social perception. In the interviews themselves, however, exposure, voyeurism and 'biological' nightmares abound and structure identities in powerful ways – often to such an extent that the fact of family belonging cannot transcend or compete with 'visible' racial belonging; one biological myth simply supersedes genetics. Sue Norris, for example, crumbles under the accusation that she is 'breeding bloody coons' and says of her own mother: 'I catch her looking at the children as if they are another species or something' (p. 222).

Attempting to allow another narrative thread, the possibility of nurturance and belonging across race and genes, Jackie Kay's poem for three voices, *The Adoption Papers*, explores myths of motherhood and identity without denying the power and reality of racial divisions. In this personal, poetic story of adoption, Kay writes from the imagined voices of the White birth mother, the White adoptive mother and the Black daughter, which allows her exploration of mixed race identity a confusion of narrative possibilities. Meditating on origins, the daughter confronts herself in the mirror, trying to read the secrets of her identity through her own image. The logic of genetics seems always to contradict the logic of parental love:

> I have my parents who are not of the same tree
> and you keep trying to make it matter
> the blood, the tie, the passing down
> generations.

(p. 29)

If nurturance does not coincide with 'natural' motherhood, the possibilities for reading the self in reference to the mother's history become fraught with contradictions. The question *'What is in my blood?'* (p. 25) is further complicated by the incommensurability between mother and racialised mirror-image:

> ... sometimes when I look in the mirror
> I give myself a bit of a shock
> and say to myself *Do you really look like this?*
> as if I'm somebody else.
>
> (p. 27)

In this way, night-longing for the 'real' mother, based on body, flesh and appearance ('She's your double she really is', p. 32), is again crossed by Whiteness, forcing another imagined thread of self-understanding through the Black father. This is a thread which becomes mediated by the physical relationship between birth mother and father, locked and conditioned by inescapable racial exposure, where Blackness threatens and fuses the boundaries between mother and father, allowing a historical narrative, spoken by the birth mother, for the daughter's face in the mirror:

> Olubayo was the colour of peat
> when he walked out heads turned
> like horses, folks stood like trees
> their eyes fixed on us – it made me
> burn, that hot glare; my hand
> would sweat down to his bone.
>
> (p. 26)

The poem allows an irresolvable tension between inherited narratives, dialogue and racial difference. Scottishness ('the land I come from/the soil in my blood', p. 29) has to exist alongside a narrative of fatherland, attested in the daughter's body by a process of imaginary mirroring:

> He never saw her. I looked for him in her;
> for a second it was as if he was there
> in that glass cot looking back through her.
>
> (p. 26)

After repeated confession to the validity of inheritance beyond the mythical pressure of genetic transference ('a few genes, blood, a birth/. . . Does it matter?', p. 20), the central conclusion, unnerved by instabilities, has to rely on a relentless meeting and conflict between Blackness and mothering. The despairing cry 'yet I confess to my contradiction/I want to know my blood' (p. 29) leads to a – socially logical – blood-tracing of Black 'cultural inheritance' through a Black political 'mother' of a different nationality from Black, White or adoptive parents:

> Angela Davis is the only female person
> I've seen (except for a nurse on TV)

who looks like me. She had big hair like mine
that grows out instead of down.

(p. 27)

This identification, allowing a form of retelling of the alienation of one's own
body through another image of belonging, is allowed to remain alongside the
yearning for dialogue with the White birth mother, figured as a longing for a
letter. The desire for written communication is a desire for a reading of her
mother's identity physically, through her own inscription:

fantasizing the colour of her paper
whether she'll underline First Class
or have a large circle over her 'i's.

(p. 34)

What both *The Colour of Love*, as a set of interviews, and *The Adoption Papers*, as
poetry, indicate is the compulsion towards racial narratives of belonging and
inheritance, which remain potent structuring forces of identity. Black cultures
of resistance as well as Black self-recognitions are not always, or ever, *simply*
inherited. Black/feminist identities, in order to gain a valid political voice,
have repeatedly and contextually to reinvent themselves in dialogue and conflict with racisms. That tension does, however, insist on the significance of
those identities which, as yet, cannot be reinvented in total, flagrant abandonment. 'Hybridity' cannot, then – except metaphorically – be merely a figure
of celebration and escape.

In conclusion

This chapter has suggested how the issues examined in preceding chapters can
be analysed in relation to the present. The overriding focus on British identities in the chapter is a way of bringing the diverse locations and histories
onto the space of the more local, specific and politically current contexts of
the United Kingdom. The preceding chapters clearly show that the local
and specific is crucially determined by a multiplicity of other spaces and
times that, within the politics of Black and African identities, are closely
related and continuously re-invoked, re-articulated and re-invented.

Notes

1 bell hooks, 'Postmodern Blackness', in *Yearning: Race Gender and Cultural Politics*
(London: Turnaround, 1991), p. 25. Further references are cited in the text.
2 Philip Rice and Patricia Waugh (eds), *Modern Literary Theory: A Reader* (London:
Edward Arnold, 1992), p. 327.

3 Patricia Waugh, 'Stalemates?: Feminists, Postmodernists and Unfinished Issues in Modern Aesthetics', in *Modern Literary Theory*, p. 344. Further references are cited in the text.

4 Toni Morrison, 'Unspeakable Things Unspoken: The Afro-American Presence in American Literature', *Michigan Quarterly Review*, 28(1) (1989). References are cited in the text.

5 Stuart Hall, 'Minimal Selves', in *Identity: The Real Me* (London: ICA Documents 6, 1987), p. 44. Further references are cited in the text.

6 Salman Rushdie, 'The New Empire Within Britain', *New Society* (9 December 1982).

7 Paul Gilroy, 'It Ain't Where You're From It's Where You're At. . . . The Dialectics of Diasporic Identification', *Third Text*, 13 (Winter 1990/91). References are cited in the text.

8 Pratibha Parmar, 'Black Feminism: The Politics of Articulation', in Jonathan Rutherford (ed.), *Identity: Community, Culture, Difference* (London: Lawrence and Wishart, 1990), p. 101. Further references are cited in the text.

9 V.S. Naipaul, *The Mimic Men* (Harmondsworth: Penguin, 1987 [1967]). References are cited in the text.

10 Sam Selvon, *The Lonely Londoners* (London: Longman Caribbean, 1972 [1956]), References are cited in the text.

11 Frantz Fanon, 'The Fact of Blackness', in *Black Skin, White Masks* (London: Pluto Press, 1986 [1952]).

12 From the Declaration of Human Rights, adopted by the General Assembly of United Nations, 10 December 1948.

13 Quoted in Bill Smithies and Peter Fiddick, *Enoch Powell on Immigration* (Suffolk: Sphere Books, 1969), pp. 55–6.

14 Address by Enoch Powell to the annual confernce of the Rotary Club of London, at the Burlington Hotel, Eastbourne, 16 November 1968, ibid., p. 73. Further references are cited in the text.

15 Speech by Enoch Powell to the AGM of the West Midlands Area Conservative Political Centre, Midland Hotel Birmingham, 20 April 1968, ibid., p. 42.

16 Sir Cyril Osborne, Spectator (4 December 1964), cited in Smithies and Fiddick, *Enoch Powell on Immigration*, p. 60.

17 Dilip Hiro, *Black British, White British* (London: Paladin, 1992), p. ix.

18 Tayeb Salih, *Season of Migration to the North* (London: Heinemann, 1985 [1969]). References are cited in the text.

19 V.S. Naipaul, *A Bend in the River* (New York: Vintage, 1980 [1979]).

20 Homi K. Bhabha, 'Remembering Fanon', Foreword to Fanon, *Black Skin, White Masks*, p. x.

21 'The jagged testimony of colonial dislocation, its displacement of time and person, its defilement of culture and territory, refuses the ambition of any "total" theory of colonial oppression', ibid.

22 Frantz Fanon, *Black Skin, White Masks*, p. 190.

23 Joseph Conrad, *Heart of Darkness*, in Morton Dauwen Zabel (ed.), *The Portable Conrad* (Harmondsworth: Penguin, 1987 [1902]), p. 573. Further references are cited in the text.

24 Ama Ata Aidoo, *Our Sister Killjoy* (Harlow: Longman, 1977). References are cited in the text.

25 Frantz Fanon, 'Algeria Unveiled', in *A Dying Colonialism* (New York: Grove Press, 1965), p. 47. Further references are cited in the text.

26 Frantz Fanon, 'The Fact of Blackness', *Black Skin, White Masks*, pp. 109, 112.

27 See Nicolas Monti (ed.), *Africa Then: Photographs 1840–1918* (London: Thames and Hudson), p. 56:

> In a very peculiar way eroticism became a medium for establishing contact, for penetrating the secrets of nature, the reality and the otherness of the continent. The seduction and conquest of the African woman became a metaphor for the conquest of Africa itself.

28 W.E.B. DuBois, *The Souls Of Black Folk*, in *Three Negro Classics* (New York: Avon Books, 1965 [1903]), p. 214. Further references are cited in the text.

29 James Weldon Johnson, *Autobiography of an Ex-Coloured Man*, in *Three Negro Classsics* (New York: Avon Books, 1965 [1912]). References will be cited in the text.

30 Pratibha Parmar, 'Black Feminism: the Politics of Articulation', p. 107.

31 Clair Wills, 'Language, Politics, Narrative, Political Violence', in Robert Young (ed.) 'Neocolonialism' (Special issue), *Oxford Literary Review*, 13 (1991), p. 53.

32 Michael Jackson, 'Black or White', in *Dangerous* (Epic/MJJ Productions Inc., 1991).

33 Kobena Mercer, 'Black Hair/Style Politics', *New Formations*, 3 (Winter 1987), p. 34.

34 Ama Ata Aidoo, 'Everything Counts', in *No Sweetness Here* (Harlow: Longman, 1970), p. 1. Further references are cited in the text.

35 For a reassessment of these debates, see, for example, Diana Fuss, *Essentially Speaking: Feminism, Nature, Difference* (New York: Routledge, 1989).

36 Stuart Hall, 'Minimal Selves', p. 44.

37 Frantz Fanon, 'The Fact of Blackness', p. 109.

38 Alice Walker, *Possessing the Secret of Joy* (London: Jonathan Cape, 1992).

39 See, for example, Mary Daly, *Gyn/Ecology* (London: The Women's Press, 1975); Fran Hosken, 'The Hosken Report: Genital Sexual Mutilation of Females', *Women's International Network News Quarterly* (December 1983). I owe these insights to Isata Kanneh, who has written and researched in this area.

40 Bessie Head, *A Question of Power* (Oxford: Heinemann, 1974). References are cited in the text.

41 Sembene Ousmane, *Xala* (London: Heinemann, 1985; first published, in French, in 1974). References are cited in the text.

42 Toni Morrison, *The Bluest Eye* (London: Triad Grafton, 1981). References are cited in the text.

43 Ngũgĩ Wa Thiong'o, *Decolonising the Mind: The Politics of Language in African Literature* (London: James Currey, 1987 [1986]), p. 46.

44 John Howard Griffin, *Black Like Me* (London: Grafton Books, 1964). References are cited in the text.

45 Christopher Hope, *My Chocolate Redeemer* (London: Minerva, 1989). References are cited in the text.

46 Nella Larsen, *Quicksand* and *Passing* (London: Serpent's Tail, 1989 [1928] [1929]). References will be cited in the text.

47 Yasmin Alibhai Brown and Anne Montague (eds), *The Colour of Love: Mixed Race Relationships* (London: Virago, 1992), p. 240. Further references are cited in the text.

48 Jackie Kay, *The Adoption Papers* (Newcastle: Bloodaxe Books, 1991), p. 21. Further references are cited in the text.

49 Adrienne Rich, *The Dream of a Common Language: Poems 1974–1977* (London: W.W. Norton, 1978), p. 75.

50 Alice Walker, 'In Search of Our Mothers' Gardens', in *In Search of Our Mothers' Gardens* (London: The Women's Press, 1984), pp. 235, 240.

51 Carolyn Steedman, *Landscape for a Good Woman: A Story of Two Lives* (London: Virago, 1986), p. 6.
52 Diana Fuss, *Essentially Speaking*, p. 20: 'It is important not to forget that essence is a sign, and as such historically contingent and constantly subject to change and to redefinition.'
53 Ibid.
54 See also the comment by Shyama Perera: 'class makes a difference . . . the middle classes are educated enough to keep their prejudices to themselves, which . . . means you have a better life', *The Colour of Love*, p. 119.

AFTERWORD

The movement between the historical, geographical and political locations visited in these chapters demonstrates the argument that theories of racial identity in late twentieth-century political narratives are vitally connected with and understood through an interdisciplinary and international crossing of borders. 'Africa' and its imagining in the literatures and debates during and after colonial domination continue to be a locus for theorising racial and cultural differences, for analysing Black identities and for exploring the relationships between race and sexuality. By uncovering often 'hidden' discursive and historical links between 'African' contexts and by interrogating the disciplines and historical narratives that have constructed Africa into a circulating textual object, I have revealed how significant these inquiries are for an understanding of feminist, nationalist and cultural debates in the late twentieth century.

My use of literary texts in these chapters is not meant to indicate a comprehensive survey of Black/African literatures, or to point towards an *exhaustive* range of texts, which could be analysed for the purposes of this argument. My reading of particular literatures discovers problems and effects that gesture towards wider concerns and which can be analysed through a range of similar texts. These analyses act as suggestive illustrations, or as methods of reading a corpus of literatures that are chronologically or thematically connected.

Using francophone texts and sources is intended as a way of further exploring important issues in anglophone sources. Frantz Fanon's Algeria, for example, becomes apparent in Alice Walker's Paris, and the relationships between Islam and African identity – evident in Freetown's history and Blyden's writings – are pertinently expressed in Kane's novel, where racial ideas, drawn from the politics of *Négritude*, align historical allegiances with the present. The connections between the politics of Ngugi's Kenya and Ousmane's Senegal are salient and emphasise the relevance of French colonialist influences to those of Britain.

I focus more particularly on narrative prose, rather than, for example, poetry, in order to foreground the importance of historical writing, consciousness and chronology. For example, reading the slave narratives as historical and imaginative texts facilitates an inquiry into the formal and stylistic features of later novels, and reading Sierra Leonean history as a complex set of narratives, from a complex set of sources, opens up a range of links, echoes and repetitions in contemporary and later narratives.

Exploring 'African-ness' from the late eighteenth century to the present, from the historical moment when ideas and productions of Africa were fomenting in lasting, violent and traumatic ways, reveals the peculiar tensions and fantasies of the modern world. 'Africa', in this enduring historical period, has never been a mere geographical location or variety of cultures and languages. The immense textual and political energies that have produced 'Africa' as knowledge and meaning have also, inextricably, formed the discourses of race, sexuality, culture and time that dominate contemporary thought.

The construction of identity in the twentieth century cannot be extricated from the overt and implicit constructions of race that emerge from Africa's metaphoric and troubled space.

BIBLIOGRAPHY

The following bibliography lists only works *cited* in the text or notes of this book.

Abraham, W.E., *The Mind of Africa* (Chicago, IL: University of Chicago Press, 1962).

Achebe, Chinua, *Things Fall Apart* (London: Heinemann, 1987 [1958]).

Aidoo, Ama Ata, 'Everything Counts', in *No Sweetness Here* (Harlow: Longman, 1970).

Aidoo, Ama Ata, *Our Sister Killjoy* (Harlow: Longman, 1977).

Anozie, Sunday O., *Structural Models and African Poetics: Toward a Pragmatic Theory of Literature* (London: Routledge & Kegan Paul, 1981).

Appiah, Kwame Anthony, *In My Father's House: Africa in the Philosophy of Culture* (London: Methuen, 1992).

Asa-Asa, Louis, 'Narrative of Louis Asa-Asa, a Captured African' [1831], appendix to the 'History of Mary Prince', in H.L. Gates (ed.), *The Classic Slave Narratives* (New York: Mentor, 1987).

Asad, Talal, *Anthropology and the Colonial Encounter* (London: Ithaca Press, 1973).

Avebury, Right Hon. Lord P.C., *On the Origin Of Civilisation and Primitive Condition of Man: Mental and Social Condition of Savages*, 6th edn (London, New York and Bombay: Longman, Green & Co., 1902 [1870]).

Barthold, Bonnie J., *Black Time: Fiction of Africa, The Caribbean, and the United States* (New Haven, CN: Yale University Press, 1981).

Benjamin, Walter, 'The Task of the Translator' and 'Theses on the Philosophy of History', in *Illuminations*, ed. Hannah Arendt, trans. Harry Zohn (London: Jonathan Cape, 1970 [1923]).

Bhabha, Homi K., 'Remembering Fanon', foreword to Frantz Fanon, *Black Skin, White Masks* (London: Pluto Press, 1986).

Bhabha, Homi K., *The Location of Culture* (London: Routledge, 1994).

Bishop, Rand, *African Literature, African Critics: The Forming of Critical Standards, 1947–1966* (New York: Greenwood Press, 1988).

Blyden, Edward Wilmot, *Christianity, Islam and the Negro Race* (Edinburgh: Edinburgh University Press, 1967 [1887]).

Brent, Linda, 'Incidents in the Life of a Slave Girl' [1861], in H.L. Gates (ed.), *The Classic Slave Narratives* (New York: Mentor, 1987).

Burton, Annie L., 'Memories of Childhood's Slavery Days' [1909], in *Six Women's Slave Narratives*, The Schomberg Library of Nineteenth-Century Black Women Writers (New York: Oxford University Press, 1988).

Brown, Yasmin Alibhai and Montague, Anne (eds), *The Colour of Love: Mixed Race Relationships* (London: Virago, 1992).

Cary, Joyce, *Mister Johnson* (Harmondsworth: Penguin, 1985 [1939]).

Casely-Hayford, Adelaide Smith, 'Mista Courifer', in Charlotte H. Bruner (ed.), *Unwinding Threads: Writing by Women in Africa* (London: Heinemann, 1983).

Certeau, Michel de, 'Ethno-Graphy: Speech, or the Space of the Other: Jean de Léry', in *The Writing of History* (New York: Columbia University Press, 1988).

Chatterjee, Partha, *Nationalist Thought and the Colonial World: A Derivative Discourse* (London: Zed Books, 1986).

Chinweizu, Jemie, Onwuchekwu and Madubuike, Ihechukwu, *Toward the Decolonization of African Literature*, vol. 1, *African Fiction and Poetry and their Critics* (Washington, DC: Howard University Press, 1983).

Clifford, James and Marcus, George (eds), *Writing Culture: The Poetics and Politics of Ethnography* (Berkeley and Los Angeles: University of California Press, 1986).

Clifford, James, *The Predicament of Culture: Twentieth-Century Ethnography, Literature, and Art* (Cambridge, MA: Harvard University Press, 1988).

Conrad, Joseph, *Heart of Darkness* [1902], in Morton Dauwen Zabel (ed.), *The Portable Conrad* (Harmondsworth: Penguin, and New York: Viking Press, 1987).

Cosentino, Donald, *Defiant Maids and Stubborn Farmers: Tradition and Invention in Mende Story Performance* (Cambridge: Cambridge University Press, 1982).

Crapanzano, Vincent, 'Hermes' Dilemma: The Making of Subversion in Ethnographic Description', in James Clifford and George Marcus (eds), *Writing Culture: The Poetics and Politics of Ethnography* (Berkeley and Los Angeles: University of California Press, 1986).

Daly, Mary, *Gyn/Ecology* (London: The Women's Press, 1975).

Davis, H.W.C. and Weaver, J.R.H. (eds), *The Dictionary of National Biography, 1912–1921* (London: Oxford University Press, 1927).

Delany, Lucy A., 'From the Darkness Cometh the Light, or Struggles for Freedom' [c. 1891], in *Six Women's Slave Narratives*, The Schomberg Library of Nineteenth-Century Black Women Writers (New York: Oxford University Press, 1988).

Douglass, Frederick, 'Narrative of the Life of Frederick Douglass an American Slave' [1845], in H.L. Gates (ed.), *The Classic Slave Narratives* (New York: Mentor, 1987).

Du Bois, W.E.B., *The Souls of Black Folk* (New York: Bantam Books, 1989 [1903]).

Ekwensi, Cyprian, 'African Literature', *Nigeria Magazine*, 83 (1964).

'Old Elizabeth', 'Memoir of Old Elizabeth, a Coloured Woman' [1863], in *Six Women's Slave Narratives*, The Schomberg Library of Nineteenth-Century Black Women Writers (New York: Oxford University Press, 1988).

Ellison, Ralph, *Invisible Man* (Harmondsworth: Penguin, 1987 [1952]).

Equiano, Olaudah, *Equiano's Travels*, ed. Paul Edwards (London: Heinemann, 1967 [1789]).

Equiano, Olaudah, 'The Interesting Narrative of the Life of Olaudah Equiano, or Gustavas Vassa, the African', a new edition [1814], in H.L. Gates (ed.), *The Classic Slave Narratives* (New York: Mentor, 1987).

Fabian, Johannes, *Time and the Other: How Anthropology Makes Its Object* (New York: Columbia University Press, 1983).

Fanon, Frantz, 'Algeria Unveiled', in *A Dying Colonialism* (New York: Grove Press, 1965).

Fanon, Frantz, *The Wretched of the Earth* (Harmondsworth: Penguin, 1985; first published in 1961, in French, as *Les Damnées de la terre*).

Fanon, Frantz, *Black Skin, White Masks* (London: Pluto,1986; first published in English in 1967, and in French, as *Peau noire, masques blancs*, in 1952).

Farah, Nuruddin, *Gifts* (London: Serif, 1993).

Foucault, Michel ,'Of Other Spaces' (originally 'Des Espaces autres', lecture, March 1967), *Diacritics* 16(1) (1986).

Ferguson, Russell, Gever, Martha, Minh-ha, Trinh T. and West, Cornel (eds), *Out There: Marginalization and Contemporary Culture* (New York, New York: The New Museum of Contemporary Art/ Cambridge, MA: The MIT Press, 1990).

Fuss, Diana, *Essentially Speaking: Feminism, Nature, Difference* (New York: Routledge, 1989).

Gates, Henry Louis, Jr, 'Criticism in the Jungle', in H. L. Gates (ed.), *Black Literature and Literary Theory* (New York: Methuen, 1984).

Gates, Henry Louis, Jr (ed.), *'Race', Writing and Difference* (Chicago, IL: University of Chicago Press, 1986).

Gates, Henry Louis, Jr (ed.), *The Classic Slave Narratives* (New York: Mentor, 1987).

Gates, Henry Louis, Jr, foreword to *Six Women's Slave Narratives*, The Schomberg Library of Nineteenth-Century Black Women Writers (New York: Oxford University Press, 1988).

Gendzier, Irene L., *Frantz Fanon: A Critical Study* (New York: Grove Press, 1973).

Gikandi, Simon, *Reading the African Novel* (London: James Currey, 1987).

Gilroy, Paul, 'It Ain't Where You're From It's Where You're At. . . . The Dialectics of Diasporic Identification', *Third Text*, 13 (Winter 1990/91); also in *Small acts* (London: Serpent's Tail, 1994).

Gilroy, Paul, *The Black Atlantic: Modernity and Double Consciousness* (London: Verso, 1993).

Gorvie, Max, *Our People of the Sierra Leone Protectorate*, Africa's Own Library, No. 6 (London and Redhill: United Society for Christian Literature, Lutterworth Press, 1944).

Griffin, John Howard, *Black Like Me* (London: Grafton Books, 1964).

Hall, Stuart, 'Minimal Selves', in *Identity: The Real Me* (London: ICA Documents 6, 1987).

Head, Bessie, *A Question of Power* (Oxford: Heinemann, 1974).

Hegel, G.W.F., *Phenomenology of Spirit*, trans. A. V. Miller (Oxford: Oxford University Press, 1977 [1807]).

Hiro, Dilip, *Black British, White British* (London: Paladin, 1992).

hooks, bell, 'Postmodern Blackness', in *Yearning: Race, Gender and Cultural Politics* (London: Turnaround, 1991).

Hope, Christopher, *My Chocolate Redeemer* (London: Minerva, 1989).

Hosken, Fran, 'The Hosken Report: Genital Sexual Mutilation of Females', *Women's International Network News Quarterly* (December 1983).

Innes, C.L., *Chinua Achebe* (Cambridge: Cambridge University Press, 1990).

Jackson, Mattie J., 'The Story of Mattie J. Jackson' [1866], in *Six Women's Slave Narratives*, The Schomberg Library of Nineteenth-Century Black Women Writers (New York: Oxford University Press, 1988).

Jackson, Michael, 'Black or White', in *Dangerous* (Epic/MJJ Productions Inc., 1991).

Jahn, Janheinz, *Muntu: An Outline of Neo-African Culture* (London: Faber & Faber, 1961 [1958]).

James, C.L.R., *The Black Jacobins: Toussaint L'Ouverture and the San Domingo Revolution* (London: Virgin Publishing, 1991 [1938]).

JanMohamed, Abdul R., *Manichean Aesthetics: The Politics of Literature in Colonial Africa* (Amherst, MA: University of Massachusetts Press, 1983).

Johnson, James Weldon, *The Autobiography of an Ex-Coloured Man*, in *Three Negro Classics* (New York: Avon Books, 1965 [1912]).

Kane, Cheikh Hamidou, *Ambiguous Adventure* (Portsmouth, NH: Heinemann, 1963; first published in French as *L'aventure ambiguë*, 1961).

Kanneh, Kadiatu, 'Place, Time and the Black Body: Myth and Resistance', in Robert Young (ed.), 'Neocolonialism' (Special issue), *Oxford Literary Review*, 13 (1991).

Kanneh, Kadiatu, 'Love, Mourning and Metaphor: Terms of Identity', in Isobel Armstrong (ed.), *New Feminist Discourses* (London: Routledge, 1992).

Kanneh, Kadiatu, 'Racism and Culture', *Paragraph*, 16(1) (1993).

Kanneh, Kadiatu, 'Mixed Feelings: When My Mother's Garden is Unfamiliar', in Sally Ledger, Josephine McDonagh and Jane Spencer (eds), *Political Gender: Texts and Contexts* (Hemel Hempstead: Harvester Wheatsheaf, 1994).

Kanneh, Kadiatu, 'The Difficult Politics of Wigs and Veils: Feminism and the Colonial Body', in Bill Ashcroft, Gareth Griffiths and Helen Tiffin (eds), *The Post-Colonial Studies Reader* (London: Routledge, 1995).

Kanneh, Kadiatu, 'The Death of the Author? Marketing Alice Walker', in Kate Fullbrook and Judy Simons (eds), *Writing: A Woman's Business* (Manchester: Manchester University Press, 1997).

Kanneh, Kadiatu, 'What is African Literature? Ethnography and Criticism', in Paul Hyland and Mpalive-Hangson Msiska (eds) *Writing and Africa* (Harlow: Longman, 1997).

Kay, Jackie, *The Adoption Papers* (Newcastle: Bloodaxe Books, 1991).

Larsen, Nella, *Quicksand* [1928] and *Passing* [1929] (London: Serpent's Tail, 1989).

Lee, Mrs R., *The African Wanderers: Or, the Adventures of Carlos and Antonio* (London: Grant & Griffith, 1850 [1847]).

Little, Kenneth, *The Mende of Sierra Leone: A West African People in Transition* (London: Routledge & Kegan Paul; New York: The Humanities Press, 1967 [1951]).

Marx, Karl, 'Critique of Hegel's Dialectic and General Philosophy', in David McLellan (ed.), *Karl Marx: Selected Writings* (Oxford: Oxford University Press, 1977).

Marx, Karl, 'The Future Results of British Rule in India', in *Karl Marx: Selected Writings* (Oxford: Oxford University Press, 1977).

Memmi, Albert, *The Colonizer and the Colonized* (Boston, MA: Beacon Press, 1967).

Mercer, Kobena, 'Black Hair/Style Politics', *New Formations*, 3 (Winter 1987), p. 34; also in *Welcome to the Jungle* (London: Routledge, 1994).

Migeod, Frederick William Hugh, *A View of Sierra Leone* (New York: Negro Universities Press, A Division of Greenwood Press, Inc., 1970 [1926]).

Miller, Christopher L., 'Theories of Africans: The Question of Literary Anthropology', in Henry Louis Gates, Jr (ed.), *'Race', Writing and Difference* (Chicago, IL: University of Chicago Press, 1986).

Miller, Christopher L., *Theories of Africans: Francophone Literature and Anthropology in Africa* (Chicago, IL: University of Chicago Press, 1990).

Monti, See Nicolas, (ed.), *Africa Then: Photographs 1840–1918* (London: Thames & Hudson, 1987).

Morrison, Toni, *Song of Solomon* (London: Triad Grafton, 1980).

Morrison, Toni, *The Bluest Eye* (London: Triad Grafton, 1981).

Morrison, Toni, *Beloved* (London: Picador, 1987).

Morrison, Toni, 'Unspeakable Things Unspoken: The Afro-American Presence in American Literature', *Michigan Quarterly Review*, 28(1) (1989).

Morrison, Toni, 'The Site of Memory', in Russell Ferguson, Martha Gever, Trinh T. Minh-ha and Cornel West (eds), *Out There: Marginalization and Contemporary Culture* (New York: New Museum of Contemporary Art and Cambridge, MA: MIT Press, 1990).

Morrison, Toni, *Playing in the Dark: Whiteness and the Literary Imagination* (Cambridge, MA: Harvard University Press, 1992).

Mudimbe, V.Y., *The Invention of Africa: Gnosis, Philosophy, and the Order of Knowledge* (Bloomington, IN: Indiana University Press; and London: James Currey, 1988).

Naipaul, V.S., *A Bend in the River* (New York: Vintage, 1980 [1979]).

Naipaul, V.S., *The Mimic Men* (Harmondsworth: Penguin, 1987 [1967]).

Naylor, Gloria, *Mama Day* (London: Vintage, 1990 [1988]).

Ngũgĩ Wa Thiong'o, *Decolonising the Mind: The Politics of Language in African Literature* (London: James Currey, 1987 [1986]).

Ngũgĩ Wa Thiong'o, *Petals of Blood* (Portsmouth, NH: Heinemann, 1988 [1977]).

Ngũgĩ Wa Thiong'o, *Moving the Centre: The Struggle for Cultural Freedoms* (London: James Currey, 1993).

Nicholls, Peter, 'The Belated Postmodern: History, Phantoms, and Toni Morrison', *Borderlines: Studies in American Culture*, 1(3) (March 1994).

Obiechina, Emmanuel, *Culture, Tradition and Society in the West African Novel* (Cambridge: Cambridge University Press, 1975).

Ong, Walter J., *Orality and Literacy: The Technologizing of the Word* (London: Methuen, 1982).

Ousmane, Sembene, *God's Bits of Wood* (Portsmouth, NH: Heinemann, 1962; first published in French as *Les Bouts de bois de Dieu*, 1960).

Ousmane, Sembene, *Xala* (London: Heinemann, 1985; first published in French in 1973).

Parmar, Pratibha, 'Black Feminism: The Politics of Articulation', in Jonathan Rutherford (ed.), *Identity: Community, Culture, Difference* (London: Lawrence & Wishart, 1990).

Perinbam, B. Marie, *Holy Violence* (Washington, D.C.: Three Continents Press, 1982).

Peterson, John, *A History of Sierra Leone, 1787–1870* (London: Faber & Faber, 1969).

Pratt, Minnie Bruce, 'Identity: Skin Blood Heart', in Elly Bulkin, Minnie Bruce Pratt, Barbara Smith, *Yours in Struggle* (New York: Long Haul Press, 1984).

Prince, Mary, 'History of Mary Prince, a West Indian Slave' [1831], in H.L. Gates (ed.), *The Classic Slave Narratives* (New York: Mentor, 1987) and in *Six Women's Slave Narratives*, The Schomberg Library of Nineteenth-Century Black Women Writers (New York: Oxford University Press, 1988).

Rice, Philip and Waugh, Patricia (eds), *Modern Literary Theory: A Reader* (London: Edward Arnold, 1992).

Rich, Adrienne, *The Dream of a Common Language: Poems 1974–1977* (London: W.W. Norton, 1978), p. 75.

Rushdie, Salman, 'The New Empire Within Britain', *New Society* (9 December 1982).

Said, Edward W., *Orientalism* (Harmondsworth: Peregrine, 1987 [1978]).

Said, Edward W., 'Reflections on Exile', in Russell Ferguson *et al.* (eds), *Out There: Marginalization and Contemporary Culture* (Cambridge, MA: MIT Press, 1990).

Said, Edward W., *Culture and Imperialism* (London: Chatto & Windus, 1993).

Salih, Tayeb, *Season of Migration to the North* (London: Heinemann, 1985 [1969]).

Sartre, Jean-Paul, Preface to Frantz Fanon, *The Wretched of the Earth* (Harmondsworth: Penguin, 1985 [1961]).

Selvon, Sam, *The Lonely Londoners* (London: Longman Caribbean, 1972 [1956]).

Smithies, Bill and Fiddick, Peter, *Enoch Powell on Immigration* (Suffolk: Sphere, 1969).

Soyinka, Wole, *The Interpreters* (London: Heinimann, 1987 [1965]).

Soyinka, Wole, *Myth, Literature and the African World* (Cambridge: Cambridge University Press, 1990 [1976]).

Spitzer, Leo, *Lives In Between: Assimilation and Marginality in Austria, Brazil, West Africa, 1780–1945* (Cambridge: Cambridge University Press, 1989).

Spivak, Gayatri Chakravorty, 'Can the Subaltern Speak?', in Patrick Williams and Laura Chrisman (eds), *Colonial Discourse and Post-Colonial Theory: A Reader* (Hemel Hempstead: Harvester Wheatsheaf, 1993).

Spivak, Gayatri Chakravorty and Adamson, Walter, 'The Problem of Self-Representation', in *The Post-Colonial Critic: Interviews, Strategies, Dialogues*, ed. Sarah Harasym (New York: Routledge, 1990).

Steedman, Carolyn, *Landscape for a Good Woman: A Story of Two Lives* (London: Virago, 1986).

Suleri, Sara, *The Rhetoric of English India* (Chicago, IL: The University of Chicago Press, 1992).

Thomas, Nicholas, *Colonialism's Culture: Anthropology, Travel and Government* (Princeton, NJ: Princeton University Press, 1994).

Vivian, Rev. William, *A Captive Missionary in Mendiland* (London: Andrew Crombie, 1899).

Wali, Obiajunwa, 'The Dead End of African Literature?', *Transition*, 10 (September, 1963).

Walker, Alice, *The Color Purple* (London: The Women's Press, 1983).

Walker, Alice, 'In Search of Our Mothers' Gardens', in *In Search of Our Mothers' Gardens* (London: The Women's Press, 1984).

Walker, Alice, *Possessing the Secret of Joy* (London: Jonathan Cape, 1992).

Watney, Simon, 'Missionary Positions: AIDS, Africa, and Race', in Russell Ferguson, Martha Gever, Trinh T. Minh-ha, Cornel West (eds), *Out There: Marginalization and Contemporary Cultures* (New York: New Museum of Contemporary Art and Cambridge, MA: MIT Press, 1990).

Waugh, Patricia, 'Stalemates?: Feminists, Postmodernists and Unfinished Issues in Modern Aesthetics', in Philip Rice and Patricia Waugh (eds), *Modern Literary Theory* (London: Edward Arnold, 1992).

West, Richard, *Back to Africa* (London: Jonathan Cape, 1970).

White, Hayden, *Tropics of Discourse: Essays in Cultural Criticism* (Baltimore, MD: Johns Hopkins University Press, 1978).

Wills, Clair, 'Language, Politics, Narrative, Political Violence', in Robert Young (ed.), 'Neocolonialism' (Special issue), *Oxford Literary Review*, 13 (1991).

Young, Robert J.C., *Colonial Desire: Hybridity in Theory, Culture and Race* (London: Routledge, 1995).

INDEX

Abraham, W.E. 42
Achebe, C. 41; *Things Fall Apart* 21–2, 23, 27, 28, 36
Adamson, W. 18 Africa: and AIDS 111–13; ambiguous identity in 30–6; Black ix; competing representations of 21–30; and death 70–1; distance/difference of 63–4; effect of colonialism on 91; and English language 59–60; essential aspects of 3–4, 42–3; feminine interpretation of 26; as freedom 132, 133; as home 116; identification with 65, 109–16; as image of war, power and destruction 131–2; journeys from 136; locating 48; looking for 2–21; and memory 125; naming 48; notions of x, 1, 23, 24, 152, 155,163–4, 190, 191; opening up of 58–9; and politics of resistance 36–42; racial splits in 60; and religion 59, 97; as symbol of origin 73, 122–3, 130; and unity with African-Americans 60–2; as victim and destroyer 110–11; as world beyond 58, 157–8
African literature: defined 37; increase in 38; independence of 38
African Literature and the University Curriculum, Conference of (1963) 41
African Writers of English Expression, Conference of (1962) 36
African-Americans: and identification with Africa 60–2, 109–16; as members of the United States 117; as writers 117
Aidoo, A.A.: 'Everything Counts' 159; *Our Sister Killjoy* 136, 152–4

alienation 165, 186; of mirror image 169–70; narrative representation of 98–9, 100–1
American/Negro split 65
Andrews, W.L. 79
anthropology 7–10, 14, 18–19, 23; fallacy 29–30
Appiah, A. 30, 40–1
Armstrong, L. 123–4, 131
Asa-Asa, L. 70, 73, 75, 76, 79
Asad, T. 7, 15–16, 44

Bai Bureh (Temne chief) 13, 91
Barthold, B.J. 58
Benjamin, W. 14–15, 16
Bhabha, H.K. 17, 30, 117, 150–1
Bishop, R. 41
Black Atlantic 62–3
Black Poor 49, 51, 71
Blackness ix–x, 103–4, 139, 151, 157, 158; as concept of excruciating visibility 166–7; and hair 158–60; as masculine 160–1; as a mask 162; as split between image and self 177–8; in white texts 168–78
Blyden, E.W. 55–6, 58–62, 65, 72, 75, 92, 190 body, the 137, 155; Black 119, 120; cultural constructions of 154–60; female 119; as hidden 156; racial/sexual signifiers of 160–7, 168, 176; and the self 184; splitting of 150–1
bolekaja critics 38–41, 46
Boyd, W. 23
Brent, L. 78, 81, 82–3
Burton, A.L. 71

Calhoun, J.C. 74
Cardinal, M. 124